Michael Wasiura

The People
In Your Neighborhood

In memory of Officer Jon Ginka

Contents

MIKE

*"**better ask somebody:** an evasive answer
given in response to an obvious question,
letting the questioner know that he/she is
out of the loop."*

—Urban Dictionary

I am from Muskegon, Michigan. Like most of the places where most Americans live, it is a place that most Americans have never heard of. It has its proud handful of celebrities with ties to the community: father of punk rock Iggy Pop (born here), mixed martial artist Tony Ferguson (raised here), disgraced televangelist Jim Bakker (born and raised here). It has its not entirely unique set of problems (shuttered factories, failing schools, racial segregation) and peculiarities (ask for a large "soda" at McDonalds, and the mother-of-three cashier is unlikely to complete your order successfully). It has its dilapidated historic mansions and its modeled subdivisions, its cookie cutter suburban strip malls and its hip microbrewery next to the rehabilitated farmer's market downtown, its picturesque lakes and its mercury warning on the consumption of fish angled from them. In short, it is like every other little known and far away microcosm that, taken together, still make up most of what America is.

I am from Muskegon, Michigan. Last November, I was asked live on the air of a meticulously-organized Russian daytime political talk show why, if The United States of America were as just and prosperous as I maintained, nearly sixty-three million of its citizens cast their ballot for a candidate who promised to annihilate the status quo. I could not muster a satisfying response. Nor could the hours of podcasts I downloaded each day to fill my ears and brain as I pushed my way back in front of the babushkas pushing their way in front of me onto the rush hour Moscow metro. Because from July 2015 to April 2016, Washington-based fellow after Brooklyn-based journalist had foretold for me the inevitable demise of Trump; from April to November, they had pointed to the polls from my home state as proof that the sum of microcosms remained within the bounds of civility and reason; and from November 8 on, they had babbled in dumb shock at the inscrutability of all those unlearned masses from all those little Muskegons sprinkled all along the Rust Belt and popping up in places from Chico east to Lowell and from Duluth down to Pensacola. Which seemed strange to me. My best friends from graduate school in Manhattan were all Midwestern transplants, and the fine-grain leather couches I crash on when passing through D.C. invariably belong to former Peace Corps Ukraine group mates who hail from every part of the union except Washington, D.C. The upper Midwest is not usually considered exotic, and its inhabitants did not usually evoke blank incomprehension from native daughters turned masters of public policy living and blogging only a few hundred miles away.

I am from Muskegon, Michigan. I went to North Muskegon High School. My mother kept the handful of clippings from the *Muskegon Chronicle* that mention my contributions to various football and baseball and basketball wins. I graduated fourth in my class, behind a future public school teacher, an orthodontist, and a real estate developer. Even though the teacher and the orthodontist and the real estate developer and the programmer and the accountant and the construction engineer and the management consultant and the geophysicist and I and pretty much all of the other professional-level people I grew up with moved away at the first chance, dammit I played football with the guys who were still here: the factory lineman and the restaurant manager and the car salesman and the sanitation worker and the cop and the tugboat deckhand. I still knew their parents and, home for Christmas, still felt silly calling them by their first names. I followed the polls all summer and fall and thought they jibed with the rough count in my head. They did. It's just that the polls were three points off, and the count in my head was three points off.

I am from Muskegon, Michigan. I do not know why my home county cast 5080 more votes for Donald Trump last November than it cast for Mitt Romney in 2012. What follows is my attempt to find an answer to that problem over burgers and beers with seventeen people living in the hometown to which I would not have returned had I not been shocked into the realization, expressed from Moscow to my mother via Skype in the early hours of November 9, 2016, that "our country is not what we thought it was, and our neighbors are not who we thought they were." This project is as much for people like my father (a long-time lawyer in town who professed not to know a single Trump supporter other than his sister) as it is for people in Park Slope and Georgetown (who may not have spoken to a Trump supporter since high school back in Des Moines), and it is as much for the grudging Walmart greeter (who has some legitimate grudges) as it is for the producer at *Fox News* (which more and more resembles Russian State TV translated into American). Because whether Trump is impeached on charges of treason after a disastrous (for him) mid-term election cycle, whether he ends his reign by anointing his first-born son Emperor Donald II, or whether he is only the precursor to whatever tragedy is to befall our country in 2037, there's something happening here. 62,985,106 neighbors willed this, whatever this is or ends up being. 65,853,625 neighbors willed against it, whatever that's worth. For everyone, it's time to get to know the neighbors again.

"Because what is history? History is everything that happens everywhere... Even what happens in his house to an ordinary man—that'll be history too someday."

—*Philip Roth*

"I am the people—the mob."

—*Carl Sandberg*

DAVE

> *"A fifty-five-year-old garbage man is a million times smarter than a twenty-eight-year-old with three PhDs."*
>
> —Louis C.K.

I didn't want my family living where we lived. I didn't like my neighbors. I didn't feel safe with my kids playing in the back yard. I had a crazy neighbor—the one's next door to us were looney. They had ducks and chickens, and they would come in my yard and shit on my kids' swing set. I built this privacy fence, and once I built the privacy fence, they felt like it was okay to stack their trash up. They had a effen pyramid of trash bags. I mean it was literally up to the branches—a mound of trash bags. They had a landfill in their back yard. Open trash. And you'd smell it. Also, they needed their septic pumped, and they wouldn't do it. During the summer, every time they took a shower, you could smell it. I'm like, "No." That was it. That and the neighborhood got dark really fast. So we moved.

The house that we're in now was quite a bit more expensive, but I said, "I'd rather be broke and have what we want." We've got ten acres. We have deer all over. I can hunt on my property. I don't have bumping rap music on one side, and I don't have a landfill on the other. We don't have to be worried that the neighbors are going to have another ghetto party on our front yard. Life is good.

I'm very happy. I've got a wife that knows me and accepts me for who I am. My kids have everything they need—and then some.

My kids can run around. I can open the door and I can let them go. They can play out there. They can do whatever they want.

Happiest I've ever been in my life is right now. Other than gaining a hundred pounds in the last eighteen months. Other than that. But that's glandular. Pretty sure. I'm pretty sure that's glandular. The wife wants me to go get checked by a doctor, but I don't get checked by doctors. Ever. Unless something's wrong. Or for my Department of Transportation physical—because I have to get that done every two years for my commercial license. Blood pressure and all that. And they touch my crank and all that. But that's it. I just don't like doctors. Never had a bad experience, but you go to the doctor, and they just tell you stuff's wrong. I'm one of these guys that don't want to hear it.

If I die tomorrow, so be it. I've got life insurance up the ass. If I die tomorrow, my house is paid for, all the vehicles are paid for, my kids' college is paid for. I mean, yeah, I want to be there for my kids, but if I did die, I'm good. I know my family would be taken care of.

I wake up in the morning, and I feel great. I breathe fine. Everything's fine. I'll keep going with what I'm doing. Something's working. I mean, what, fifteen hundred years ago, life expectancy was thirty-five years old? I figure I'm beating it right now. That's historical understanding. Most people don't know that. Back then, people were like four foot eight and a hundred and twenty pounds. Now I'm six foot tall and three hundred pounds, but who's counting? They drank mead, I'm drinking flowing water from the Rockies. My Coors Light has got to be healthier than the mead they drank, right? I stick to the light beer now. No more Stroh's. Got to watch my girlish figure.

So I still drink. That's all I do now. I work and I drink, but I work more than I drink. Oh god, I work constantly. Constant work. Two jobs. For like forty, forty-five hours a week, I'm a "sanitation engineer." I drive a truck. Pick up seven hundred houses a day. Trash. It's hard, crappy, dirty, nasty work. You're picking up diapers, cat shit, dead animals. But I don't have anybody to answer to. I've got one job: stop, stop, stop, boom, boom, boom, pick up, pick up, pick up, drive. You just have to drive the truck and throw the trash. It's kind of boring, but it ain't bad. I've got the Sirius XM radio deal on my phone—I get to listen to Howard Stern a few hours a day. And for not going to college or anything, I make more at that job than most people I know with bachelor's degrees. Then I cut hair on the side.

I'm not saying that I'm lucky and I have a great job. I'm a fucking garbage man. It's not like I fell into a lavish lifestyle. But I've got money in the bank. I've got everything paid for. I don't have to worry about my electric bill. I don't have to worry about food for my kids. If my kids need something, it's not like, "Okay, let's go to Walmart and get you Walmart shoes." It's, "I'm gonna order you a pair a sweet Under Armour cleats for soccer." I'm just comfortable right now where I'm at. And none of that would have happened if I hadn't met my wife. Without her, I'd have ended up in jail.

No question, meeting my wife was the best thing that ever happened to me. She brought structure to my life when it was in shambles. She's the one that got me turned around, got me on the right track.

Not a lot of my friends know that I went through some bad times. My parents got divorced when I was fourteen or so, and really, after that was when I started to fuck up in school. Fifth, sixth, seventh grade, I had As and Bs. Normal. All my tests were good. But after they got divorced, I fucked around, you know? Didn't think of future life back then. It was all one day at a time. I didn't think about my future. The year I got kicked out of North Muskegon, I had a zero-point-six-seven grade point average. They told me, "If you miss any homework assignment or fail a test, you're done. We're going to just expel you." So I thought, "Might as well just walk away."

That's when I went to M-Tec—Muskegon alternative ed. I went to school there for a little while. The students would smoke pot with the teachers out on the sidewalk. We'd literally smoke pot with the teachers on the sidewalk. They didn't give a shit about us. We got leftover lunch from Muskegon High School—cold, soggy lunch. We were just throwaway kids. It was like a school of rejects. The students were from any school around here that kids got kicked out of.

It was me in khaki shorts and a polo shirt walking into Ghettoville down by Frontier Mart, and I ended up getting in trouble there. Some black guy picked a fight with me and I decked him in class—knocked his ass out in the chair. All the people were jumping around like *"Daaaaamn!"* They're all jumping around, and I walked out. I walked out and I said, "I'm done with school." That was horrible. They shouldn't have put me in that school. But I had no other choice. That was my last option, and I blew that one.

My dad kicked me out of the house when I was sixteen. I'm not saying my parents gave up on me, but when they got divorced, they kind of gave up on everything really. My dad got remarried, and me and my step-mom didn't get along at first, so I moved to downtown Muskegon. When all my friends from school were still juniors and seniors at North Muskegon, I was living in downtown Muskegon, Grand and Seventh. Ghetto.

At that point, I worked part-time once in a while—Papa John's, doing pizza. Fifteen hours a week, max. While I worked at Papa John's, they were going to throw me in jail for writing bad checks, and the reason why I wrote bad checks was to get food, because I had no food at the house. I'd write my own employer a bad check to buy a small pizza at the end of the night.

So what do you do when you're in the ghetto and you're seventeen and you're broke? You sell drugs to get out. I'd bring a quarter pound of weed to a North Muskegon party and sell it and make money. That's all I had. I had no other way to make money. I always hung around with guys from North Muskegon and never portrayed that my life was so horrible, but oh god it was bad.

I was destitute for a while. There was a point where I didn't eat anything for a week but a can of green beans. And then coke. That's all I did. I mean, it was terrible. It was a horrible, horrible life I lived. I remember, I didn't have a can opener. I remember taking a butter knife and forcing open this can of French style green beans. That's what I ate for a week. Literally a week went by without anything else to eat. It was bad, man. It was bad. And every couple days, I did a thousand dollars-worth of blow. It was free because I was selling it. I would have a pile in front of me—a big, beautiful pile of coke. That was just a really, really horrible part of my life.

I stole a bag of tea candles for heat one night. Because I had nothing. I had two thousand dollars worth of cocaine in my pocket, but I didn't have any cash at certain moments. I'd go to Meijer's and pick cigarette butts out of the fucking ash tray so I could smoke something. You watch somebody put half a cigarette out, you're over there like "boom." But that's where I was before I met her. I mean, it was bad. I didn't even tell my friends how bad it was.

I was bad. Robbing people—people I knew. Selling them fake drugs. Telling people you'll get them a pound of pot, then whipping them in the face with a bar and breaking their jaw and stealing their money. I mean, it was bad. It was the horrible, horrible, lowest low point of my life.

It was bad. Busting light bulbs out of ceilings, smoking coke with straws. Smoking coke out of a light bulb: You take a normal light bulb—a round light bulb with the screw-in bottom. Take a Phillips-head screwdriver, and there's a little lead part that makes the contact for the power to run through. You grab that with any kind of cloth and you hold that so just the screw part's sticking through. You take the Phillips-head and stick it in there, then you take a hammer and you pop it through. You dump everything out, you rinse out the bulb, and all you're left with is the metal screw-in part and the glass. Well, you dump the cocaine in there, and you heat it up, and you stick a straw in there, and you smoke it—smoking coke. Just, again, stupid shit you learn when you live in the ghetto.

But that was when I hit rock bottom. For a little while it was, "Oh this is fun, this is fun, partying." Then I started doing more, selling, doing it and doing it and doing it, and then it was just like—boom: twenty years old, living in a shed. Literally. In the winter. With tea candles I stole from Meijer's for heat. With a sleeping bag over me. Trying to stay warm. At that point I was like, "Wow, this fuckin sucks." That was really the changing point in my life—just sitting there thinking, "Well, I've already pissed away my high school education. That's gone." That was rock bottom. So I started working.

I got a shop job. Temp. Office furniture. Knoll Group. Where my dad worked. Powder coat. Sprayed powder coat. I worked on and off. In, laid off, back in, laid off again. Then I got an apartment. I was living in downtown Muskegon in a $290-a-month, all-utilities-included apartment. Working through Manpower. I slowly started building from there.

Did that for three years. Never missed a day of work, because they would fire me if I did. Three years temp. Ten bucks an hour. No benefits. No vacation. Nothing. Never late. Nonstop. I stuck with it for the chance of getting hired in, because once you get hired in there, it's twenty, twenty-two dollars an hour. Never missed a day of work.

That's where I met my wife. Funny story: When she came to work, we called her "Miss New Booty," because that was right around the time that song came out, *"oooh I found you, Miss New Booty."* I didn't know her name. I just called her "Miss New Booty" at work. She was the new one with the donkey butt.

Well, it was right before Christmas. I was in paint line on System 3. I worked with this black guy—big goofy fucker. Ghetto as shit. And this girl came in, and she talked to him, and all of a sudden he goes, "Damn, that big-booty bitch out there at unloadin wants to know what you're doin after work." He goes, "I think she wants to hang out with you." Then her friend came in. Her friend asked me out for her. She goes, "What are you doin after work today?" This was right before plant shutdown. She goes, "Well, all of us are goin up to Dog House Saloon. Why don't you come with us?" We were working third shift. It was seven in the morning. And I said, "Alright." I went up there, and that was it. We had a couple beers. From there we went to Mibar and played pool. She dropped me back off at my apartment, because I didn't have a car. We hung out every day after that, and we've been together basically every day since.

As soon as I met her, I stopped smoking pot. I stopped using any kind of hard drugs. Everything just stopped. She's really the one that saved me from my downward spiral.

We got married, then we both got laid off, and that's when I said, "Alright, I'm gonna go down to barber college." Both of us moved to Lansing, and I went to barber school. Got her knocked up. She moved back a month before I graduated. Had my son. Graduated. Moved back to Muskegon. Had kind of a hard time of it, but my big plan was, "I'm gonna open a barbershop." Got ahold of this guy—older guy. He goes, "I'm gonna retire." So I said, "Okay." I started cutting for him. Well, it was like forty or fifty bucks a week. I did it for six months, then I had to tell him, "Hey, you know, I've got a family I've gotta support. I've got a family." So I quit that, started working again at a shop through Manpower. My wife was working there too. She got hired in, and I didn't.

Then her cousin got hired in at the garbage place here, and he goes, "Hey, I might be able to pull a string, get you a job." I said, "I don't have a commercial license or anything." He goes, "Let's just get you in the door first." I got an interview, and they hired me before I even had my license. They go, "You need to hurry up and get your license." So I took our mortgage payment that month and hired somebody to give me a training. You have to do a pre-trip and a post-trip—inspecting the truck, make sure it's street worthy, all that. I basically gambled a mortgage payment on that, and I passed my test. Got my CDL, started working.

I didn't listen to anyone really before I met my wife. When I met her, I had a four hundred credit score. It's funny, because now the roles are reversed. We had a joint checking account for a while. Both of us had a debit card, and I'm like, "Man, you know, we're making a lot of money, and there ain't no fuckin money here." We were struggling to pay our bills. Bills were in shut off. It was like, "That don't make no sense." So I get the printout of all the stuff: it's two dollars here, three dollars there, swipe, swipe, swipe, swipe. She doesn't pay attention to it—she just swipes. So now I took over all the money. I do everything. I give her a hundred bucks a week spending money. I literally went from so irresponsible with money—I mean bad—to a really good budget now. I learned from my mistakes, and now I've taken the step to where now I'm in control of all of our finances. Not saying that she's not responsible, but she's a swiper—*whfft, whfft, whfft, whfft.*

Like, at our last house, our mortgage payment was $720 a month. I had a vehicle worth half of what I have now, she had an old car that we had no payment on, and we were still broke. Now at our new place, we doubled our mortgage payment, we both got new vehicles, and we're more comfortable than we've ever been. Yes, I have a second job, but I'm kind of proud of the fact that I run the money in the house. I've got a pretty cushy bank account. I'm not bragging about money, but from where I was to where I am now? I'm proud of it. I've got a seven-eighty credit score. Everything's good.

So why did we move? There was a ghetto party in our front yard, and it was bad. Me, my buddy Zach from work, his now-fiancée, and my wife—we're sitting in the back yard at my house, just having a fire, hanging out. Casual. Drinking. The kids are inside in bed. Then, all of a sudden, there's a lot of traffic. I said, "Holy shit, there's a lot of traffic out here." I walk around the fence, and it was like the Muskegon Heights was dumped into my front yard—literally hundreds of people walking in my front yard. I go out there and I said, "Hey, get off my yard." Now they're yelling at me—"Fuck you, motherfucker." They were speaking to me in a way that wasn't friendly. It's my home. My children are in there sleeping. I said, "Okay."

I walk inside and I grab my .45 and I grab my .40 pistol and I put them in my back pocket. Now I'm back in the front yard. Me and my buddy are standing there. There are hundreds of people on my grass. And not to be racist, but they were dark. Then this car pulls in through my grass that I just spent eight thousand dollars on. He pulled into my yard, through my grass, and parked in my driveway. Headlights facing me. I said, "Get the fuck out of my yard." My wife called 9-1-1. She's like, "You need to get here. There's a car here threatening my husband. He's gonna shoot somebody." The dispatcher is on the phone, "Tell your husband to calm down, put the guns away..." My wife's saying, "No. He's not gonna put the guns away. He has them drawn. He will shoot somebody." While she's on the phone, the guy in the car shines his bright lights, and they start opening the doors. I said, "Okay." So I pulled both the pistols out, and I have them hanging by my side. They're looking, and they're looking, and they pulled forward a little bit, and they revved their engine. So I lift my arms and I start walking towards their car, and I'm screaming so that the dispatcher on the phone can hear me, "You better get someone fucking over here, cause I'm gonna shoot somebody in the face." They peel out, back up. Meanwhile, my wife is crying, because these guys were going to get out of the car until they saw that I had the pistols pointed. So I told her, "Get the kids. Go to your mom's house." She loaded the kids, and my wife had to drive through people to get out of her own home. That's not how it's supposed to be. Not acceptable.

All my friends left. Now it's just me sitting on my front porch with the pistols. Meanwhile, there's still literally hundreds of people standing right out there on my lawn, and I'm sitting here thinking, "Okay, I've got fourteen rounds in this one. I've got nine rounds in this one." I'm like, "I'm gonna take at least a dozen people out with me." It's like fighting zombies.

Well, an hour later, seven state cops start walking up to my house with flashlights, and I'm fucking drunk. Drunk. Sitting on a chair with two pistols in my lap. The cops come up to me, they go, "Hey, are you armed?" I said, "Yep." He goes, "You need to put those away." I say, "I'm not putting anything away until these people are out of my yard." And he tried to get tough with me, like, "Put em away. You can't have a firearm when you're drunk." I'm like, "No." Because I know the law. I'm defending my home now. I said, "Yes I have booze on my breath, but I was not planning on holding a gun when the night started." He goes, "Well, nevertheless, you've been drinkin." I said, "Yeah I have been. I'm pretty drunk." He goes, "You can't have a firearm when you're drunk." I said, "I picked my firearm up only after people threatened me in my yard with my children sleeping inside." He said, "Well, you gotta put em away." I said, "Ah, I know my rights." I had a concealed carry permit; I'm licensed to hold a firearm. So he came up, checked all my stuff, and he said again, "You need to go inside." I said, "I'm not going anywhere." I said, "I'm going to sit on my porch until you guys clear this up, and once it's cleared, then I'll go inside." He goes, "Okay." They left. They left me there drunk on my porch with both my pistols.

Well, it took seven police departments—with helicopters—to finally get this party under control. There was like eighteen hundred people.

The next morning, I woke up, and I told my wife: "Call a realtor." The house sold in twenty-two hours. It was a beautiful house. It was our first home that we bought. When we moved in, it had sand in the front yard, sand in the back yard. I brought in semi loads of black dirt. I put a sprinkler system in. I put fence up. I built a barbecue pit. It was pristine. Nicest house on the block, by far. But I said, "We're out of here. My kids ain't gonna live around this shit."

That's the problem with this town now. Now everybody's all empowered, and white people are all of a sudden the enemy of everybody. You can't walk around. Random people will say shit, yell shit. There are random shootings all the time. They just shoot people. You can't even drive around anywhere in the heart of Muskegon. If it's not broad daylight, you can't go through there.

Complete one-eighty from when we were kids. In high school, we used to take Kirk's van down to Frontier Mart to get crackheads to buy beer for us—and they wouldn't rob us most of the time. They'd buy ten forties and you'd agree to give them two, and everybody held up their end of the deal. I mean, Nick—valedictorian of our class, Judge's son—he would drive to Frontier Mart and negotiate with crackheads. You do that now? White kids down there? You get shot. That's a little, miniscule thing, but it all ties into the same idea: It's not safe in this town. The drug dealers and the poor people and the violent people are now all empowered, and it's dangerous. And you can't even speak out about it, because everybody's so liberal now. You speak out about anything, and you're a racist. You're blackballed. You're done. You can't say anything.

But I'll say it: No one has work ethic. My buddy, the other day he went to Walmart and watched a guy walk out with two shopping carts full of pop. He's like, "What the fuck's this guy doin?" My buddy's watching—the guy opened every fucking one of them in the parking lot, dumped them out, went inside, and returned the cans for the deposit. He bought them with a Bridge Card. That's what this country's coming to, and that's bullshit. Everybody gets mad, "Oh, you're cutting off benefits." Benefits are for people that work.

Another story: Me and my wife had just had our son. We both got laid off. He was two or three months old. No money to pay his bills. I went and applied for food stamps. Denied. Denied. I said, "Well, we're both jobless. We have no money." I said, "I can't feed my family." So they gave us an exception for a month. They gave us one month worth of food stamps. We still couldn't pay our bills, but we went and bought food. Next month, we reapplied. Denied. Shut off. That's it. Really? I can't get anything? I can't get formula? We were both laid off. There was nothing we could do. We tried to get jobs, but it was 2010 when the economy was still shit. So we had nothing. Denied.

I just don't understand how this system works. You can sit, you can not even try to get a job—like my sister—and go on welfare and get so much money, but then people that actually work and try and try to do something get shut down. That's a huge reason why I was pissed off for a long time. We went and sat in that filthy building in Muskegon, feeling like shit because I needed help—help that I'd been paying into now for years and years, taking taxes out. Then when I need it for a couple months? Nope, denied.

And it's not a racial thing. My nephew and my sister—who is a fucking scumbag—live in the Heights in my mom's rental house. My sister sends her scrawny little white kid—my nephew—to the Heights, and he gets the shit beat out of him all the time.

She doesn't work. She doesn't even try to work. She gets Social Security for my nephew because his dad's in prison for life. She goes, "Why would I work? I can go get a minimum wage job working forty hours and make less money than I get for sitting around all day. Why would I go work?" And I really have no argument to answer her back. Really, why would she work? You're giving her eighteen hundred dollars a month for nothing. And food stamps on top of that. And assistance for her bills. It's a fuck ton. She has a comfortable life doing nothing. Why would you go work?

My sister takes advantage of the system—rapes it. The system needs limitations. My sister needs to get cut off. She's an able-bodied person. She lives within a quarter mile of many businesses that are hiring. Meijer's is one of them—a hundred yards away. There's no reason why she can't work. That's what pisses me off the most—just laziness.

I mean, I saw her today, and I can't even stand to be around her. I can't even listen to her. The way she's raising my nephew, it's just—it's unacceptable. I told him the other weekend, I told him straight out, I said, "Your mom's a scumbag. Your only shot is going to the military." I said, "You got no other shot." He's fifteen, and he doesn't even know how to tie his fucking shoes. He came over here to work—split wood, stack wood with me last summer. I said, "I'm gonna pay you. I'm gonna pay you really good. You come over here and help me split and stack wood." Well, he pissed out after like an hour. So I told him, I said, "You know what? I don't want you to do any more work." I said, "You sit here, and you learn how to tie your shoes, and I'll give you fifty bucks." And he did it, in front of me. I said, "I wanna see you untie and tie." He did it. Five, ten times or whatever. I gave him fifty bucks. For nothing. Which I shouldn't have to do. A week later, he came out again—he had forgotten how to do it. He's fifteen years old and he doesn't know how to tie his shoes. He doesn't know how to ride a two-wheeler. How can you raise a kid like that? That's my sister.

I hate to see what this country's going to look like in fifty years, because everybody's entitled now. Everybody wants something for free. You've got kids crying over an election. That's something to cry about? Because your candidate lost, you need grief counseling? At a university? Pansies. That's what this country's raised.

What's the symbol of this country now? It used to be the broad with the muscles with the do-rag tied on making steel while her husband's across the world kicking Japs asses in the Pacific—Rosy the Riveter. Now what is it? It's a bunch of people with their hands out wanting something for free. I can see why other countries have a bad view of the United States, because the United States used to be something back in our grandparents' day. Imagine what it's going to be in fifty years.

Everything's just going to shit. The whole country's going to shit. You look at these World War II vets, people that really had a hard life, that really had a fucking terrible life—Great Depression and all that. I look at my wife's grandma—she saved onion bags. The bags that her onions came in: she saved those and used them again. Now you've got people taking their Bridge Card and buying two carts full of pop and dumping it in a parking lot? I have no sympathy for those people. None. Everybody's way too privileged around here, and that's why everything in this country is just dragged down. That's where all our money goes. Are there people that need it? Yeah, when me and my wife needed it, we really did need it. And we got shut down. Yet they're just giving it away to people that refuse to work because they make more money not working.

Something needs to change, because the shit that we're doing ain't working. It's not. We're just getting taxed and taxed and taxed, and shit's getting worse and worse and worse.

And I'm a pro-government guy. You want to spy on my phone? Spy on my phone. Whatever makes everything generally safer, I'm fine with. You want to put a camera in my TV? Watch me. I don't care. That's how it should be. Without our government, we're nothing. We are protected by this big entity that is the United States Government. If you don't like it, go to Somalia and see how you like it. Get your iPhone in Somalia? Ain't gonna happen. You'll be living on the street with beetles crawling in your ass and be starving because there's no food. Big government's good as long as it's not wasteful. But now there's too much of the "gimmee gimmee gimmee gimmee gimmee." That's what's going to be the downfall of this country.

I love Trump. I don't know why everybody's saying he's racist. I don't get it. He says stupid shit because he's a normal person, not a politician. He's not programmed. He's kind of like me. He says stupid shit. I consider him more—not down to earth, because he's a billionaire, but he's a normaler person than a normal politician. He's not focus-grouped. He didn't use his whole career to learn how to speak to the masses. He shoots from the cuff.

And really, what we've been doing hasn't been working. It's been the same shit for years and years and years. Why not try something a little bit different? Why not try a businessman? He's a businessman. He ran many successful—and failing—businesses. Which happens. I just think it's something different. Try something different. It's a breath of fresh air. I voted for him. My wife voted for him. Everybody I know voted for him. Try something different.

It can't hurt anything. I don't think it can hurt anything. I mean, maybe World War III will start because he blasts North Korea, but I'm okay with that. If things keep going the same way they've been going, we're not going to be here anyway. I can't imagine when my kids are my age trying to raise kids. I'm going to tell them to move.

Talking to a guy at the barber shop today about spanking kids. Everybody's scared to spank their kids. You know what? I pulled my kids' pants down in the middle of Meijer's and spanked their ass. I will pull my kids' pants down and spank their bare ass somewhere, and if someone wants to get in my face about it or call the cops about it, call them. If a cop walked up to me, I'd tell him to mind his own business. I don't beat my kids; I would never beat my kids. But my kids are going to toe the mark. When I was a kid, I should have been smacked a lot harder than I was; maybe I wouldn't have been so messed up for the first ten years of my adolescent life.

That's the problem—it all starts with the kids, and there's no accountability for anything in this country anymore. Everybody runs free and does whatever they want. At my son's soccer practice, you see kids running around crazy. My son started acting crazy.

I went out there, and I told him, "You listen to your coach. You do what you're supposed to do." Everybody else is running around stupid, not paying attention. They're little kids—yeah, that's fine. But there needs to be structure. There's no structure in this country anymore. I'm stern with my kids. I love them and I'll coddle them, but there's a time to be stern.

There's a difference between loving your kids and spoiling your kids—I mean literally ruining them. I've got two real smart kids. Smart as shit. My son is so smart. He knew how to read—full books—before kindergarten, because I chose to pay fifteen hundred dollars a month to send him to an early learning place. I just don't know how you can't rip the skin off your own body to give everything you can to your kids. I work two jobs for my kids, to give them the best I can give them. Which ain't the best, but it's: a warm house; it's somewhat good food; it's a quiet place to play. They're going to go to college, and I'll work another job if I have to. I will do everything in my power to give them what they need. It costs fifty grand a year to go to school? Okay, I'll figure out a way to do it.

And I'm not one of these parents that goes, "You can be the president if you want." If they wanted to be the president, I'd encourage it, but if I've got any advice for my kids, it's this— and I tell them this all the time, I tell them straight up: "If you don't go to school, and you don't get a job, and you don't do what you're supposed to do, then you're going to be living on the street with nothing." I don't sugar coat stuff for my kids. And I wish shit wouldn't have been sugar coated for me, because my mom was kind of like that—"Oh, it'll be okay. It'll be okay." It's not going to be okay. I tell them, I say, "You want to live on the street? You want to be homeless? You want to sleep in a shed in the winter?"

I lived a shitty life for quite a while, and I'm really, really happy where I'm at. I'm really happy. Yes, I wish I would have bit the bullet and went to school. I wish I wouldn't have fucked around in high school. My dad made good money. I had everything there. I just fucked off. And I've learned that there's people a lot smarter than you are in this world, and it's best to heed their advice, because all of a sudden, you'll find yourself being twenty-five years old with no education and no future except for the future you decide to make by working hard for yourself to make up for lost time. Don't think you know everything, because you don't know anything.

That would be what I've learned. That's my life lesson. I really fucked up. I did a lot of shit I really, really regret from fifteen to twenty-five years old. Because again, until you're a little bit older, you don't really know what's going on. You've got a general idea, and yeah, there are some cases that are different, but you've only got one shot at life, and it just makes everything a whole lot easier if you don't fuck it up. My life's half-gone, but this is by far the best point of my life so far.

I love it where I'm at. I love it. In the winter time, you know what I do when I piss outside? I piss swear words—"ass." Sometimes, if I really got to piss, I'll try to throw a "fuck" out there. You know— juvenile shit. I still feel like I'm sixteen. I still feel like I could go out and shotgun some beers and then drive around in the Toyota Corolla and listen to Jay-Z Hard Knock Life. It's the little things, you know? It's the little things. Sitting out here in my quiet woods. No thumping rap music. No screaming. Not a damn sound. Dead quiet. That's why I moved out here. That's why I work two jobs: for the three hours a day I've got to myself out here. Not saying I'm anti-social or anything, but I like it out here.

LYNN

"Thou shalt love thy neighbor as thyself. There is none other commandment greater."

—Mark 12:31

In Muskegon, when you walk down the street, somebody's going to look at you and say, "Hi!" It's not that way in all communities, but it is here. We really are that Middle America that so many people talk about.

Muskegon is a handshake community. When I worked at the *Chronicle*, every day there were many subscribers that were coming in to pay their bill. They didn't want to do it online; they wanted that personal connection. We didn't have answering machines for a very long time, because the editor wanted somebody to be a voice on the other end. That's how you engage. And to me, that's always been the way how a community should be led.

I got started at the *Chronicle* because, when I became a single mom, I needed to get a part-time job. I had four children at the time, so I wasn't looking for a full-time job. I needed to be a mom first.

I went to the *Chronicle* and got started in production. Mostly I was involved in design—the building of the ads and the building of the pages. When the advertising representatives would bring us the ads, we would get them ready to go on the pages.

Before I moved to full-time, I worked Tuesday through Thursday, because if my children were not with me on the weekend,

I would miss them terribly. I had Monday and Friday off. What other place would do that for you?

The *Chronicle* was an unbelievable place to work. It was a family. When I run into former colleagues, it's a hug. It's just still that way. We took care of each other there. If there were people that were financially down, we did collections. We did great things for each other, and we did great things for the community.

As the paper was growing, we provided special sections for the local schools—anti-bullying materials, or sections on history, or science, or literacy. We would get sponsorship, and all of these materials would be given to classrooms. Classrooms that could afford it would get it for the price of the newspaper that accompanied it, and classrooms that couldn't would get it free.

The *Chronicle* was wonderful in its service to the community. We were not just a newspaper. We put together events like Student Showcase at the Frauenthal Theater, the Chronicle Seaway Run, things like that. We organized events and worked with volunteers. And I was involved in that.

Then advertising went down. Social media really took hold, and then there were all of these new avenues for advertising. After that, new and younger leadership came in, and so new and younger ideas came in, and that's when consolidation started.

As things started to consolidate, I started doing more—car sections, visitors guides, that sort of thing. At the end, I was engaging writers for articles and then working and setting up those sections. I did a little bit of writing myself there, but it was more engaging others. If there was a story that needed to be written, I would do it, but I had by that time many friends that had been writers—now they were freelancers—so it was easy for me to call and say, "Hey, we're doing this section. I really want a story on this. Would you be willing to do it?" And they were so generous. They would come in and write most of the articles for those little sections.

Then, in February of 2010, I got the nod that it was my turn. I was six years too young and two and a half years short on time in to be able to retire. Sometimes life takes you in a different direction.

Now I'm in the non-profit world, involved with feeding kids. There's over nine thousand youth in Muskegon County that are nutritionally insecure, and to understand what that means, I challenge people to do this (and I have done this myself): "I want you to eat lunch, and then wait until breakfast the next day. Where does your mind go?" By evening, the need is so basic that the only thing you can think about is survival—"When am I going to eat next?" A lot of times, when you're hungry, you're very edgy— you're angry. Hunger can be quite a barrier, and our organization is just scratching the surface with the youngest kids—where the greatest impact can be made—so that they can be more successful in school and in life.

The schools that we serve are determined by the percentage of free-and-reduced price lunches among the student body. The two schools that we're currently serving are at ninety-eight percent and one hundred percent, and on our waiting list there are eleven elementary schools that are at seventy percent or higher.

What do I see as the impact of what we do? Test scores are higher. In 2013, we started serving the second, third, fourth, and fifth graders at one of the elementary schools in Muskegon Heights. We couldn't start serving all the students until December 1st, because we had only secured so much funding, but we still had some money, and the principal was such a supporter that he said, "Why don't you start serving the second and third graders now, and we'll start serving the fourth and fifth graders in December?" He wanted to do that, to touch those kids. Well, in fourth grade, in October, you take the MEAPs—the Michigan Educational Assessment Program standardized test. And then you take them again in the spring. So they took the MEAPs in October, we started serving them in December, and they took it again in March. Their test scores increased by twenty-one percent—the highest in all of Muskegon County. The principal said he was one hundred and ten percent sure that the sack suppers helped to make that happen. That's huge impact.

When kids have the stability of knowing where their next meal is coming from, discipline in the classroom is also unbelievably better. In Nelson School, when we started serving them, there was over an eighty percent drop in after-school suspensions and over a sixty percent drop in write-ups.

We had an event, and one of our directors asked one of the teachers, "Tell me what hunger looks like at Orchard View." The teacher went on to explain that she had this little boy in her third grade classroom that was very charismatic. All the kids loved him. All the kids wanted to be his friend. That was the first week. The second week it was still: everybody wanted to be his friend—just a good kid. By week three he was grumpy and kind of short with the other kids. And week four, he was almost lethargic. So the teacher was wondering, "What's going on?" She thought that this could be a discipline thing. Well, then the next month came and this boy was charismatic again and all the kids wanted to be his friend. That's when she realized that it was not a behavioral problem—it was a nutritional problem. His family had got their food stamps. That's what hunger looked like for that little boy.

But what I've seen is not only statistics that let me know we're impacting the community—I've actually had the privilege of seeing the kids when they receive the sack suppers, and of talking with the teachers. I've seen the need and the impact of stability in a child's life—it changes who they are. I am fortunate to be that leader, but I am more honored to be working side-by-side with people that believe in this mission and are having such great impact in the community. That's why I'm here.

We have about two hundred and ten volunteers that come in our door every week. We have all these businesses that are supportive. We have law enforcement that helps us deliver. So it is a community taking care of a community problem. We have kids from schools come in, so we even have kids helping kids—one out of five kids is nutritionally insecure, but five out of five kids can help. And these kids want to help. They don't want to just receive. They want to be part of the helping process as well.

And so do their parents. That's what I've learned: there's so many reasons why children are hungry. There's two-parent working families that still have barriers. I know that first hand, because even after I got remarried and we were a two-parent working family again, our children always had enough food, but our children did get free-and-reduced lunch.

Things are different from when we had our children and we were low-income, because the cost of transportation, the cost of insurance, the cost of housing, the cost of education—all of those things have gone up. Child care costs are unbelievable for those working families. The reality is that the cost of living is different from what it used to be, and it's too high even for some families to meet with two parents working.

It was much easier for me too, because I worked at the *Chronicle* and they had different things for the families to do. Even though we were low-income, our children never even knew that, because they could still go to Michigan's Adventure and ride the roller coasters once a year through my work; we could get a couple tickets to the symphony at the Frauenthal and take one of the kids. We had that ability for them to experience things. Plus we were involved in all the sports.

When my oldest son was in Pony League, my husband and his cousin were the head coaches, and they wanted me to coach with them. I'm an athletic mind, and I was very athletic when I was younger. The dream was always to be the first woman football official, but then the children started coming, and so that didn't happen. But when my husband asked me to help out with baseball, I said, "Okay." I was the first base coach.

Then later, when our youngest son was seven or eight, we were looking for coaches for his team. I'm a very old-fashioned woman. I was born in 1960. My father worked at Campbell — Wyant & Cannon, and my mother didn't. Mom stayed home, dad worked; you knew your neighbors, you played outside till it was time to come in—it was that real Middle America family. So I was a firm believer that there needed to be men leadership, but there wasn't anyone else prepared to step in and be the head coach, and so I took on that role. I had men assistants, because I wanted the boys to have mentors. These young boys needed to have men around them—especially those that did not have fathers in their home. There weren't a lot of those, but there were some. They needed men around them. They didn't necessarily need another mom. But I helped out where there was that need.

I had a little different philosophy when you work with those younger kids. My philosophy as a baseball coach was: first of all, you engage the parents. I said, "I'm going to tell you right now, that I'm probably going to go up to your son and put my arm around him and give him a kiss on the top of the head, so if you aren't comfortable with that, this probably isn't the team that you need." Then, if their child needed to go to the restroom in the middle of practice, the parent grabbed their child's glove and they took that position until the kid got back. So engaging them, talking to them, making them a part of it—it's a lot harder to be angry at someone who you've worked with and who you know and who you like than it is to be angry at somebody who you don't. Because of that engagement, when Coach Lynn would say, "I need you to not do that," if their child did not react right away, then the parent would be very supportive of me. The parents became part of the team as well.

I think that one of the most special things that ever happened to me was just a few years ago when the father of a child that I coached fifteen years before stopped me in the gas station and said, "I need you to know that you were the best coach that my son ever had." That meant a lot to me, that this shy little boy was able to get something out of baseball. Those are the really important things. I think if you've never had much money—and I didn't grow up with it—then you learn what's important and you learn to live within your means. That's what I've taught my children: "Find something you love to do and live within your means, and then you will be happy."

Even today, we're lower-middle income. When my husband and I got married, he was a DJ. He was in radio in the military. *Good Morning, Vietnam*—that was my husband. That's what he did. He was the Lonn Man. He was there when they closed Rock 95 down, then he went to WKBZ, then his final radio job was WCXT in Oceana County. That's when we realized that we were not able to support the family with him in radio. It was not do-able. I had the four kids, and then we had two more. So that's when he got re-trained and went to work at the hospital. He's been at Mercy Hospital for the last twenty-six years.

He is now a chief steward at Mercy, and so he's been able to play a role with the employees' union there. I am a firm believer in a good union. Key word there is *good*. It's not just that management is fair, but that the workers are responsible workers. Unions don't always have to protect people that are not good workers; they should be about promoting fairness. But with Right to Work and stuff like that, I feel that I have watched things go from good and fair to many people working fifty-five hours a week for less money. At the *Chronicle* back in the '80s and '90s, everyone wanted to be salaried, because if you worked overtime, you still got time-and-a-half. Now salaries, if you get a salary, that just means that if you work over forty hours, you're working for free.

I'm scared as I watch more and more people work longer hours, be away from their family longer, live more stressed lives, because more stressed lives causes even more divorce, more divorce causes more stressful financial situations, and that leads to more kids that don't have their bills paid and maybe don't have the food they need on their table.

So am I concerned about where America is? I think that there's some trying times that are coming. The cost of education was a hardship for most of my children. In 1978, I could go to the Career Tech Center at Muskegon Community College and get all the training I needed in one semester. I only needed one semester at college to get started in a career, and after that career came to an end I could still make that transition from the newspaper into the non-profit sector because I had all those years of professional experience and leadership and support from my bosses. I think that will be a little different for my children.

If the question is, "Am I concerned that Donald Trump is our leader?" then the answer is, "I'm anxious to see what he can do." Daggone it, he's got to get off the Twitter. He's like a middle school girl on there. But I'm a person of second-chances, so I would just say, "Back off and give him a chance." I had to quit listening to the morning show that I used to watch for years. I can't even watch it now. ABC News. I can't. Because it's just all about him. I don't want to hear about it. I am angered by the fact that President Trump is spending so much time warding off punches in the gut from people that just won't let him breathe.

Normally I'm one of those people that are really a Republican supporter because of my moral beliefs. That's more where I stand as a person. Like I said, I'm an old-fashioned woman. I'm not this big women's rights activist. I'm mission-driven, and my mission is children. I'm very proud to be a right-to-life supporter, and feminist groups tend not to be there. I didn't do cartwheels over voting for either one of the candidates this year, but you have to vote, and I voted for Trump. I voted for Trump because of the Supreme Court.

It's not something we really talk about around here. A lot of the volunteers are pretty vocal about being anti-Trump, and that can be uncomfortable. It's just one of those things that you don't discuss at work, because it only distracts from the mission.

I have lived my life to be kind, to treat others the way I want to be treated, and to think of others first. I spent my life trying to be a really good person—a good Christian—to care for others above myself and be "inclusive" and all of these new words. Those are things that I was taught to do, but those weren't the words that were used.

Words change over generations, and so all of these words that are challenging whether I did it right or not—that has been very challenging for me personally. For example, I think of "compassion" as a good thing, then I hear other people say, "Compassion is enabling," and I'm like, "What? No. Time out. No. True compassion is not enabling." These are things that have really come into my life and caused me great anxiety—words like "empathy" and "bias." Those kinds of misunderstandings can be really hard.

I think the generation coming up needs to learn how to really listen to their elders. Every generation comes in—just like mine did—and we have a vision of what we think is the direction that things should go in. I'm sure the generation that came before me was concerned about me—that's just the rite of passage, I guess—but still, the greatest thing I learned how to do was to listen to people older than me. I learned more, not only from their successes, but through their ability to tell you what they wish they could have done better. If you engage them, you're going to learn from what they did, and it will make your job easier. That's the biggest thing that I learned, and it's something that I continue to do. Because they have so much to give to us. They really are so important. We can't do it without their knowledge. You don't need to re-invent the wheel. And so sometimes, I think that the new generation really needs to close their mouths and open their ears just a little bit more, because there's so much more that they can learn. That will make them better people, better leaders, and it will make the community stronger.

That's really what this is all about: building stronger communities. In this community, I think that people care more about the well-being of the person next to them than they do about where they're getting in life, and that's why Muskegon is such a wonderful place to be a part of. I think that we care about each other individually. I think it matters to people here whether or not kids have food; it matters to people whether or not someone has electricity; it matters if someone can't get to work because their vehicle broke down; it matters whether or not, when somebody's sitting on the side of the road because he's homeless, you look him in the eye and say, "Hi." That matters here. It matters because it's our responsibility. And what I haven't seen change in the last forty years is that caring. I'm really proud of the community that I live in. It continues to care, even when times get tough.

BILL

"There is a close bond between these two elements—freedom and productive industry."

—Alexis de Tocqueville*

You look at Muskegon forty years ago—there were huge industries around. All the foundries: you had Lakey Foundry; you had West Michigan Steel; you had Campbell — Wyant & Cannon; you had Clover Foundry, which was in my mom's family. There were all these manufacturers that made things— Lift Tech and Sealed Power and Bennett Pump and Continental Motors. You could come out of high school and step into a job that would bring you up into the middle class. Now you can find a job making twelve, thirteen bucks an hour doing something, but how are people supposed to live on that? You've got all these people who are a paycheck away from going over the edge. I've seen that change take place.

I was born here in Muskegon, but I didn't grow up here. My dad's family is from the Grand Rapids area. My mother's family is from here. All German. My great grandmother was from Germany, came over on the boat. Great grandfather was born here in Grand Rapids. He was a tinsmith. My grandfather was the first one in the family to graduate from high school. Then his son—my dad—graduated from Muskegon Heights back in the day. He graduated in '42, then went right into the service. He was a medic. Went through

D-Day and the Battle of the Bulge and then came back and went to Harvard—Harvard School of Government. He actually graduated with Henry Kissinger, in the same class. He and my mother got married while he was in school. My older brother was born while they were still in Boston, and coming out of there, Dad got a job with a brokerage firm—it was Paine Webber, now it's UBS. He moved back to Muskegon to work. I was born in '51. Dad died in '52 of polio—there was a big epidemic in this area of polio back then. And so it was my mother, my brother and I. We were here until '59, when we moved to Greenwich, Connecticut, where my mother had a sister. I was actually the backdoor neighbor to George Bush Sr.'s dad, Prescott Bush. He was a Senator, and I was his paperboy. And this was back when paperboys didn't just throw the paper up on the porch—they placed it in different places. At Senator Bush's house, we put it on the kitchen table. Every morning, I came in the back door and put his newspaper on the table.

We left there in '63 and moved to just south of San Francisco. That's where another sister of my mother's lived. I finished high school there in '69. Within weeks after I finished high school, I was in the Navy. While I was in boot camp, my mother remarried to a gentleman who she had known here in Muskegon. They had gone to high school together. Actually, he had married her best friend, but she had passed away of cancer, so he called my mom and they got married. I stayed in the service until '73. I was stationed mostly in south Texas, in the aviation division—I fixed airplanes. When I got out, my mother and her husband were in Ohio, so I went to school at Ohio University. That's where I met my wife.

I got a degree in art—photography and painting. I came back up here just to earn enough money to go back and get my master's, and then I kind of got into manufacturing. I've always been mechanical, and I really enjoyed it. I got started working for the same company that my grandfather had worked for. My cousin was the president, and I started doing engineering work for him. I was there for eight years, and the company was going to be sold, and I had the opportunity to buy a small machine shop, so I bought it. Went into a lot of debt. I was pretty naïve—didn't know what the heck I was really doing. It was kind of a fluke.

I bought it from a guy who had bought it as an investment and really wasn't hands-on. Sales were something like fifty grand a year. No business survives on that. It took several years to get the thing turned around and get it rolling. A lot of it was just: I had more time than money, and so I was just there all the time. A lot of it was just plain luck: maybe I was at the right spot at the right time. I was close to shutting it down. It had been about a year and a half, and the guy that I bought it from was also financing—he was carrying the note, and I was making payments to him. One day we had lunch, and he said, "So what're you gonna ship this month?" I said, "Ah, it's not too good. We're only gonna ship about ten thousand bucks." He said, "Any horse's ass can ship ten thousand dollars." And I said, "Well, if they got the sales, yeah."

I had quoted a job—a little turn part for a company called Morbark up in Winn, Michigan. They make woodchippers. And so I called this guy, Ira Bateman, and I said, "You know that part I quote? How is that?" He said, "Oh no, that didn't fly. We're not gonna do that one." He said, "You do any milling?" I said, "Yeah." He said, "Well we been tryin to cut these parts here for days, and we got one done, and it's not right. We need some help. I'll Fedex you the drawings." There were no faxes back then, so I got the drawings the next day, and I kind of had an idea that these were pretty expensive parts, so I quoted him and he said, "Can you come up?" I drove up there and I walked out with a sixty-thousand-dollar order. I thought I'd died and gone to heaven. We started making these parts for them, and that's the company that saved my bacon.

Then things finally started to roll. All of a sudden, we were doing a hundred and fifty, two hundred thousand dollars a month. We were running out of space. But that was just luck. That and the fact that we were able to do the work. But you sit there and you look at the forks in the road: if not for this, then what would I be doing? Just in life in general, you know? Had my dad not died, I'd have grown up in Boston (he was being transferred to Boston). Had my mother not remarried, I'd have gone back to California and wouldn't have gone to Ohio and wouldn't have met my wife. There are all these little forks in the road as you go through. You've got to take what you're given and make what you can out of it.

Because things are always changing. Twenty-some years ago, we had an opportunity. I met this guy at Shaw Walker (they're still over in Norton Shores; somebody bought them and they have a different name, which escapes me, but they're still in town). Anyway, this guy was in charge of their tool room, and they had a machine called a Savinini. It was an Italian machine that moved sheet metal around. It had a plunger that would come down and move the metal around so that a punch could punch holes in it. And there was a shaft about a foot, foot-and-a-half long, and it was designed—in case something happened—to break so as not to damage the rest of the machine. Well, SavininI was charging them three hundred dollars apiece when these things broke, and the problem was, usually you didn't break just one, you broke two. So every time they bumped the machine, it was six hundred bucks—and they had several of these machines. This guy from Shaw Walker came to me, and he knew we did some machining, and he asked me to come in. He said his guys had been trying to duplicate this shaft. He said, "It's been eight hours, and they still just can't get it." They were all on manual machines in their tool room—their tool room was kind of antiquated. Well, I looked at the shaft, and I said, "We'll have you a sample back tomorrow morning." This was around five o'clock in the evening, and we had a second shift working. All he said was, "This is what I want," and at nine thirty the next morning I handed him a brand-new shaft.

I think I charged him thirty-one dollars, and I could have made them all day long and done so well at thirty-one. It was just ridiculous. But it was the technology. It was the machine we had in our shop that allowed us to do that. Those guys in his tool room were so frustrated. They were true machinists. I mean, they knew how to cut metal. They knew the feel of it probably much better than what my guys understand, because guys now on these big CNC machines, they don't have the feel. They understand, and they know as much as they need to. But the artisans, the machinists before? Man.

One of the things I see, kids today say, "I'm a CNC programmer." Well, you're playing a video game, in essence. Kids love to do that. But you don't understand what the machine is doing. "Why are you running it at that speed? Why don't you want it faster? You can't do that, so you have to run it slower." They don't understand cutting metal; they understand programming machines. And so the cutting metal part is what we really have to get an understanding of.

The progression of the machines—they'll chew gum, they'll whistle, and they'll jump up and down all at the same time. It's high-tech. When I first came up here, almost forty years ago now, I got put in a machine shop as a management trainee, and when you started to make the machine move, you'd turn a crank. Back then we had what was called NC—numerical control. You had to program the whole thing, and it was actually a paper tape. So I would hand-write a program, then I would type it into a machine that was called a flex writer, and then there were these big rolls of paper tape that would feed through with a series of dots, and the spacing of the dots and the number of dots would make up a code, and you fed that into the machine. Every time that program ran, you had to run that paper through there. Then, the next version had some memory, so once you put the tape in there, it could repeat that program. Then we got to the CNC—computer numerical control—where you could program it right at the machine. Before, we would take a drawing, and I'd look at it and figure out what it's going to take to make this thing, but now, with the software we use, you pull the drawing into the computer. You pull the geometry right off the page and program it automatically. Now that's the forging.

It's phenomenal. Years ago, when I worked at Westran, I was in the inspection department, and I had to do everything with a height gauge: bring it up, touch off, bring it down, look at the dial, write it down, then do the math. Now, with the vision systems for inspection, you can pass a part under a system that will inspect it completely in just a matter of seconds—all of these dimensions, and very accurately. Our laser scanner takes hundreds of thousands of data points in thirty seconds. The whole thing is progressing so rapidly that you just don't need as many people on the floor.

And you don't need the same kinds of skill sets. My neighbor when I was first in business down in the Norton Industrial Center was a pattern maker. He made wood patterns. To make a casting, you started out with what was called a wood master. They would take a paper drawing, look at it, and out of a chunk of wood they would machine this model. Then from that wood model, they would make a steel mold that would separate so that you could pour in metal to create the shape you wanted.

Well, every other year I go to this show in Chicago. It's called the machine tools show. IMTS—International Manufacturing Technology Show—but we just call it the machine tools show. A few years ago down there, I was watching this machine that does something called LOM—laminated object manufacturing. A sheet of paper is about eight-thousandths thick, and what this machine did was it took a sheet of paper and laid the paper down, and it did a cut with a laser, and then the machine pushed the paper down under force. Then another sheet came in, and it laid it down and cut it and pushed it down and glued it to the previous sheet. Then it laid another one down and cut and glued it down and laid another one down and over and over and over again. It would build up about an inch an hour, so over the course of twenty-four hours, you could build up something twenty-four inches. When it was finished, you pulled the whole block out, and because it was all perforated, you just broke off what you didn't want, and here was this valve body sitting there that was a wood master that was printed with paper in a day. All that was left to do was sand it, and it was done. In twenty-four hours. This guy—my neighbor—it would have taken him weeks to make that. I saw that and I came back and I said, "Ron, you gotta see this." And he retired. He closed up. Not just because of that. He was getting on. But he could see the writing on the wall.

The pattern maker was this artisan—part science, but so much of it was art to get that thing done. Now it's a drawing that you can sit there and feed into the computer. You still have to make the patterns, but now the computer is what you start with. You don't need the master. You start with a model, you put that data into the computer, and it just sits there and cuts it. You go right from the drawing to the pattern. Period. Nothing in-between. No hands.

For me it's fascinating, but it's also a tad frustrating, because of the speed at which this stuff changes. You learn one thing, and then you've got to learn the next thing and the next thing. When I was thirty-five, forty, forty-five, fifty, that was one thing, but now I'm sixty-six almost and I'm sitting here thinking, "Shit, I don't wanna learn any more of this. I wanna learn to do something else."

But I enjoy making things. I love it. To say you can take a chunk of metal and casting and turn it into something that's used? That's really a gratifying thing for me—to see a truck go down the road and say, "I got parts on that." We got sent a video from SKF, and there's this train going down the track, and I said, "We made that." That's cool. I love that.

Except, here in town, we don't really make the finished products anymore. We still have some component manufacturers, but there are no more large industrial producers. That's a change. When I got started, that's where my customer base was: all local customers, all local companies. Lift Tech, Clark Floor, Sealed Power, Bennett Pump—that's who we did work for. They supported all of these smaller shops. But they're gone. The companies we do work for now, they're: Caterpillar, not manufactured here; Harley Davidson, not here; John Deere, not here; SKF, not here. My son Nik is heading to California on Sunday to meet with two customers who we think we have a pretty good chance of making product for. Go find customers in California—that's what you have to do in this area now in order to survive in this business.

Muskegon, the one thing about it, you know, it's a gorgeous place—and I think it's changing finally—but there's just always something wrong. Forty years ago, when I came back, everybody said, "Muskegon's just about to take off." Well, it's still on the runway. I came back when I was twenty-seven, and they had just finished building the mall downtown. They had demolished the old Western Avenue and put in the mall, but it just never seemed to do what they wanted it to do. And as soon as the new Lakes Mall was built out in Fruitport Township, things went from bad to worse as far as having something to bring people downtown. When they finally tore down the downtown mall, my daughter, Stacy, was back for her first summer from University of Detroit Mercy. She was working at an architectural firm, and they looked at Muskegon and they called it little Beirut, because that's what it looked like. It was just rubble. And now you've still got big hunks of Western Avenue that are just sand. They use the lots for volleyball tournaments in the summer—sand volleyball. My daughter-in-law opened up a yoga studio down there, and on either side of the yoga studio you've got piles of dirt. I guess there are some buildings that are in the planning stage to try to bring some stuff back, but it's not there yet.

I do think there's a lot of good things starting to happen. The thing that's impressed me recently is that there's a lot of young energy. I'm not the young energy anymore, but kids—young adults—in their mid-to-late thirties, they're really doing stuff downtown. You've got stuff going on at night. We go to yoga, and there's no place to park because everybody's going to Unruly Brewing or Pigeon Hill brewery or somewhere. There's a lot going on, and that never was the case before. There are a lot of young people who have got some great ideas, and they're willing to stick around because the quality of life in Muskegon is so high in terms of the natural beauty, but I'm saying this from a North Muskegon perspective—not living in the inner city.

So here's a tangent: I spent twelve years on a charter school's school board. I was one of around six local businesspeople who were trying to get a millage passed for vocational education in Muskegon, because all the schools were doing away with it—they needed room for computers, everybody had to go to college, times were changing, all of that.

We wanted kids to have some other options. When I was a kid in California, we had a foundry in our shop. We had an auto shop. We had electric. We had drafting. We had woodshop. Vocational education was a big part of schooling back then, because most people sort of understood that not everybody was going to go to college—and in California, college was free. It was free. You just had to pay for your books.

Anyhow, we tried to get this millage passed, and it failed twice, so we just went ahead and started Waypoint Academy. I thought, "How the hell do you start a school?" You know? Well, we got this company from out east that ran for-profit schools. We got them in here, and we tried to get people interested and educated in more hands-on type activities. You still had to pass your solid academic classes, but the kids that we were trying to get were those that were more interested in some kind of real-world training. We went out around and we went to churches and we had open houses and we talked to people about coming to the school. We tried to introduce them to the trades.

We ended up getting a group of kids that were just so totally challenged from all aspects: socially, academically, legal issues. Then the company that we hired, they did a horrible job. Just terrible. They didn't hire the right staff. They didn't have really a clue of what they were going to do with the group of kids that they got. They were so overwhelmed with problems. It wasn't like these kids were going to just come in and sit down and learn. We had parents fighting in the hallway. After a week, the principal was just hiding in his office—he wouldn't come out. It was like the inmates were in charge of the asylum.

But we did get the thing rolling. We fired that company and hired our own principal, and we did it ourselves. It was mostly just force of will. We had to expel kids. We had to get the thing under control. The remediation that we had to do was just tremendous.

But you know, we had some kids that came in and just clicked. They were so successful, because they were in a different environment where they were able to be themselves. And so, for a few years, after we got things ironed out, it went really well.

But I got a real rude awakening about the reality of so many families in the area that are so challenged. We had kids coming in in the seventh grade that read at a second-grade level. We had kids that had been held back and held back. We had seventeen-year-old freshmen. Some of these kids, the best thing that happened to them was coming to school. They didn't have a home life. They didn't have the support. They would be the first ones there in the morning—as early as they could get there—and then we had to ask them to leave at night, you know, "We're locking the door," because they didn't want to go home. We had homeless kids. We had a lot of homeless kids—homeless with their family, homeless by themselves—and we didn't realize it at the time, until things started unraveling with them a little bit.

Anyway, each year we added a grade. We started with seventh, eighth, and ninth, and we added a grade every year until we got up to twelfth. So after four years, we had our first graduating class.

Then, No Child Left Behind was passed by the federal government, and that mandated that the overall school had to measure up to a certain standard. The problem was, every kid that we got came in with such a deficit with regard to their learning achievement— I mean three, four years behind—that the authorization had to tell us, "You guys aren't cutting it from an academic standpoint." Never mind that we were making progress with the kids—every time we got new kids, we were back in the remediation business. We were just on a slippery slope, and we saw that the handwriting was on the wall, so we closed the school.

I was pretty upset when it happened. It's a double standard. I asked, "What are you gonna do with these kids? What are you gonna do with them? They're gonna be in jail if we're not taking care of them somehow—educating them in just the basics." It was an experience.

More than anything else, that's the thing that opened my eyes to the challenges that so many families in this area face. From that perspective, Muskegon has got a lot of hurdles to overcome. You know, all boats rise supposedly, but if you're not in a boat, it can be kind of tough. That's the thing that I get worried about. You sit there and you look at all these people who are just a paycheck away from just going down.

My average wage for my guys is twenty-five to twenty-six dollars, plus benefits. I've got a ton of guys making sixty-five to seventy-thousand dollars a year. But the ability of people to manage their money? It never fails to amaze me that some of the guys are just hand-to-mouth, regardless of what they're making.

You've got a breakdown of a society. When I was growing up with a single mom, there were very few single moms. Now we send checks to the friend of the court for child support—I've got guys sending them to three women. How do you survive? And I'm sure that's always happened, but there are just so many people right on the edge now. You look around and you have to say, "Things aren't as rosy as some people think."

And then on the other side of the coin there's this idea that all these people are coming in here from Mexico and taking our jobs. Well that's so much crap. We can't find people now. Manufacturing isn't dying, but it's changed drastically. Trump saying, "I'm gonna bring back all these good jobs," that's so much bullshit, because what's taken the jobs is the technology. Policy might have had some impact, but technology is the biggest part. When cheap labor can't compete with technology, that's when the jobs are lost.

For example, I just today got feedback on a job we quoted recently. My competitor was trying to manufacture a similar part in China, and it failed. It was a really complicated part, and they weren't able to do it over there. That's work that was going to leave if they could have offshored it, but they just couldn't do the job over there. We see a lot of work like that coming back from China to the foundries because of their quality control in certain types of technologies. Caterpillar casting technologies is one—if you get a bad casting, you may not know it until it breaks, because there can be problems internally, problems metallurgically, mechanically. And so production is coming back, but I don't see large numbers of jobs following it. The technology just doesn't require that many people.

Case in point: We had a cell in the middle of the shop, and it took five guys to run that cell before we got a robot in there—then it took one guy. That's it. The robot loaded and unloaded the machine and put the part in the pods, then we assembled it. When we automated that, we didn't lay anybody off, but we were so much more efficient doing it that way. Machine vision now: Where before you would have just a pile of castings sitting in a gong waiting to be machined, now this robot with machine vision can come in and look at the damn part and—*wkch*—it recognizes how it's lying there, and it goes and grabs it. Then it'll set it on an intermediate station so another one knows exactly how it's going to be presented to it, and it takes off. Those are the things that are causing the good jobs to go—what were considered good jobs.

We still need people, and we can train people, but these machines are extremely expensive, and they're very complicated. You have to have a head on your shoulders to operate them, and it's difficult to get somebody interested enough to really get into it. You have people walk in the door, and they're looking for a job. So I say, "What do you wanna do? What do you wanna do as a career?" And they say, "Aaah, I just need a job." There's no forethought as far as what this is. Back in the day, when you had vocational education and people had some exposure to the trades, then they had some understanding of what we do. That's increasingly no longer the case.

We have openings, and we can't find people. We just had a temp. We normally bring them in through the temp agency, keep them on for ninety days, and then we hire them. If we're going to keep them, we don't keep them as a temp—we hire them in and give them benefits. We had this guy—hell of a good worker. He'd been here a month and a half, and right in the middle of a shift, he said, "You know, I think I'm gonna go to Louisiana." He just walks out the door. We're like, "Shit, he was a good worker." He was a good worker.

We've had these discussions internally—you used to just bring people in and say: "This is what we want you to do. Now go do it." Now we have to treat millennials different. So we have a welcome kit. We give them a hat. We give them a t-shirt. We bring them up and we put them in a classroom for two or three hours, and we kind of talk about what we're going to do. Then we take them down on the floor and let them work for a few hours. We do this for a week, this touchy-feely stuff. It's a different animal.

So by saying, "These twelve million people are freeloaders," that's so much horse crap. They're trying to make a living just like everybody else. And where the heck are we going to find people to replace these people with? Trump drives me nuts. And I couldn't vote for Hillary, but I didn't vote for him, and that's the first time in my adult life that I didn't vote for President. Every time I see him on TV, it's just so surreal. I'm just like, "Is this really happening?" It's nuts.

But it's not too tough to understand. Like I said, if you walk out of here, unemployment is real low. Anybody can go work in retail for ten bucks an hour. But when you get outside of North Muskegon and see all these people who are just one paycheck away from going over the edge, is it really such a shock that they'd vote to blow the whole thing up?

KURT

"America loves an underdog."
—*well-worn cliché*

North Muskegon? That just wasn't my style. I came into North Muskegon in middle school, so I didn't grow up with nobody there. I was kind of the juvenile delinquent of the school. I was raised by my mom, and my mom was pretty lenient on me, so I did what I wanted and ended up where I was.

What haven't I gotten into? I've done anything and everything under the sun. I fell into some bad habits. When it comes to narcotics and stuff, I've done everything except for heroin. I've seen people overdose. I've seen people get stabbed, shot. I've seen it all.

Actually caught my concealed weapon while I was still in high school. I was dating this girl and got pulled over going to pick up her prescription. Cop was like, "Your car smells like marijuana. Mind if we search it?" I was like, "I don't care. I ain't got nothin here." Well, they search and they found a dagger about six inches long from tip to handle, but seeing how daggers are illegal in the state of Michigan, they got me for a concealed weapon. I was like, "Fuck, I didn't even remember I had that knife in there." I had took it from a girl I used to date, because she was a cutter. I took the knife from her so she had one less thing to cut herself with. Didn't even do no jail time for that one. I was seventeen years old.

Then caught my home invasion because I had someone who owed me money and wasn't paying me. I went and got my money, and they called the cops. That was right after graduation. I got locked up for my home invasion on September 14th, 2001.

I got out and I fell on hard times. I had my hands into everything. I had black market guns. I was selling drugs. Stealing cars for money. The guy that I was working with had people in Grand Rapids and Detroit that he'd take the cars to. They'd basically take them to a chop shop. They'd strip the cars down, change out the VIN numbers, and resell them. The way it goes is, you can steal a brand-new car, buy a wrecked version of the same make, model, year, color and everything of the car you stole, take them to the shop, switch out all the VIN numbers, and you've got a brand-new car. It's got the rebuilt title, but nothing is wrong with it, and you paid a fraction of the price for it. And for the guys who are stealing them, you can get a couple hundred dollars, or you can get a couple thousand dollars. It all depends on the kind of car you took.

But what got me busted was, I was out joyriding. I was on the east side of town, over by the townhouses on Marquette. Me and my buddy were out drinking and didn't feel like walking home and so—"Ah, fuck it. There's a car. That's an easy one right there." Popped the lock, got in there, popped the ignition out. Boom. We were out driving around in that thing all damn day. What got us busted is, his dad's girlfriend happened to have the same car at his house, and I was going to take it up there and switch out the VINs and keep the car. I parked the car we stole in the old ramp down there on Clay. I was painting the hood the same color as her car's to make it look a little less conspicuous. Soon as I got done spraying the hood, then the cop comes in. Just doing a routine check. I took off running, because I was already on probation for home invasion. Got around by Jefferson Towers to find the cops with their guns drawn, and I just dropped to the ground like, "Yep, I'm not goin nowhere." The cop that arrested me was the same one that got me for the home invasion. He was like, "Let me guess, you're smokin that fuckin crack again, aren't you?" I looked at him, I was like, "Guess what, fucker? I'm sober this time." He was like, "Hey, you know what they gave me for throwin your little punk ass on the ground?" "Ah, what'd they give you?" "Oh, they gave me my own office." I was like, "Oh, they gave you your own office for bein a dick, huh?" Yeah, I was a mouthy fucker.

I did two years across in state prison. The judge was Nick's dad. I've seen Nick since I got out. They were on the trolley party bus thing for someone's wedding or something. He told me, he was like, "My dad didn't want to send you to prison, but with the guidelines and the points you've had with your juvenile, basically he had to. But if it was up to him, he woulda just gave you probation." In all honesty though, I'm kind of glad he did send me to prison, because it opened my eyes up to a lot of things. I've been clean ever since. I haven't touched nothing—just my beer and my Jack and my liquor—but drugs I haven't touched since oh-one. I have sixteen years. My car theft, joyriding: it was all stupid shit. Learned from all of it.

I found a job within a week after getting out of prison. I just got out there, busted my ass. I was putting in applications anywhere and everywhere, from shops to restaurants. I actually got hired in right on the spot at Arby's on Henry Street. The manager looked at the application and he was like, "Oh, you're on parole, aren't ya?" I was sitting there thinking, "Fuck." I say, "Yeah, I am." He says, "That means you gotta work, huh?" I'm like, "Yes, sir. It does." He says, "Alright. Be here tomorrow at seven a.m." I'm like, "Okay, I'll be here."

I worked for a while there. Lived with my dad. I had to live somewhere, and my step-dad didn't let me go back to my mom's because he didn't want a felon in the house. Hypocrite—his son's been in and out of prison three times now. But I lived with my dad.

I worked at Arby's. I worked at Henry Street Grill. And I was going to college full time, studying culinary arts.

I got screwed over by my dad. Got kicked out because I decided to go out and have a birthday drink for my twenty-first birthday. Well, seeing as how I was on parole, I'm not supposed to be drinking. My dad called my parole officer, parole officer called the cops, the cops come, give me a breathalyzer. I blew point zero six. But I'm not supposed to drink at all, so they lock me up for the night. Got out, all my stuff was at the end of my dad's driveway. Alright.

I ended up staying in a program called TLP—Transitional Living Placement. While I was there, I was working two jobs and going to college still. I was the first person to complete the program. Got money saved up. Ended up getting my own house.

Met my first wife. Ended up having a kid—had my oldest. We split up and she moved down to Lansing. I stayed up here.

I stayed up here for a while. This is home. Didn't have no place to go, because the house that we had—the city came in and condemned it saying the landlord never should have even rented it out. Stayed where I could. Slept down at Heritage Landing, down in the little tunnels that the kids crawl through. I done crashed down there at night. I would stay at friends' houses when I could.

I ended up moving down to Lansing with my ex-wife. Started working things out. Lived down in Lansing about a year and a half. We split up. I ended up coming back home. Lived with a friend. Ended up moving back down to Lansing again because I found out she was pregnant. She was going to have an abortion, and I told her, "If you have an abortion, you will never hear of me or speak to me again." She didn't have the abortion.

I ended up living down in Lansing for about five, six years altogether before I moved back up here. Down there I worked for a shop called Peckham Industries, sewing military clothing. Shit job. I literally worked on a sewing machine for seven dollars an hour. Twelve hour days fucking seven days a week. That was money. Got me by.

Then my ex-wife ended up having my kids taken from her. I fought about two years to get custody of my kids, because the judge was like, "Reunification with mom, reunification with mom." Well, mom kept dating (if you don't mind my language) niggers that would like to beat her ass. And she continued smoking pot. And the court finally got fed up with her shit and said, "Reunification with dad."

Well, at that time I wasn't working. I was on unemployment, and they told me I needed a job and I needed a bigger place if the kids were going to live with me. This, that, and the other thing. I found another job, but I was basically living at that time in the VOA, which is a homeless shelter in Lansing. I worked first shift, so I would get out of work at like two-thirty, go back to the shelter, sign in so I had my bed for the night, then from three to eight I'd walk around the corner to the titty bar and sit in the titty bar until I could get into the shelter at eight o'clock. Got free drinks from the dancers that I knew.

I fell into a really bad depression. That's when I caught my DUI. Me and this stripper I was fucking around with, we killed a fifth in a half hour—sitting there in the car just passing a fifth back and forth. Stopped at the store, she bought another fifth. Sitting there passing it back and forth. It was winter out. I went to go stop—ended up sliding into someone's rear. Cops show up and I'm sitting there with my tire iron trying to pull the fender out of my tire so I can take off. They gave me a breathalyzer—I blew point one six five. I was over double the limit.

In court, they tried holding that against me, and I was like, "You can try to hold it against me if you want. Legally you can't because of the fact that I am over the age of twenty-one. It's not in my stipulations that I cannot drink. The case is not against me, it's against my ex-wife. And another fact: my kids were not in the vehicle with me." But my kids got taken.

Ended up getting a house. Got my kids back. Then the job
I had started cutting hours back and I started pulling back on my
rent. I was actually in Muskegon visiting my mom and was told by
a buddy that was staying with me, "The landlord showed up and
slapped an eviction notice on the door." My mom told me, "Go down
there, pack up what you can in the van. You and the kids can move
back home." Been back in Muskegon ever since.

B ack here I've had a few jobs. Being a felon, it's not easy getting a decent job in this town. I moved back in oh-nine, and
basically it was temp jobs all the way through. I had a job when
I was fighting for custody of my daughter, and they had a policy:
"No cell phones on the shop floor." Well, I was fighting for custody of my daughter with Child Protective Services—fighting her
mom for custody. I had my phone on me, and I went into the bathroom, because I got a message from the caseworker. So I texted
her back. I'm sitting there in the stall texting back and forth with
CPS. Get done, come walking out—there's the plant manager and
my shift supervisor standing right there. Plant manager looks at
me, he's like, "You done texting?" I looked him dead in the eye
and I said, "Honestly, to tell you the truth, no I'm not." He looked
at my supervisor, he's like, "Well, he's your employee. You can do
with him what you want." I look right at them both and said, "You
know something? I'm in the middle of a custody battle fighting
for my daughter through CPS right now. You guys can do what the
fuck you wanna do with me." I was like, "Jobs come and go, but
my daughter ain't goin nowhere." I was like, "If you wanna fire
me, fire me. I'll get another job within a week, but my daughter
comes before anything and everything. My kids come before my
job." Family before everything, that's how I've always been. My
boss told me, "You know, I understand where you're coming from,
just don't make it so often." But they slowed down at the end of the
year, so they ended up letting me go just because it slowed down.

I've been hired in at my shop now for three years. Been there three and a half years, because I did my time with the temp service. Started off at ten dollars an hour as a temp—I now make seventeen, and when I work my weekends or when my team leader's not there, I make eighteen twenty-five. For having just basically high school education, I think I'm doing pretty damn good. I got my truck payment, my payment for my bike, and the payment for my old lady's Acadia, and with insurance and everything, that's eighteen hundred bucks a month. The old lady asks me, "Why's your truck all loaded and my Acadia's just got economy features?" I'm like, "That's cause I'm the one bringin in the money." My boss will always ask me, "You wanna come in early? I need your help coverin second shift." I'm like, "Yeah, I'll be here." I've got no problem working. If I didn't like my job, I wouldn't come in. I love what I do.

The tool mold area is my department. We do everything from start to process. We build the mold and get it approved for production—make sure it's up to our spec. We've got our CNC area, and we do what's called low-pressure casting. So what happens is, there's a mold, and the machine sucks the air out of the mold, and when it sucks the air out, that pushes the metal up out of the crucible. It's all sand core. Some of the molds, we'll run them anywhere from five thousand shots all the way up to thirteen thousand shots. It just depends on what product it is, because some of the molds won't last as long as other ones running. It also depends on who preps the molds. If you've got someone who can't prep for shit, then you can have a mold that should run for nine thousand shots that gets pulled at four thousand shots because it's too thick on pyrostain. Each mold is supposed to have one to two mills of pyrostain, but some guys'll ice blast them. They'll spray the shit out of them—ten to fifteen mills. Then we have to take the old molds and sit there and sandblast them until it's back to bare metal. We tear them down. We fix them. We clean the pins. We basically do a complete rebuild of the molds when they get taken out.

We make steering knuckles for anybody and everybody. The part gets casted, robot picks it up, takes it up to a quench tank to cool it down, puts it in a trim dye, from the trim dye it'll go to a saw plate, from the saw plate—after it's cut—it goes down to the chute, operator grabs it up, runs it through x-ray and makes sure it's up to spec, then we send it out to get machined. The parts alone, before they're trimmed, weigh about thirty-five pounds. Each one.

We used to do parts for Tesla. We've got a mold somewhere around the shop that we've done for Ferrari. We've got four or five machines that run parts for Mercedes. We got one that's just dedicated to Corvette. We've got eight machines dedicated to Ford— those machines run nothing but Ford. That contract we have with Ford is like a twenty-five, thirty million dollar a year contract. Our Ford line's running seven days a week, because they want fifty-five hundred sets. It's money.

If I'm not at work, I'm at home passed out, because I'm a third shifter. I'd rather work third shift than any other shift. I get to spend time with my family. First shift? I'm not a morning person. But third shift? I get home, get the kids off to school, sleep until they get home, get some time with them, take an hour nap before I have to go in to work, and be at work from eight o'clock at night till six thirty in the morning.

Life's good. The kids go to Orchard View schools. They play soccer, football. My step kids play tee-ball. My daughters, when they get old enough, they'll do cheerleading. We live just south of Apple Avenue, east of the highway, not far from Parslow Park. I'm right across the street from that park. Kids want to play? "Take your asses down to the park." They're old enough.

Sometimes I do worry about my kids growing up here. When I was younger, Muskegon was nice. It's kind of going to shit now. Ninety percent of the shootings, it's black-on-black crime. Motherfuckers shooting people over stupid shit. It's stupid. "Oh, you talked shit about my brother. You're dead." Stupid. Fucking put the fucking guns down and man up. Throw bones like back in the day. You know? I've thrown my rounds. I've thrown my rounds plenty of times.

The violence around here is getting fucking ridiculous. A few years ago, this guy I worked with got murdered in cold blood. His brother's car was stolen from DJ's Pub over on Henry Street. He went chasing after them and got shot for it. He was on his motorcycle chasing them down. Some of the thiefs were riding along in a different car behind the car that got stolen, and they ended up firing off two clips at him—hit him in the back. Police thought it was just him wrecking his bike that killed him, then when they did the autopsy, they realized he had a bullet hole in his back. Probably the largest funeral that I've been to. He had probably a good three-quarter-mile-long row of bikes going behind him to his resting place. All because someone was stealing his brother's car.

So I worry about my kids growing up here. I do. And yet again, I don't, because I've been raising my kids not to take shit from nobody. I took a lot of shit when I was in school. I never fought back; I just took it. I don't do that no more. I got into the cage fight stuff kind of as a way to let out aggression—legally. So raising my kids, I tell them, "Don't take shit from nobody." If somebody starts something with you, it's like, "They start it, you finish it." I've already had my oldest out of school a couple times. People mess with him, he fights back.

I'll leave my kids in a car. I was at Rent-a-Center over here on Apple. Left my old truck running, had my oldest in there. Run in there real quick, take care of this bill, and I'll be out. Hand him my knife, I say, "Here's my knife. Here's how to open it. Anyone comes up to my truck, you pull the knife on em." I come back, he's sitting there with the knife out. He's like, "Dad. I had some black dude come up to the truck. I pulled the knife on him." I'm like, "Good boy."

I love my kids. They're good kids. And they know their daddy don't put up with no shit. Daddy will put a foot in the ass. But I love my kids more than anything. I have all my kids on me—literally. All my kids are tattooed on me. I have my boys on my right arm— they picked out the colors of their stars, and when I went to go get touch-up done, my oldest actually helped with needle. I got my younger daughter with her footprints from the hospital on the right side of my chest—older daughter with her footprints on the left side. Then I have my life and death, my grim reaper, my grandma and my grandpa that passed away, my key (my old lady has the lock on her foot), my Iron Cross, my Confederacy, and then I got my cancer ribbon for my mom and for my little brother. Anarchy one is on my back.

The Confederacy—there's a guy at work who don't like that one. But the Confederacy isn't about racism, it's about states' rights. It's about freedom from tyranny. So I showed the guy at work, I showed him articles about how many thousands of African-American people fought for the Confederacy in the Civil War. Because it's not about racism or white supremacy, it's about freedom and protecting your property from anybody who's trying to take it.

I'm not racist—I am racist to a point. You know, my sister's biracial. I love her to death, but there's a line. There's a line between black, and there's a line between niggers, and before they changed the meaning of "nigger," it used to be an uneducated, lazy black. Well, now it's considered a racial slur, so my wife will get on me all the time about saying it. But I'm not doing nothing wrong. All these motherfuckers doing these shootings around here are niggers. Plain and simple. Lazy motherfuckers that just want to sit on their ass and do nothing. They want to live in public housing and they want hardworking people taking care of them. They want all the freebies they can get. That's why they didn't want Trump in office.

Honestly, I have no problem with Trump. He wants to build the wall, I'm all for it. Keep the motherfuckers out. I'm not working to support people that want to come into this country illegally. My tax dollars—I'll pay for the police, but to illegally give food stamps and

Medicaid and cash assistance to illegal immigrants? Shit. I'd rather have my tax dollars go to help pay for law enforcement. I saw that over in Detroit, they got people parading up and down the street with ISIS flags. Some of the bikers are talking about heading over there to put a stop to that—Bikers Against Radical Islam. I'll ride over there with them. If we don't have enough money to pay law enforcement to take care of shit like that, then somebody else is going to have to.

We really got to step it up. They've got the State Police coming into Muskegon Heights. The State Police are helping patrol Muskegon Heights, but it still ain't helping. The violence around here is getting fucking ridiculous. I actually want to get out of the city part and get more into the country. I'm tired of hearing the fucking sirens all goddamn day. I wake up hearing the sirens.

I've got motherfuckers trying to get into my garage. I told my old lady, I told her, "Next time you see a motherfucker trying to get into my garage, take the shotgun and put a bullet in his ass." She's all scared—"But I can't do that." I was like, "The fuck you can't. He's breaking into our property. It's protecting our family."

I had a thirty-gallon trash bag full of beer cans, bottles, pop cans, that sort of thing—stolen out of my front yard. Didn't know who the fuck it was. Well, I was at work covering second shift. I got a call. My old lady's like, "I just had some black dude trying to get in the garage." I was like, "What the fuck?" She described him to me and I was like, "I know who that motherfucker is." I hadn't seen him for a while. So I caught up to him at Walmart. He come right up to me saying, "I'm, yeah, um, I'm tryin to tryin to find a job, um, seein if anyone needs help with yardwork or anything." I looked at him and I said, "You motherfuckin nigger. You stay the fuck away from my goddamn yard." He looks at me, he's like, "Don't fuckin come at me." I was like, "You don't know who I am, do you?" He's like, "No." I'm like, "I'm that house over by the park." He's like, "You're that house?" I'm like, "Yeah, I'm the house whose garage you were tryin to get into." He says, "I didn't try to get in no garage. I, I, I took the bag of cans, but I never tried to get in your garage." I'm like, "You're a motherfuckin liar. My wife caught you. She came out the door. My neighbors came chasing after you. You come near my house again, you leavin in a fuckin body bag." He said, "Don't fuckin talk to me like that." I said, "Miles, I know who you are. You're a fuckin crackhead. Your whole family's a fuckin crackhead. You come near my house again and my wife's already got permission to put a bullet in ya." I haven't seen him around my house since.

I've been through thieving, stealing. I did the shit myself. And honestly, now that I'm older and wiser, I can't stand a fucking thief. I hate the motherfuckers with a passion. I've had people ask me, "Do you regret your past?" No. I don't regret my past. My past is what made me the man I am today. If I could go back and change it, I wouldn't go back and change it. Because if it wasn't for me getting in trouble—getting locked up—ten to one I'd probably be dead right now. Everything I was into when I was younger? I would have been dead. No lie about that.

NATE

"I think my mistakes became the chemistry for my miracles."

—T.D. Jakes

I grew up in the Nelson neighborhood—the inner city. Of the guys I grew up with, some are in prison, some are dead, and the ones who aren't dead or in prison are still out there selling dope—in their thirties and forties. Almost all of us came from single-parent homes. All of us had parents that were addicted to drugs. In my family, it was just heroin for my mom, and then my dad did heroin and crack. They got divorced when I was young. Almost all of our parents—at least the dads, if not the moms as well—had been to prison. You put all that stuff together, and what have you got? You got a bunch of delinquents running around. Everyone drops out and works at a factory or sells dope.

I'd already got introduced to the drug game in junior high. Seeing all the other guys around you that are selling drugs—it's attractive. Those guys have money. The girls are around them. It's like, "Sssh, this is cool." You know what I mean? There's no real way to gauge it. There's no frame of reference to say, "Oh, that probably might not be a good thing to do. I could end up in jail." All you see is this half over here: the money, the drugs, the girls, the street fame.

In ninth grade I said, "I don't need algebra class. I can count money. I'm gonna sell crack." I remember taking my lunch money, and I got a double-up. I bought ten or twenty dollars worth of rock, and I doubled my money. I'm like, "Man, that's easy." You know? I'm thinking, "Man, I'm gonna figure this thing out." I didn't know it at the time, but I got that broker's mentality. Hustling was just an attractive thing. I loved the challenge, I loved the money, I loved all the stuff that came with it. And I did it. I got discipled by the older guys—I let them teach me how to do it the right way.

If you didn't know, you would think, "It's easy. It's just sellin drugs. How complicated can it really be?" But there's a lot to learn. Like, if you're selling crack and the crackhead pulls up in the car, how close do you get to the car, and what do you do and don't do? As an example, when you walk up on a car, you never spit your dope out and put your hand close enough to the window where this guy can bump your hand to knock the dope in and pull off. You've got to wait until you see the money and count it out. And the whole time you've got to be looking down the street, making sure the police aren't turning the corner.

If you keep your dope in your mouth, make sure you double-wrap it—just in normal plastic baggies. It's got to be double-packed so it doesn't break, because you don't want the cocaine to get in you.

Never keep more than ten rocks on you, and always keep you a soft drink. That way, if there is a raid that happens, you swallow the dope. You never want to have more on you than what you can get rid of—what you can swallow. It was just those little things you had to learn.

You move up a little bit, and then there's trap houses. You've got guys with walkie talkies—they don't have dope on them, but they ride their bikes around the neighborhood. Their whole deal is just to direct crack sales to the trap house. They find a customer and they tell him, "Go up into the alley. There'll be someone standin at the back door." Then they take the walkie talkie and call the runner, "Hey, there's a guy comin. He's got a blue truck. He's legit." The runner comes down to the back door, and he's peeking out. He sees a blue truck come through the alley and he goes, "*Whoop.*" Then the guy who's looking for the drugs knows, "Okay, that's him." You never let them in—never let them see who's who, except for the runner. It's all that stuff that goes on behind the scenes that you learn as you get out there. You learn how to maneuver out there.

You're constantly on the lookout for intruders: for the police undercover, for people just coming into the neighborhood—they may appear to be a drug user, but they're really an undercover cop. You're constantly having to keep your spider senses turned on. You're constantly having to read people. It was always, "Who is this dude? Where did he come from?"

There's a slang term for the streets—it's called "the game." In "the game," you can be whoever you want to be. That's why everyone has nicknames. Whatever the person's nickname is, that's the image that he's created of himself. That's what he wants everyone else to view him as, but it's really a counterfeit version of himself. When he creates this image in his mind, he creates these new rules that he lives by: "Oh, I won't tell. I'm tough. I'm this. I'm that." But in reality, that's not actually who he is. It's false. And the friends that he has are not really his friends—they're just a benefit to him.

The only reason I may hang out with this particular person is because he sells drugs, and he has his own money—he's not a peon, he's not a lackey, he's not a flunkey. This is someone who has respect on the streets, so I want to be known as being acquainted with this person. But trust only goes so far. As long as everything is playing along according to the game and to who I am, then we're good. But as soon as things start playing out the way I don't want them to and it comes down to something where it's between me and you, then you got to go. It's all a part of this illusion that we enter into. When you're in it, you're thinking this stuff is real when it's not. It's a counterfeit version of real life, and yet it has real consequences that go with it. It can literally change the rest of your life.

In '95, '96, there really wasn't a lot of gang activity in Muskegon—not in a serious sense. You had your little cliques, but they weren't a threat to anyone. It wasn't like they were killing each other at the time. We would ride our bikes over into the Wood Street neighborhood, into the Jackson Hill neighborhood—we would play basketball, and everything was cool. We weren't from that neighborhood, but the mindset wasn't, "Beat them up if you see them."

In '97 was when things really began to happen. I remember one of the first fights that our neighborhood got into with Wood Street. It started over something stupid—over some ninth graders and their girlfriends. It was just something stupid. But after all that, now you had groups forming—you had the Amity Group, or the Jackson Hill Black Gangsters, or the East Park Projects, or the South Side Heights. Now there was a group of people that identified themselves with that name and that area of town, and all of a sudden, there was a lot of fighting whenever we would see each other.

October 10 of '98, some older guys from our neighborhood had gone to a club—a night club called The Palace—on Sixth Street in the Heights. While they're there hanging out, they end up getting into a big fight with some of the guys from Wood Street. It happened over a girl, believe it or not. One guy from my neighborhood was dancing with a girl whose boyfriend was from Wood Street, and — Boom! A big old clash happens. The next thing you know, they're fighting. Then they separate, and everyone takes off.

Every time we would get into it with Wood Street, they would always come back shooting. Never hit anyone, but they would always come back shooting.

That night, there was four of us that were hanging out. Me and some of my buddies went to a football game at Muskegon—we were selling drugs, doing our thing. And I remember, at about two o'clock in the morning, I had started getting hungry, so me and one of the other guys said, "We're gonna walk up to Shell gas station and get something to eat." We went up to Shell's—up there on the corner of Third Street and Muskegon—and we got some Hot Pockets. We ate, make a couple phone calls, check in with some people—some girls—girls said, "Naw, we don't have a ride tonight. Let's catch you guys tomorrow." We ate, and we walked back to the neighborhood.

On our way back, we heard a gunshot. Sitting there thinking, "Man, you think those guys came into the neighborhood?" "Nah, I don't think they came." We just kind of brushed it off as a fluke. Didn't give much attention to it. Kept walking. We get back down into the neighborhood, on Mason Street, and there was a guy whose name was Chip, and he was sitting there, and he was mad, and he ran up on us, and he said, "Which one a you guys shot at my truck? You almost killed me and my cousin." I was like, "What are you talkin bout, man?" And he was like, "One a y'all shot at my truck." And during that time, while he's arguing with me, my best friend— Ted—he and another guy walk out from the side of a house, and they say, "That was us who shot at you." So Chip turns around and starts arguing with them. They say, "We thought you were those guys from the Wood Street neighborhood." So picture this: it's three in the morning; it's dead silent out; people are asleep; and here they are out in the middle of the street yelling at each other about why Ted was shooting at Chip's truck.

After about five minutes of that, I sparked up a cigarette, and down the street half a block, on Fifth and Mason, there was this car pulled up to the stop sign. I looked at it, and I knew something was out of place. This car—it just didn't fit right in this neighborhood. It turned left—coming towards us up the street—and we all stopped and backed off the curb and looked at the car as they rode past us. They rode by real slow, and we just stared at them. You could tell that there was several guys in the car, and they were looking at us too.

Chip and my buddy go back to arguing over the situation. The car goes up to Sixth and Mason, and then they take a left. I remember thinking that these guys were going to come around the block—that they were just going to see who was out here, and then come back and shoot. When they went up to the corner, they took that left, and I stood on the corner looking through the block to see if I could see them coming on the next street over. I was looking, and there was no cars coming. Then all of a sudden, here this car is—with its lights off—coming from behind the houses in the alley. So I automatically knew then that it was these guys, and I said, "Man, here these guys go again. Right here man." Everyone turned around and looked, and then we all took off running. Me and Ted, we were the last two that took off, and you could just hear, "Pow, Pow, Pow"—gunshots just going off. Then somebody yells, "Get on the ground!" So we're jumping on the ground, but as we were jumping on the ground, we were in the bent-over position, and the bullet struck Ted in his right butt cheek. It travelled through his inside and it came out his esophagus. As we're going to the ground he's like, "I got hit." It sounded like the wind got knocked out of him, because the bullet had pierced his lungs. And at the time I'm thinking it's probably just his leg. I'm thinking this kind of stuff happens in the movies. We get down, and he's just staring at the grass—he's crunching the grass. And the guy is still shooting. The bullets are hitting the house—we had run off along the side of this abandoned house. I can hear him still shooting, so I'm laying there, and I don't get up until I hear the gravel kicking up in the alley as they're driving out. Then I'm up and I say, "Come on, man. We gotta go." He's not responding though. So I flipped him over on his back and I said, "Come on, man. We gotta go, man. The police are gonna be comin." He didn't say anything, and as I'm trying to pick him up, he took his last breath—literally. It was one of those things where it happened so quick and so unexpectedly, you're thinking that this is not really real. It's not really hitting me. I'm like, "What in the world?" Chip had come running back and tried to help me pick him up, and I said, "Man, he's dead, man." I said, "We'll call the police."

Chip went to the house next door to call for the ambulance, and they wouldn't open up the door. Obviously. They were in the neighborhood. I'm sure they just heard those gunshots. They're not going to open up the door. Chip runs back and he says, "Man, they won't open up the door." So I ran up the street, down a bit to where one of my other buddies lived, and I banged on the door and his mom came to the door and I said, "Call the police. Ted just got shot." She said, "Okay." I ran back down there, and Ted had dope on him, so we took the dope and money and different things—got that off of him—and by the time we did that, you could hear the sirens coming from the Fire Department.

We took off running and left him there, and we ran over to his mother's house to tell her. It was a few blocks over. We woke her up. Told her. You can just imagine. You get this news that your son's been murdered. She just flipped out. We walked her down there—she wanted to go down to where the body was at, so we took her down there, and by the time we got there the ambulance and the police and everybody was there. Funeral was a couple days later.

Between the Wood and Mason Street beefs, he was the first one that got killed. That was the first killing between the two neighborhoods: October 10 of '98. After that, it just escalated into what's going on today.

A little over a year later, another guy from our neighborhood was murdered, at Nubby's Lounge on Sherman—shot in the back of the head. Over stupid stuff again. That was over someone stepping on his shoes. Really? But when you're in that mindset, no one's going to say, "Oh, I'm sorry. I didn't mean to do that." "Don't worry. It's all cool." No. It's a pride thing. Every person's pride is in competition with the next, and when that's the case, now there's no common sense. Before it was just like a movie thing. I had never met anyone who had been killed or shot or any of that stuff. Now it was like, "Man, this is really real. This isn't the movies. This is really real." And so when it hit that close to home, it changed the whole landscape of everything—the violence, the anger, the lines you're willing to cross.

At the time of Ted's death, we were just low-level drug dealers. I hadn't gotten into really making a lot of money other than a hundred dollars here, a hundred dollars there. But now, after Ted got killed, now this anger part came in. Now I'm walking around with a gun all the time, because now it's real that you can actually get snuffed out. And it comes with the territory—when you start picking up guns, you start doing things you didn't think you'd ever do. I opened up a new door, so to speak, and once that door opened up, it just became normal and common to do different things, and eventually I went to prison for armed robbery.

There were some guys from another neighborhood down in our neighborhood, and I did a robbery—this was Thanksgiving of 2000. It wasn't until a week later that one of the victims that was there told the police that she had discovered that I had been a part of this, and she told the detectives. The detectives came to my mother's house real early in the morning and got me. I was up getting ready to eat breakfast and heard the knock on the door. Peered out the blinds to see who it was, saw that it was the police, but I assumed they don't have any concrete evidence—there's no gun, they don't have any of the money and things that we got, so I'm thinking, "Well, if they don't have that, then they really don't have a case." But I didn't know that this lady had told on us.

I ended up getting arrested that day. Got taken down to the courthouse and then was booked in at the Muskegon County Jail. I found out there that they had a delivery of cocaine charge against me too, so after sitting in County Jail for ten months during the trial and all that, then it was off to prison for seventeen-and-a-half to fifty.

I went to prison on September 14th, 2001. Friday. It was right after 9/11. I went to Riverside Correctional Facility in Ionia, Michigan. That was the reception center—quarantine. You go do your psych evaluation, find out what security level you'll be at, do all your tests for diseases and all that kind of stuff. They want to see if you're a looney toon or not. I mean, think about it: you're out here shooting people—they want to make sure you're working with a full deck upstairs.

It's also to see if you need meds. A psych will meet with you. They ask you questions, and they see what your evaluation is. They diagnosed me as being anti-social. They said I just didn't want to go with the program of society, which was true—I didn't. I thought I had it all figured out, dealing drugs and all that stuff. I didn't have to be on no meds or nothing. They just said, "There's nothing else wrong with you other than that you just don't want to go with the program. You know the difference between right and wrong, you just don't do it." Didn't change anything on my security level. Still had to go to maximum security because of the amount of time I was doing.

While I was at Riverside for quarantine, I remember the only books that we had were these testimonial books from this group out of Fort Worth, Texas called Chaplain Ray Prison Ministry. These were testimonial books of men who had been to prison, gotten their life right while they were in prison, surrendered to God, came home, and just did some real powerful things in ministry. Those were the only books you could get. You were on twenty-three-hour lockdown. You can only look out the little window in your cell door for so long. Then either you could read these books, or you talk to the brick walls. So I read those books. And when I was reading them, I didn't realize it at the time, but they were planting seeds in my mind—giving hope of, "Man, you can get out of here and change your life." All these different things were coming into my mind. But I quickly forget about it. I put it in the back of my mind and picked up where I left off—smoking weed and doing my thing.

Then I got transferred to maximum security in St. Louis, Michigan, and after I was in two years, I ended up getting a visit from my appellate attorney. She came to the prison and met with me, and she said, "I think we have something we can do." See, I got sentenced to five-to-twenty years on delivery of cocaine; I got sentenced to twelve-to-thirty years on armed robbery and felony firearm. But she's sitting here telling me, "There's a technicality in your sentencing. The delivery of cocaine has a mandatory consecutive sentencing clause attached to it. Because of the mandatory consecutive sentencing clause, the instructions to the judge on that say that the delivery of cocaine sentence has to be the last sentence imposed upon you—it cannot be the first one." But I had got sentenced first on the drug case, then on the armed robbery/ felony firearm. You understand? So she said, "Now, in order for it to stick, the delivery of cocaine had to be the last sentence imposed upon you, because it runs consecutive to another term or imprisonment." So she says, "We're gonna file a motion to see if we can get you some of this time back." I said, "Oh, perfect. That'd be wonderful." Obviously, I'm pumped. Then she explains, "Now, the judge doesn't have to go with this, because you agreed with the sentence. You signed the paper. We're really on the mercy of the courts, but we'll file the motion to see what he'll do."

So at this time, I remember leaving the control center from meeting with her, and now all of a sudden it was like, "I want God in my life." You know what I mean? It was like, "If you're gonna do somethin, show up now and do it." There was a part of me that was beginning to get tired of all this whole mess. It was like, "How many times are you gonna get in a fight and do all of this other stuff? This is stupid. We're just doin this just to be doin it. By the time I get out, I'm gonna be thirty-seven years old. I'm doin this for what? This is stupid." I was just getting worn out from all this, so I was like, "Man, God, if you can get this five years taken off, I'll give you my whole life, man." And half of me is blowing smoke up His butt, but the other half is that I'm really just starting to get tired. I just want to get out. That was kind of the posture of my heart.

Several months later, October 14th, 2002, my lawyer goes back in the courtroom for oral arguments to argue our case. I stayed at the prison, and the whole time I'm praying, because in the penal system, it's not common to give time back. It's understood: they're not going to be wasting a lot of time and money going back into cases just because there's a technicality or something in how the paperwork was filed. But my attorney argues the case, and the judge sides with us. Which was amazing. Then, thirty days later, I go in for resentencing. Then I got the paper in the mail from the judge saying that it was flipped from consecutive to concurrent, so it was official. And for me, it was like a supernatural act of God. You're going down from seventeen-and-a-half to twelve-and-a-half with good behavior.

After that, I ended up signing up and going over to the church. It was on Saturdays that they had services. I go over there and some guy's preaching—coming in from the outside world—and at the end of the service there were these tables in the back with all these books on them. After the service I remember I go back there, and I'm looking for a book that talks about The Bible, because every other place that I had been locked up, it was just King James Version Bibles—"hither thou go thine unto thee." I'm thinking, "Who can understand that mess?" I had dropped out in ninth grade. I didn't even have my GED at the time. Reading that, it was just like, "bluh-bluh-bluh-bluh-bluh-bluh." You know? It didn't make any sense.

In my mind I thought, "Well, I just need a book that talks about The Bible." So I go back there, and I'm looking, but I come across this Bible, and it had a dove on it, and it said "Set Free" on the inside. I pick it up, and I read a couple verses, and it was a Contemporary English Version Bible. I said, "Oh, okay. This is more my speed right here." And so I got it, and I took it back to my cell, and I just began to read a chapter or two a day, and out of all this time that I had been incarcerated, this was the first time when the condition of my heart was really sincere. Before that, you know, you're sitting in the cell on twenty-four-hour lockdown, The Bible is the only thing in there, you'll pick it up, probably read a couple of verses, then—"Ah, I can't really get into that." But this time it was different. The posture of my heart was different. Really, I was looking for a real answer to the dilemma that I had found myself in—not just getting out of prison, but this dilemma in life. "Man, here I am. I'm making dumb choices that are leading me here. Obviously, somethin's wrong, and if things keep going at the rate they're going, this is gonna be me for the rest of my life: in and out of prison like some of these other guys who are in here in their fifties and sixties. They grew up in this place."

So I get that Bible, bring it back, and for the next six months I'm just reading like a chapter or two a day, and this was the first time that it just came alive on the inside for me—this reality that Jesus was a real person who walked this earth: who literally did miracles, died on the cross, was raised from the dead. Just internally, it became like a living understanding of it. You know how you just know when you know something? You might not be able to adequately explain it to someone, but up in my head I just knew it, "Man, this is it."

I just stayed like that for five or six months. I'm still reading, just becoming more convinced that this was Truth here. And I remember a guy came on TV—a televangelist—and he was preaching about Judgement Day. He's talking about how all of our choices have consequences to them, and it was just so crystal clear to me. I just knew that, "Man, there's gonna come a day where I'm gonna end up givin an account for all this stuff that I've done." Internally, I just had a sense like, "What if all this stuff really is real, and I step out of time into eternity, and what this guy's talking about really is real?" He talked about Hell, but it wasn't fire and brimstone. He did it in a way that just kind of made you ponder, "What if all this stuff really is real? What if something happens in the yard and we get into it with another group and I end up gettin stabbed to death and then I step out of time into Eternity and I really never have given my life to the Lord? What would it be like? Eternity is too long to be wrong." That was a rude awakening.

But now it was the next month, and I was still smoking cigarettes, still trading war stories, still talking negative about women—all the stuff that comes with the whole lifestyle—and I'm like, "Man, I can't keep doing this. This is the same old mess. I can't keep doing this, man. I can't." I thought that way for about another month. Then there was a guy who came on TV by the name of T.D. Jakes. I remember this was right before I went to chow that night. Jakes came up on the TV, and the title of his sermon was "Bad Boys and the God Who Loves Them." I remember, as soon as he started speaking, it was almost like one of those sermons where you feel like someone tipped the preacher off that you were there, because he's reading your mail to you type of deal. As soon as he opened up his mouth, one of the first things he said was, "The next ten years of your life, God is gonna do a work on the inside of you." As soon as I heard "ten years," I'm thinking, "I've got ten years left." I literally had ten years, one month left on my sentence when he's saying this. So I'm thinking, "Man, he's speaking to me." That grabbed my attention. And all throughout that sermon he just began to talk about the different men that God had used to do some extraordinary things. I remember him talking about Moses and David, and how Moses had murdered an Egyptian man, but God had used him to write the first five books of the Old Testament, and David and Bathsheba and that whole ordeal and sending Uriah out to be killed. He talked about the Apostle Paul and how he'd made it his mission in life to destroy the Christian faith—had casted his vote that Christians be placed in prison—but then God turns around and uses him to write two-thirds of the New Testament from a prison cell in Rome after his encounter in Damascus with Jesus. And I remember thinking, "Man, I kinda fit in with this group a dudes." Because before that, I had cooked this thought up in my mind that Saint Peter and Saint Paul: these are holy roller dudes—these guys didn't do anything bad; these guys were handpicked from birth to be the righteous preachers. And looking back I'm like, "Well how come no one ever talks about these guys like this?" All this religious stuff was always just, Saint Peter, Saint Paul, Saint This. But T.D. Jakes just began to really unpack the heart of the Father—that we can't go too far that his arm is too short to save us, and restore us, and rebuild our lives. It gave me so much hope it was ridiculous. It just pushed me over the edge where I was like, "I've gotta do this."

I didn't do it right away. For a couple days, it was like the war was going on inside of me. I really weighed it. In the heat of the moment, you see people run to God, and I didn't want to do that. I counted the cost—"Is this really what I want to do? If I do, I have to come all the way in on this thing." Really, the war was going on on the inside to where it was like, "Man, Islam really has to be the true religion. That's where Jesus is from is the Middle East. Christianity started in America, so how can that be right?" At the time, I didn't know anything, but I couldn't get away from the Truth that was coming alive on the inside of me. There was this deep conviction that, "That is it." You just know it when you know it: That is it.

Two nights later, I remember coming off the big yard like, "Man, I just can't keep livin the way I'm living. I've gotta give my life to God." And that night in my cell, I just came to a place that was transparency before the Lord. Just broken—in a good way. It was an unorthodox prayer. It wasn't one of those things you learn in Sunday school. I was just like, "Look, man. I'm tore up from the floor up. I know I'm screwed up. And if you can take my life and you can do something with it, then you've got me for the rest of my life. You become King, and you call the shots. You tell me what I can and can't do." And I remember, as soon as I finished praying, I just kind of internally felt this Holy Spirit saying, "Get everything that's in yourself that don't line up with the word of God, and get it out." I remember grabbing my cigarettes and flushing them. My magazines that I had. Books. My music—I had all the rap music and stuff. Got rid of all of it. Threw it in the trash. Flushed what I could flush. It was the first night since I was a kid that I went to sleep with a clean conscience.

When I woke up the next morning, this is what kind of sealed the deal: I was brushing my teeth and washing my face—I was getting ready to go to chow—and the first thing in my mind as I'm washing up, I'm thinking, "Man, you got the saved last night. You're a Christian." I remember thinking it felt strange even thinking that. All of a sudden, I'm a holy roller in my mind. "Hey, you're a Christian now."

I could feel the difference. I noticed that God supernaturally delivered me from cigarettes, as if I'd never even smoked before a day in my life. There was an umpire of peace that came on, and the cuss words wouldn't even flow out my mouth anymore. For me, that was a big deal. I think it was the Lord doing that just to kind of put his fingerprint—his seal—on this, so that I would know that something really did happen on the inside and I'm not just going crazy. It was like it just came over me. It was just like, "Okay, the storm's over."

And it was real. I remember, that night, I went out and told the guys I'd been hanging with, I said, "Look, I gave my life back to God last night. I'm not with this stuff anymore." They thought I was going crazy, but while they were laughing and everything, I just walked away and introduced myself to the Christian brothers there on the yard. They gave me the right hand of fellowship, and I began to get discipled by those guys. From there, I just had a real hunger for the Word. I just wanted to get into The Bible. I wanted to renew my mind. I just wanted to get filled up on this stuff. So I did that. Wrote my girlfriend, told her she had to go. Then really just kind of disconnected myself from the outside world for the next ten years—went on a mission to discover who this God was that I met in my cell that night, and who Jesus was. I just had a ferocious hunger for that, an appetite. It was crazy.

I had the opportunity of pastoring a couple of churches on the inside—one for five years, the other one for three. It became a mission field and a training ground. I think of Moses sometimes, of how Moses, after he left Egypt, he went to the desert, where he met Jethro and his daughter. He hung out there in the wilderness for forty years, and during that time of being in the wilderness, God calls him back to Egypt and says, "Okay, here's what I have for you: You're gonna lead the People out of Egypt. You're gonna go to Pharaoh and you're gonna say, 'Let my People go.' You're gonna be my mouthpiece." Then, after that, Moses spends another forty years in the desert. Experientially, God used those forty years with Jethro to prepare Moses for the next forty years that he was going to be wandering with the children of Israel. It was kind of in that context that the Lord was preparing me. He just used prison as a training ground for me to become a student of the Word. While I was locked up, I got an opportunity to really sit back—really evaluate my life—and I got my life right with God. I remember telling the Lord at the very beginning, I said, "Man, you shine the light of your Word on every area of my heart, and whatever you call a weed, it's a weed. Let's deal with it in here before I get out." And we did. It was there in prison that it began, me dreaming with the Lord about going home and what we were going to do with the ministry and the church-planting and all that stuff. And now, here we are today, living out what I was sitting in my cell dreaming about all those years.

Now I'm working with men and women coming home from prison, so that time that I spent locked up wasn't wasted. You know, being a former drug dealer, I've got that broker's mentality. I'm a communicator. That's my gift. I'm a visionary. I've still got my ability to hustle, and I've still got my ability to recruit, so I was like, "Look here, Man. Here's my gifts. What are we doin with em?" And it was like He said, "Here's what I've called you to: You're gonna go back in and help clean up what you helped mess up."

I actually had a real smooth transition. My dad had cleaned up his life, and I got to stay with him, so having the support there was huge. You'd think after twelve and a half years it would be a big culture shock, and I think it was in a sense, but for whatever reason, it didn't affect me in a way to where I would get anxiety or depression. For me it was like getting a new toy—I had never been on the Internet. I didn't even realize I could vote. I would have voted for Trump, but I didn't even know I could. You used to have to wait seven years from the time you got out, and I was still under that impression. Then I talked to one of the guys who just came home, and he goes, "Yeah, I went to go get my license, and I signed my voting card." I'm like, "How did you do that?" He was like, "We can vote. Soon as we get released, we can vote." Well, I didn't know that. But like I was saying, for me, getting out was exciting. I didn't know anything about e-mail, Facebook—all that stuff. This was all brand new. But I had developed a mindset of being a lifelong student in whatever I was going after. For me it was, "Show me how to do this, man. Show me what I do."

Soon as I came home, I looked at what degrees they offered at Grand Valley that would transfer from Muskegon Community College. I looked at the business degrees, and there was a liberal studies degree in business leadership that had a primary focus in the non-profit sector. I knew that with ministry-related stuff and prisoner reentry, I was going to be going into the non-profit world, and I had to learn the professional behavior so that I wasn't just floating with just the street guys. I wanted to be able to go into the boardroom and talk with donors and investors and different people to help support the cause. So I signed up to five classes—full load— and did the work-and-study program at the same time.

I had only been home ten months, and I had an elementary school building given to me—Grace Christian Academy. It was offered to me by a church in there that was dying out, so I got in contact with another guy and proposed him a plan: "Hey, let's team up and plant a church together." So we did. And then me and another guy, we were talking and dreaming about doing a prison ministry, and I knew that I wanted to do both, but I couldn't do both by myself, so me and the one guy were over here with the church, and then me and the other guy were over there with the prison ministry. We took around eighteen months and developed the relationships, built a launch team, went the whole nine yards, did it right. Then, on September 19th, 2015, we planted the church, and on March 1st, 2016, we planted 70x7 Muskegon.

God used all the bad things I saw and I did. He took those and used them to draw me to Himself. And now, because of that, I get to share my story. That's part of it. That's part of it that helps other people—just being able to identify with the other guys that have been through the same thing. Because you can't give away something you don't have yourself. The fact that I've been there and that I can relate helps me give them hope. One of my passions in life is helping men and women—returning citizens—with how to win the war of staying out, and we're doing it in a way where it's not your normal church way of doing it. In a sense, it's kind of contextualizing the Gospel for the returning citizens.

What does the Good News look like—what does it sound like—to those coming home from prison? It doesn't sound like John 3:16. We're not just hitting people over the head with a Bible verse. Instead, it may start with just a hug and a cup of coffee and a "tell me about you. What do you need?" "Oh, I need a job." "Okay, let's work on that." In that process, we're developing relationships and earning the right to speak into people's lives.

At 70x7, we focus on three primary things: employment, recovery, and education. We have an employment specialist whose primary job is to work with employers that will hire people with felonies. We've got a real good success rate on jobs—probably about ninety-five percent. Then we have recovery services, because a lot of people coming home from prison have drugs attached to their crime in one way, shape, or form—either you were selling, or you were using. Then we have an education track: some folk have to get GEDs, some go back to college, and then we have connections with the trade programs in Muskegon so that they can either do welding or CNC training or truck driving, and they're all paid for while they're on parole.

The guys who take part in that, some of them choose to come to church with us on Sundays—they want to know the God that we serve—and others don't, which is cool. We're going to love on them regardless. Jesus said, "Love your neighbor as yourself," not, "Love your neighbor, but only if they agree with you." We follow that philosophy. And in that, we've been seeing a lot of fruit.

A lot of people are coming into contact with who they were designed to be and rediscovering their purpose and what their destiny really is. They're realizing that just because you've been to prison and you have a felony, that doesn't determine how far you can go in life. You're the producer, and you're the director of your own film. In the end, if it's a flop, you've got yourself to blame. But if it's a hit, you've got yourself to credit.

We talk about dreams. Everyone puts dream boards together. They have to look out five years into the future, and they have to come up with a destination. Because if I don't know where I'm headed to, then anything's an option—yeah, I can smoke weed; yeah, I can drink, yeah, I can fight; yeah, I can put my life in jeopardy; yeah, I can go to jail; yeah, I can do all these things. Why? Because I don't know my purpose. I haven't found my tribe—and until I find my tribe, I won't find my purpose. We help them figure that out: "Who are the people that I was created to be around? Who are the people in this room who have a destiny that interlinks with mine?" We help them walk through and discover that, and once they do—once they realize what they're here for and what they were created for—it's like the light comes on. We help create the core values, and now it's like: "Any decision I make that doesn't line up with my dream board, it's a no." Now the question isn't, "What's wrong with it? What's wrong with smoking weed?" Now the question is: "What's right with it? How is doing that helping me fulfill my dream?"

I heard someone tell me one time: "Bad never gets better, it only gets worse." But I'm still hopeful. That's the reason that I'm doing what I'm doing. Because, especially for the guys coming home from prison who have younger kids, if they get on their feet and get their life together, the impact that they can have on their kids by being legit husbands and fathers has ramifications beyond just our lives. We have the potential to break that cycle of defeat so that their children don't have to cycle on through it like we did.

I'm confident that through what we and a number of other organizations are doing, there's still hope out there. I don't think I'll ever get to a place where we'll lose hope, you know what I mean? I consider my situation and how the Lord brought me out of all that mess—He could do whatever he wants to. Just last year, we were able to bring my dad on as our teaching pastor at the church. Me and him went from being out on the streets together to now running a ministry together. That's a pretty cool story right there.

But there's still a lot of work left to be done. When you're going through the Heights or through parts of downtown—areas where I know there's drug sales going on—I can pick it up, because I've been out there. Some guy looks like he's just walking down the street, but I know the walk, and I know the look—"You're the eyes on the floor." To someone who's not acquainted with that lifestyle, he may just look like a normal guy out for a stroll, but I can tell by the way he's dressed and by the way he looks what kind of mission he's on—if he's going to buy dope, or if he's going to sell dope. I see his eyeballs, and I see he's paying attention to every car coming down the street and it's like, "Why are you watching these cars so closely?" Well, he's watching out for undercovers, seeing if there's undercover cars in the alleys, seeing where the cruiser is at, seeing if they're staking out a place. That's a whole other world out there, and it's still out there.

SARAH

"There but for the grace of God go I."
—*humbling proverb*

I didn't know how rare it was to grow up in North Muskegon. I grew up in privilege. In high school, I had like five different friends that had swimming pools, and it was just so normal. In my friend circle, it was people who were basically all leaders—who wanted to make a difference in the community. I didn't have to worry about someone coming in the house and stealing something. It was very safe. I had never heard the words "human" and "trafficking" used in one sentence before. I didn't know it existed. I lived such a sheltered life.

Then I studied social work in college, at Baylor University. Someone did a presentation on human trafficking, and he talked about how there are more slaves today than at any other time in history. As he kept on going in his presentation, I'm like, "What? If this is this big of a deal, I need to get more educated on this. If there really are more slaves today than at any other time, then what the heck am I doing?"

Well, in the process of studying about the issue, I ended up watching a movie, and in this movie, there was a really short scene, and for whatever reason, it got me. There was a woman who was trafficked from Russia into the United States and was forced into prostitution, and she was looking into a bathroom mirror, and you could tell: she just wanted to die. She was in this cheap motel bathroom, and she was just staring at herself, and you could tell that she was contemplating suicide. So I go back home after I watch this movie. I'm in my apartment, looking in the mirror in my bathroom, and I asked the question, "Why?" I ask, "Why is that not me? If so many people are victims out there, why am I not one of them?" I began to ask the question, "Why is my life so good?"

I began to get angry. I had a conversation with God about it. I was kind of yelling at Him, like, "It's not fair! Why are some people given this amazing life?" I mean, my parents are still together. My dad's a doctor. He was paying for my college education when I know that so many other people have to work really hard for it. I just kind of came to this place: "Why have I been given all of this when other people are literally given hell to live in?" I was so upset at that.

Of course, at the same time I'm like, "Thank you, God, that that hasn't happened to me." But I still had this wrestle in my heart, and I just heard, "Sarah, when much is given, much is required." So I'm like, "Okay. Okay, God, I'm in. Whatever it looks like." I prayed the prayer, "Would you break my heart for the things that break your heart?" And He completely wrecked me. I was a weeping mess on my floor in my bedroom, crying out to Him and just seeing more of his heart for women who have been forced into prostitution.

That is when I got a heart for the issue. That was my junior year of college. Then I ended up taking a class on human trafficking my senior year. It was the first time they offered a class on it. We talked a lot about the definition, about what trafficking looks like in other countries, what it looks like here. We talked about labor trafficking, sex trafficking. Standard class: we read articles, wrote papers. But it was heart-wrenching. You would leave a crying mess. It was awful, some of the stuff that you would learn. I think to understand the reality of the issue, you have to see the ugliness of it, even though a lot of people don't want to see it.

After I graduated from college, I still didn't know what I was going to do with my life. I was in AmeriCorps—I was a tutor at a school in Waco. I did that, and I did a discipleship training school in my church, but I really didn't know what I was supposed to do. Then I went to this Bible study and I was asked the icebreaker question: "If you had no fear, and money wasn't an issue, what would you do with your life?" Instantly, I heard myself say, "Share the Gospel, and open up a home for girls who have been victims of sex trafficking." I looked down, and I'm like, "Where the heck did that come from?" I really didn't know that that was inside of me. I knew I was passionate about the issue, but I had never thought about opening up a home someday. Then the lifegroup leader said, "You're called to do nothing less than that." I'm like, "Could I do that? Am I supposed to do that? Is this my calling?" I just began to really question, "Is this what I'm supposed to do with my life? He said I'm called to do nothing less than this."

Well, my parents moved to Ethiopia. They were serving as medical missionaries, and they asked me to come live in their house in North Muskegon. I originally had told them "no," because I didn't want to move back to Michigan and be in the cold. I liked Texas. But I knew my mom was praying for me pretty hard, and one day I was walking home from a friend's house, and I started singing this song in my head; it was, *"I speak through your mother, I speak through your mother."* I was just singing this out loud as I'm walking—*"I speak through your mother."* I stop, like, "Why am I singing this? What the heck? Where is this coming from? God, is this you?" And I really felt like I was supposed to pray about moving back home. So I did. I had a friend praying with me too, and as she was praying she was like, "Sarah, this is strange, because I keep on hearing *Michigan*. I cannot get the word *Michigan* out of my head." I'm like, "Alright, I'm moving back home."

I moved back home in July of 2010, not knowing what I'm sup- posed to do—I'm just supposed to be in Michigan. A couple months later, I'm in Grand Rapids at another Bible study, and this girl is sharing with me how her dream is to open a home someday for girls coming out of trafficking, and my body literally jerked when she said that. It was like, "Wait. What do you want to do?" She told me again and I was like, "Oh my gosh, that's what I want to do!" Right then she said, "You need to meet my friend Amanda, who's doing that in Muskegon." I'm like, "What? There's an anti-trafficking organization in Muskegon?" She tells me, "Yeah, they're working to open a home for girls eleven through seventeen who have been victims of trafficking." "And it's in my hometown?" "Yeah." "Oh my gosh."

So I got connected with them, and I started volunteering in the thrift store. For over a year, I was a volunteer, then they hired me on full-time as their communications director. We're still working on getting the home open, but I work a lot with adult survivors who are coming out. I do a lot of mentoring, case management, connecting them with other resources. I'll make phone calls across the country trying to find them a place to go if they need to. It's really just about being the extra support for them as they're trying to recover from what happened to them. I've also done tons of awareness events. I speak a lot in the community about what human trafficking is, and about what it looks like in Muskegon.

Sometimes it looks like a child being pimped out by a family member for drugs or for rent money. Some of the girls I work with, they were pimped out at four years old and used in pornography. And these are local people. One girl, she was four, and her dad sold her to support his drug habit. That's one way how it happens.

Another way is through drug addiction. A girl gets addicted to drugs, she'll meet a guy, and he's like, "Oh, well I can help you get what you need." He becomes a boyfriend, and then he eventually pimps her out. One of my clients, she was originally addicted to drugs—and there's always a back story of how they got to that point—but because of her drug addiction, she was selling herself to get the drugs. That's not trafficking; that's just prostitution. But it changed when she met this guy who said, "Oh, baby, I'll be able to help you with that. I'll set up your clients, and I'll help you make some more money." This boyfriend became her pimp, but there came a point where, if she didn't make so much money every night, he would beat her up. That is when it shifted from prostitution to trafficking, because she couldn't refuse anyone anymore—now there was force and coercion involved. She had no choice in the matter. She was beaten up multiple times. Now, thank God, that pimp is in prison. We helped get him caught. He had pimped out three of our women who we work with, and we know that there were more women he was pimping out on the streets, mainly in Muskegon Heights. That was our first human trafficking conviction in Muskegon County.

Another one of my girls, she met her pimp at a strip club. She was dancing—underage—and the guy wooed her. He became her boyfriend. He promised her that he was going to help her make a lot more money dancing at other clubs around the country. He painted this beautiful picture of travelling. On the first stop out of the state, she was gang raped in a hotel, and it turned into a sex-trafficking situation. He had her pimped out at the Super Bowl in New Orleans a few years ago and had her all across the country doing that. She managed to get away, but he comes back to Muskegon for like two weeks a year, and when he's around, she's terrified—she doesn't want to leave her house. She doesn't want him to find her. We're trying just to come up with a plan so that she feels safe. We do whatever we can to help.

My day varies. A lot of it is just meeting with survivors and saying, "Hey, I love you. We want to help you." Sometimes I'm going to jail to visit them because they caught some drug charge or theft or whatever it is. Sometimes it might be going to court with them. If someone is trying to get their kids back, we supervise visits. We work with the other social workers, and we try to do the best we can to help her get her children back.

It really varies from person to person, because some people we work with are fresh out of the trafficking situation, and others were trafficked as children and now they're in their thirties, forties, fifties, and they're trying to deal with the trauma that happened to them when they were a child.

Some of them have a lot of mental health issues. They're paranoid, or they have thoughts of depression, or they have thoughts of suicide, or they've been diagnosed with schizophrenia. We have donors who have stepped up to say they would be willing to pay for their counseling, and we have a couple therapists that we partner with, so if their insurance doesn't cover the counseling process, then our organization will pick up the tab to help them in that way.

The outcomes for survivors vary. Some go to prison. Some are addicted to drugs. Some have been re-trafficked—one of my clients, she was re-trafficked at fifty years old, and so now she's dealing with that. Others get a degree in social work.

One survivor wants to open a house for women who have been out on the streets and who have been to prison—she wants to help them. A lot of them, they want to help those who have been in those situations. The majority of them do. One woman, she has a ministry to help boys that have been abused. She's really passionate about helping boys so that they don't become pimps or buyers. That's what she does. A lot of them, they're moms. They work. They're trying to do the best they can do with the lives that they have. It varies. It really does vary from person to person what they do. A lot of it depends on their support system.

For the majority, I feel like—the one's that I work with, those who are farthest along in their healing—they want to help somebody else that's gone through it, because they want to prevent this from happening to someone else. And if it does happen to someone, they want to be there to help them out, to say, "Hey, there is hope. You can get past this."

When the Hope Project started, they didn't think they'd be working with people from this area being trafficked. They thought it would be a home for minors from other places. But then the more awareness generating we did, the more survivors came forward, and it was like, "Oh, wow. It is here too."

I don't know if I was completely shocked at that. I was reading a lot about the problem. I knew that it was out there. For me, it was more like, "Okay, we have it in our city as well. Our city is no different from anyone else."

But I love Muskegon. I think it's a beautiful place to live. The lakes make it a gorgeous place. I think the people are great here too. I feel like it's an exciting time to be here in this city—things are moving forward. I know other people look at Muskegon and think, "Oh, that's where all the crime happens," but they haven't experienced Muskegon for what it really is. We have the amusement park, we have the State parks, we have the beach, we have suburban areas, we have the urban, we have farmland. It really is an emblematic American town.

I love living in America. I think we have a wonderful country. We have a lot of areas to grow in, but I think—overall—I love being here. The political situation: it's a mess. I think we have a long ways to go. I'm not someone who gets into the politics and all of that, but we have a long ways to go. This past election, I felt like there was so much conflict. It felt like, if someone found out I voted for this person, it would be like, "Oh my gosh, I can't believe you voted for them." Or, if I voted for another person, it'd be the same thing the other way—just depending on who I was talking to. So I decided to keep the peace. Nate doesn't even know who I voted for. I just felt like, in order to keep the peace with family groups and friend circles, my policy had to be, "I'm not going to tell anyone who I voted for." Because, again, there were people who were so strong one way, and people who were so strong the other way, and they would see me as one way if I voted for this person, or they'd see me another way if I voted for that person, so in the end I was like, "I'm just going to stay out of that and not tell people."

I'm a peacemaker. I see some things that are happening in the background, but I speak Life over our city and over our country. I don't talk a lot about the negative. When people talk about the negative, my response is to say, "Alright, let's talk about the solution to that problem. Let's find the solution, and then let's do what we're supposed to do to make it better."

JON

A lot of times, as a police officer, you're almost like a social worker a little bit. Like, for example, I get called yesterday because a mom can't get her eight-year-old son to mind her. She can't get him to go to the hospital for a mental eval— because the eight-year-old wants to kill himself. We get there and she's like, "He's not listening to me. He's not gonna stay in the car until the hospital." I'm like, "Okay, what do you want us to do?" The kid's eight years old. He's like this big. What do you want us to do about it? Then the kid starts yelling and swearing like, "You fuckin jackasses, you get the fuck away from me. I hate the fuckin police. You suck dick!" This is an eight-year-old kid saying, "You suck dick." I almost started laughing, because, dude, it was funny. It was like, "Are you kidding me? You're eight years old and you talk like this?"

I think a lot of things today, too, the parents a lot of times are afraid to discipline their kids. And they weren't afraid back when I was growing up. My mom had a wooden spoon, and I tell you what: if you messed up, you got the wooden spoon. Or if you had to deal with my dad? I remember. Oh, I was scared. But that's why my generation has more respect for other people; it's because we were raised more correctly. We had discipline. This mom yesterday, all she did was stand there like, "Oh, settle down, it'll be okay, we need to go to the hospital." Never once yelled at her son or smacked him or whatever. If that was my son, he would've been smacked. I mean, I'm sorry, but that's discipline. You need to know that you can't act like that. If you don't discipline them, then they're going to find out that they can get away with a lot more.

You wouldn't believe how many times we get called by parents saying their child won't listen to them. It's like, "What do you expect us to do? We're not social workers. We're not here to give you guidance on how to treat your kid. You can discipline them." But I think they're too afraid that they're going get in trouble for child abuse, and that's not the case. So a lot of the time they'll call and they'll just expect us to take care of the problem. It's like, maybe by painting us as the bad guy to the kid, they'll make the kid afraid of the police. They threaten the kid, "Okay, if you don't listen to me, then I'm gonna call the police." But we're not there to be the bad guy either. We're not supposed to be there as someone to fear. It's really unfortunate that's what they grow up with—fearing us—because then they end up hating us. It's a bad cycle like that.

It's not just problems between parents and kids, it's also problems between adults and adults. Pretty much every domestic we go to, they don't involve violence. They just involve chirping at each other. Verbal arguments. Like they got some kind of long-term, deep-seated problem that they're trying to work out, and they think that by calling the police it's going to make everything better. It's like, "Well, we can only come put a bandaid on it for tonight. We're not a long-term fix. You need to figure out your own problems." Like I said, a lot of what we do is social work, especially as far as domestics and trying to calm situations down.

I don't think it's bad. I mean, obviously, we're there to help. I would never discourage someone from calling. But there's a difference between someone that really needs us because their husband's drunk and going on a rampage in the house, and a mom or a dad who can't control their nine-year-old or ten-year-old. There's a difference there. But when I say it's a lot of social work, that's what it is.

That's why working in Norton Shores, people say, "Oh, you're a Norton Shores cop? You must have a nice cushy job, because you're dealing with the rich." But not all of Norton Shores is rich. I've been in houses in Norton Shores that you would not want to step foot in. Literally. You're talking about bugs and mold growing on the trailers. We have six trailer parks in our city, and some of those trailers are just—I'm not trying to put down trailer parks, but—some of them are just like they don't give a shit. They'll leave shit out. There's bugs. I've been through ones where they don't clean up after their cat, so they've got shit all over the place. Some of the places you go to, it's unbelievable that people could live there. Just the smell alone. What makes someone want to live their life like that? I don't know. It's interesting. It's something that a sociology professor would want to study. It's interesting to me, but I don't have the answers.

Norton Shores is kind of odd, because the city is split up in half. There's the west side, where there's huge houses—there was one that Michael Jordan was looking at buying in the early '90s off of Lake Harbor Road; it's this huge, log-cabin type mansion. So if you're working the west side, you're going to be dealing more with, maybe, underage drinking parties, domestics where the husband and wife get in arguments, stuff like that. Then, if you go to the east side, it's lower income, so you're dealing with more of the hardcore crimes—stabbings, shootings, stuff like that. I've been at a lot of stabbings. You've got that dichotomy. We cover a lot.

For three years, I did undercover narcotics on the West Michigan Enforcement Team—WEMET—and I can talk about that, because I'm done with it completely. It's a multi-jurisdictional narcotics enforcement team, but you can only be on that for three years, then you have to go back to your department.

We investigated drug dealers. How our job worked was: people will call in complaints; you'll get anonymous tips; you cultivate confidential informants (people who have been arrested with drugs and want to, essentially, snitch on their dealer); and then there's cases you build with that. Ideally, the case ends up with you going undercover and buying the drugs from the dealer. That was always the best-case scenario, because then, when you bought it as an officer undercover, you charge them directly with the sale. If I'm the one buying undercover, then—boom!—they're hit with the delivery charge automatically.

Then you show up in court—even though you're undercover—and you identify yourself as a police officer. It was really weird at first. I had a long beard, long hair. So picture this: a big bearded man who looks like he's probably from Iraq—Homeland Security guy told me I could go in and work undercover in ISIS for them—I go into court, and you have to go up there on the stand. You swear in, "Detective such and such, City of Norton Shores, currently assigned to WEMET." You got the whole courtroom watching.

The first couple times it was so weird, because I'm thinking, "Oh crap, now all these people out there in the courtroom are gonna know who I am." But you know what? I have never—ever—been called a cop during a buy. Ever. Now, I've had people recognize me in the courthouse—leaving or coming in or stuff like that. But whenever I've done a buy, people have never recognized me. And I had that same hairstyle for at least two years. It was kind of weird, you know? But drug dealers, all they care about is money. That's what drives them. They're not the brightest people.

The last guy that got murdered in the Heights—what was it, a couple weeks ago? He was sixteen years old, and he had seven hundred and eighty bucks in his pocket. He was gunned down with assault rifle rounds. If you're going to kill someone, that's pretty heavy duty. It's crazy, man, but I guess that guy was known to flash his money around. It's like, "Okay, if you're gonna do that, you oughta expect to get robbed—or worse."

My work was pretty much all in the Heights and the City of Muskegon. That's where most of our cases were. And it's ridiculous. It's like a different culture over there—I mean like a culture where it's okay to deal drugs. You're talking about eighteen-year-old guys walking around with a thousand dollars in their pocket like it's nothing to them. And no job. To a parent there—if you tell a mom or a dad that their kid got arrested for drug dealing—it's almost accepted, because they're making money. There are some good parents out there that will be pissed off, but on the whole, it was a culture shock for me.

Especially the houses. Being on WEMET, we had the opportunity to go into some of the houses where the drug dealers lived, and maybe eighty-five, ninety percent of the time: kids live there. Young kids. I could not believe it. They had roaches walking all over. There was mold on the plates because the food on them had been just sitting around in the kitchen for so long. I was just like, "I cannot believe that anyone could live in that." Child Protective Services would have their hands full—they do have their hands full in this county. But it's so odd that it's isolated to this area when you've got the neighboring communities that are actually really nice. I don't know. It's like people don't care about their community over there as much as they should. And all of it is not too far from cozy little North Muskegon. Just across the lake.

So yeah, North Muskegon. The Village. I came here in second grade. Mrs. Wieman's class. I always thought school was great. It was nice living in a smaller community where you could jump on your bike and go visit your buddies. It was before you could just text each other, so you had to call up the house phone, you know, "Hi! It's Johnny, can you come over and play?" Those times were a lot different. Video games, Simpsons episodes, swimming pool. It was awesome. I had a great childhood. Sports. Football up until ninth grade. I kind of regret not finishing football through high school. I'll have dreams now that we're back on the varsity team. In my dreams, I just decided to stay, decided to continue to play. Then I wake up with the regret, like, "You know what? I didn't do it." I mean, I loved playing hockey, but still. That's one regret from high school. Still, man, some good times anyway.

After high school, I stayed here and commuted to Grand Valley for five years. I actually worked across the lake here at the Water Resources Institute, because originally my major was going to be natural resources management. When I was younger, around eleven or twelve, I wanted to be a police officer—bad. My cousin Jack, who lives over in Detroit, had just graduated high school—'95—and he was sworn in as a Detroit Police Officer. Eighteen years old. I remember talking to him just shortly after that, and some of the stories he had, I remember, that's what I wanted to do with my life. I wanted to be a police officer. Then, towards the end of high school, I kind of changed my mind about that. I don't know exactly what triggered it, but I changed my mind. When I went to college, it was for natural resources management—at first.

Well, I started working in that field a little bit as a college student, doing GPS-mapping of wells and working on different projects and stuff like that, and I realized, "This shit's kinda boring. I don't think I'm gonna like doing this the rest of my life." So halfway through, after two years of college, I decided to go back to my first passion, which was law enforcement. I started taking criminal justice classes, and right then I realized, "I really like this. This is what I wanna do."

That was right around then that I met Tricia. When I met Tricia, she had a daughter, who had just turned two. Then we were together, and she ended up getting pregnant and we had our second daughter. I still had two more years left of college. She was living with her parents at the time, and her parents moved to New Mexico, and so she moved in with me at my parents' house. So we had my parents, we had the two girls, and we had her and me. It took me an extra year, but in five years I graduated. Then, when I graduated, we got married, and I signed up for the police academy.

I was a big guy then—not as big as I am now, but I was a big guy. I was working out and running, but I was not prepared for the police academy. The very first day I went, I got through half of the day, but when we started doing the workouts, I just couldn't do it. I dropped out, and that was probably the lowest point in my life. Here I am: this is what I've studied for, this is what I've wanted to do, this is what my future was going to be, and I couldn't finish day one of the fricking academy. That was a real low point.

Instead of just giving up, I decided I was going to start exercising two times a day. I came back here—I still lived with my parents in North Muskegon—and I started exercising two times a day. I lost thirty pounds in four months, and then I enrolled in Kalamazoo Valley's police academy.

That one I almost gave up on my first day too. This was worse than Grand Valley's academy. This was more militaristic. We had drill sergeants that had been actual drill sergeants in the Army together. They knew what they were doing. They were having us with the bags over your head marching, doing lots of pushups, everything till you pretty much just wanted to give up. I almost gave up again, but I was like, "You know what? No. I remember that feeling four months ago when I gave up." I told myself there was nothing I will ever give up on again in my life. The academy was eighteen weeks. I stuck it through and ended up graduating.

After that, I was working as a security guard for a couple of months, and then the opportunity came up where I could get a part-time job in New Era as a police officer—get sworn in. It was two or three shifts a week, eight hours at a time. There were barely any calls. Mostly traffic stops. I had one call for cows running loose in the road, and there wasn't much I could do about that.

After four months, I get a call back from Norton Shores, and they want to hire me. I went to work there, and after a year on the force there, I knew that this was what I wanted to do for the rest of my life, so that's when we decided to buy our house in North Muskegon. We got it for a good price—fixer upper. It's right by the school, so the kids walk to school. Our youngest had Mrs. Wieman as her second-grade teacher, so it was like full circle.

Part of the reason I wanted to come back to North Muskegon was the school system. I wanted my kids to have the same type of upbringing that I had, in a small community. There's something to be said for that.

That being said though, we're not immune to a lot of the stuff that's going on around here. Even before I was on WEMET, crystal meth was making a pretty big appearance in Muskegon County. It started out in the rural areas, then it started creeping up into the city, and by the end it was actually showing up a couple of places in North Muskegon.

Good case in point: if you go down Ruddiman towards the lake, right across from the old Harbor View, there was a house there. It's brand new now as the result of a meth explosion—a big fire. This was one of my cases I got to investigate. (It just so happened to be on the day of the night of the father-daughter dance, so I wasn't able to go; my dad had to go in my place, but that's just a little side note.) We get called there because there was four people staying at the house: three of them were meth heads, one was just a raging alcoholic—they would give him alcohol, buy him beer and let him stay as long as he cooked their meth or whatever. Well, early early one Saturday morning, one of the meth heads was in the basement, and she was trying to do a "recook" on some old meth. She had this chemical liquid with lithium and pseudo-ephedrine and all that, and she put it in a glass jar. To heat it, they use Coleman fuel—like for camping. What you do is, you heat up the chemical liquid, and you try to pass off some of the evaporants and filter out the meth. Well, she was putting the torch to the glass, and she didn't realize—she was being dumb—she didn't realize that it was not a Pyrex glass. So the glass jar shattered, and the liquid and all this Coleman fuel got on her arm and started on fire. She flailed around, the fire started to spread rapidly in the basement, and it ended up burning up the whole house. They all escape. She's the only one with injuries—bad burns. They bring her to the hospital.

We do an investigation, because we're trying to figure out, "How did this fire start?" We were pretty sure the fire had something to do with the meth lab, but no one was talking. No one was saying, "Oh, this is what we were doing when it happened." Anyway, I was finally, in the end, able to get her to confess that she was trying to do a recook, and that that's what happened. It burned down that whole house.

Then they rebuilt it brand new. I guess one of the people's parents were pretty wealthy. They had bought that house for him so that he could drink, because they didn't want him having parties at their house. For a while at least, that house that burned down was kind of the party house in town. I was going through the garage as part of the investigation, and I remembered how when we were in high school, Kirk would have parties, and he used to have us sign the wall in his basement. Well, out in the garage is where this kid would have people sign when they had parties, and I remember I recognized some North Muskegon names.

I worry that people in a place like North Muskegon have a false sense of security when it comes to what's really going on out there. One of the worst things I've seen is what drugs like heroin has done to people's lives. You talk about an epidemic going on now? It's heroin use, and it's in Muskegon County bad. The hospitals were telling one of our lieutenants that they get three-to-four overdoses a day—friends dropping off their friends at the front door and leaving.

And it's not like it hasn't hit us close to home. Brian Miton died of an overdose—I graduated with his sister. Brad O'Shea—I graduated with him—he was addicted, and he shot himself. I saw the pictures: blood splatter, brain splattered all over the ceiling. It was a shotgun that he used. It was bad.

I've had crazy stuff that I've seen. I had one where I was the first on the scene on the highway where these two kids—they were probably like eighteen, nineteen, twenty—they ran out of gas, so they went and stole gas from a neighbor's there. Well, one was filling the tank, and the snowplow came by. The snowplow didn't see him, and it just crushed him. We get there, and both of his legs are severed completely off. One is up by his head, and the other is still attached to the snowplow, which is like twenty feet away. The dude's eyes are wide open—I remember that; he's just looking straight up. I remember trying to calm his friend down. His friend's like, "You gotta do somethin for him, you gotta do somethin for him." I'm like, "The paramedics are here. They're doin everything they can." I didn't want to tell him his buddy's dead, so I just said, "They're doin everything they can, man." That was one of the worst—probably the goriest scene I've seen.

I take that back. I got called to an industrial accident where a guy had jerry-rigged this press machine. The company makes pressed styrofoam boxes, and this guy was fixing a machine. He had jerry-rigged the safety mechanism on it, and he got inside the machine, and something set it off. He was literally crushed flat. It was—oh, it was nasty. Then I had to go tell his wife what had happened. It was her second day of work at a corporate office, and she thought I was kidding at first. She said, "You're joking. You've gotta be kidding me. There's no way." Then, when it started to hit her? That's the worst part: telling a loved one that their loved one died.

To do it, you've got to kind of like go into a certain place in your head. You've got to prepare, because you know they're not going to believe you at first. Then they're going to cry—they're going to be hysteric. You've just got to prepare for it. You go in there kind of like with a blank mind and tell them, "Hey, I'm very sorry that I'm the one to have to tell you this. There was an accident at your husband's work, with a machine, and he ended up, um, passing away as a result of the accident." I didn't want to tell her he was squished like a little bug, so I said, "Well, there was an accident, and your husband passed away." That's not normal. You don't plan to hear that your loved one has been in a traumatic accident.

Luckily, I haven't had to do too many of those. There's been a few, but most times when there's an accident, the family members have already been contacted, either by friends who heard about the incident, or, if they're at the hospital, the doctors will tell them. Like one time, this older lady ran a red light at Sherman and Lincoln, and there was a motorcycle that had the green light, and she T-boned the motorcycle. There was two people on it: the guy who was driving it, and his girlfriend, and the girlfriend ended up getting ejected— flew off the bike like twenty feet. She had a full helmet on, but it broke her neck, and she died instantly. I remember, the driver on the motorcycle didn't even know her last name. He was like, "I only started datin her recently." *Oooh.* That's not good. But somehow her parents were at the hospital, and the doctor was the one who told them she had passed away, so I didn't have to do that.

You've probably heard this: police officers have a very dark sense of humor. We do, but it's a coping mechanism. We don't make fun of a tragic situation like "ha ha," but if we're talking about what happened that day, we will joke about stuff that would make other people say, "That's a sick bastard." We do it because, if you don't, then that's how it gets to you. If you don't joke about certain things that we see and do, then it will get to you. It will bother you. It will fuck with your mind. But when you make the jokes, it's kind of like blowing off steam. It gets it out of there, and you can move on.

Because really, I became a cop to help people. It isn't glamorous, but that's what I wanted to do. So when I see police officers doing the wrong thing, that breaks my heart, because I went into this line of work to help people. But what also kind of hurts is some of the things that people do in response to that—some of the blanket statements that people make against the police in general—especially now with the political climate. Because I love this country. I love it with my heart and soul. My brother is a Staff Sergeant First Class. For me it's God, family, country. In that order.

Say what you will about the president—I respect people's opinions. I don't love the guy. I don't love Trump, but I voted for him, and I'm going to support him. So when it comes to some of the response to Trump's election: you have the right to protest, but rioting is criminal. Breaking into stores, looting stores, breaking shit—especially in your own community? You're not going to get your point across. It really irritates me when some of the people out there are calling it protesting when what they're really doing is rioting. Burning cars, vandalism, disrupting traffic—there are reports of ambulances not being able to get to hospitals in time because people are "protesting" by shutting down traffic on highways. I mean, that's ridiculous. How do you think the civil rights people got their way? Not by rioting. Peaceful protest. Martin Luther King.

I'm not saying every police officer is a saint, because they're not—we're not. There's going to be bad apples. There are. There are bad cops out there—cops that are overzealous, cops that are way too quick to use violence, cops that are way too quick to use force. But what I think happens now is, the media sensationalizes a lot of it. The media kind of blows it out of proportion. If you look at the stats, it says that use of force against African-Americans by police is not on the rise, but the media's attention to it is. So if something happens over in Bumfuck County, you're going to see it on the national news now, whereas before you might not have ever heard about it. And when you see it, a lot of people will only see: "Black man shot by police." What the media might not say right away is that the guy had a gun in his hand. If people were to see the whole thing and see the body cam, then they'll see: we had to do what we had to do. Watch what that guy was doing beforehand, and watch why I had to react the way I did. I'm going home at night to my family. At the end of the day, we go home, and we take our badges off. We're humans. We have a job to do just like anyone else. But all most people see is the headline: "Black man shot by police."

The big elephant in the room in regards to the police is racism. That's huge. It's huge right now. Some people think racial profiling is what really drives us, which, I mean, for me? I can't tell who's in the car in front of me. Usually I'm behind them when I'm running a plate. And then, whether it's a white guy or a black guy, to me that doesn't matter. If someone broke the law, they broke the law. Four or five years ago at our department, they said that we were arresting too many black guys, and I was like, "Hold on a second. Hold on a second. We're not going out and looking for black guys to arrest. We're responding to calls. We're making traffic stops. And if it happens to be a black person, it happens to be a black person. If it's a white guy, it's a white guy. We're not targeting black guys and letting white guys go." So I always thought that was silly. To me, my job is my job. But in the culture, police are racist. If you talk to an average minority, they're afraid of the police.

Case in point: I get called to another car accident. It happened on Henry at Sherman. It's a black guy and a white woman, and I guess he was furious. He was yelling, threatening her, banging on her window, whatever. By the time we get there, he's in his car, and I knock on the window, and he doesn't roll it down. He looks at me and he goes, "Get the fuck away from me." I'm like, "What? I need your driver's license, registration, and insurance, sir." He says, "You get the fuck away from me right now." That's all he would say. I was like, "Okay, I need your license, or you're gonna go to jail." And he just started getting more mad—screaming. He'd get on the phone for a while, then he'd get off, screaming, telling me to get the fuck away from his car. I'm like, "What? Is this dude on drugs or something? What the fuck?" Well, it turns out, a couple minutes later, his dad shows up on the scene. And his dad was real decent. He was like, "Hey, you know, I'm real sorry. My son had a bad experience with the police. I'm here to calm him down." So he calmed down a little bit, but he was still very disrespectful—"Ah, I hate the fuckin police." Whatever. He told me what happened with the accident. He obviously was in the wrong. He was leaving the Shell parking lot—he was turning left—and somebody was waving him on, but there was another car in the other lane that kept going, and it crashed into him. Technically, he has to yield the right of way to all oncoming traffic, even if someone's waving him on. Which is kind of crappy. I get that. But anyways, I go back and I'm doing my ticket and my partner asks the dad, "By the way, I'm just curious, what bad experience did your son have with the police?" And what he told me was ridiculous. I thought "bad experience" meant he got the shit beat out of him. But it was: his cousins were fighting out in front of his house. He came out to break them up. The Muskegon Heights police who responded obviously didn't know where he lived, so when they said, "Can you go back to your house?" he started yelling at them, "I live right here." He started yelling. He wouldn't listen to them. So they put him in handcuffs and put him in the back of the cop car for like ten minutes. That was it. That's someone that I would consider to be a snowflake—a little overly sensitive.

I don't know if I'll ever really understand it. I mean, growing up in North Muskegon, who was the first black person I got to meet? It was Rod. Ninth grade. Turned out to be a great friend. Haven't talked to him in a while, but I still consider him a great friend. I would say we were tolerant of people, but I think it would have been nice to have a little bit more of a diversity. And it has become more diverse, which I think is good. It won't be such a culture shock if kids—when they're younger—start realizing, "Hey, we're all the same. We're all humans. Just because you have a different skin color doesn't mean you're different."

A couple weeks ago, I had an African American I was talking to. He was an ex-Navy guy, and he had numerous cousins on the Chicago Police Department. He goes, "You know what? You guys have a pretty bad rap right now. You have it pretty tough. In the military, we knew who our enemies were. We knew, when I stepped foot on the ground with my assault rifle, the enemy was the bad guy on the other side that didn't speak the same language as I did. We knew who they were. But you guys, as cops, you don't know who the enemy is sometimes." And then he also said, making the point to me, "A lotta black people may not support you guys in the police right now, but I want you to know that I am one black person that does." To me, that meant the world. It made my whole day. I'm kind of a sentimental guy. I thanked him.

ROD

Big deal. Did I cry? Oh yeah, I cried. I'm not going to lie. I cried. Because you don't know what the outcome's going to be. It's a change of cultures. Sometimes the path that you take, you think that you know, but you really don't. You really don't. You don't have a clue. Things can circle on you really fast. When it happens, you think, "What just happened? What did I just do?"

I never would have thought, not in a million years, that that would have been my decision—to take my child out of Muskegon Heights and move him to North Muskegon. I never would have thought that. No way. I thought, "He's gonna graduate from Muskegon Heights, like his pa did, and like his grandpa did."

My parents went there, then I went there. And it was a pretty strong school. Out of my class, we have doctors, lawyers, judges. We've got all kinds of people that went on to be real high up in education. I graduated from Muskegon Heights in '78, and by the time I was there it wasn't really that diverse. It was more of an all-black school. There were maybe five or six white kids, and they kind of stayed in a little shell by themselves. Everybody pretty much got along, but you could tell that there was a gap, that there was a difference.

Growing up around here was totally great for me. Sixth Street. As a kid, we played football after school. We played basketball all the time. It was always outside, "rippin 'n runnin." There was no video games. No such thing as a video game. There was black and white television. We had three channels. You wasn't glued to a television, so everything you did was more creative. I built an ice rink in my back yard. My dad thought that was kind of different, that I would want to ice skate. But we spent all of our time outside. Muskegon Heights—it was just a nice community neighborhood. There was no crime at all—very little, very little. You could leave your house open. You didn't have to bolt nothing down, didn't have to chain nothing down. Everybody was like family.

My parents were born in the South. My mother's family is from Shreveport, Louisiana. My dad's is from Birmingham, Alabama. But they met up here. Got married at sixteen.

The foundry is what brought my grandparents here—during the War. My mom's dad worked at Continental Motors. Thirty years in there. Hard Worker. Healthy man. He lived to be ninety-four years old. He would hunt, fish. He shot squirrels—bring them home, clean them, cook them. He had a garden in the backyard. He knew how to live off the land. My grandmother would can, so they ate a lot of stuff that wasn't in the store. That's probably why he lived to be ninety-four. He always had that kind of stuff that didn't come out of the store. Grandpa killed it and brought it home, and they cooked it and ate it. Grandma gardened and canned. They always had their garden at their house over there on Wood Street. Her cabinets were full of preserves. That's different. People live a lot longer eating like that.

Not everybody though. My mom passed when I was six years old, and my dad remarried, so my step-mom raised me. My mother died from asthma. There was a ton of pollution around here. When I went to junior high, we would walk along Sanford Street, so we walked by Campbell's every day—CWC—and we would see that smoke. That's what you breathed every day walking to school. You'd breathe that smoke all the way. Big clouds of smoke. Black. Just going up into the air. We breathed all that every day.

My brother worked at Campbell's for a minute. He got out of school, became a teacher's aide, but then he went to Campbell's and got a job. He worked at Campbell's eight days. Got his first check and he said, "There is no way. I ain't gonna work like this." He worked eight days, came home and said, "Brother, I can't do it. It's too much dirt." He said, "I can't do a job like that." So he left there. The money was good. He said, "I don't care how good the money is." He said, "There ain't no dirt like this."

My dad was a supervisor at West Michigan Steel. He hired in there at eighteen years old and put in thirty-some plus years there. My step-mom didn't work much. My dad pretty much took care of us himself. He retired from the plant several years before it closed. Now that's just open land down there.

I think that's what's really killed the Muskegon area is those jobs moving out of here. I think they should have left those jobs for anybody that wanted to get them—with or without a high school diploma. Because not everybody's going to get an education. Not everybody's going to be smart. Some people are going to need those decent-paying jobs to raise a family, so when you take those jobs away from here—and now they've moved them almost all away—a man can't live on nine dollars an hour. By himself he can, but he ain't going to have no family. No decent home, no decent car. But that's what's happened to Muskegon.

It changed people's opportunities. Now, to get a job, you have to have education, which a lot of kids don't have. That's where crime steps in, because people see that they can make more money doing stupid stuff like selling drugs. Why would you take a nine-dollar-an-hour job when you can make a lot more money doing it the other way? That's what's happened to this little town, and we knew that would happen once the industry started moving out of here.

Nowadays, if you can't pass a little test, you get no job. I graduated in June '78 and was hired in almost immediately at Alcoa up in Whitehall, and when I hired in, there was no test. All you had to have was a diploma. But now, if you can't pass a test, you can't even get interviewed. And the test has got math, so a lot of people can't get that kind of job. It's a decent paying job, but a lot of people just can't get those jobs, so they end up making nine dollars an hour, and that's what's really took this area down to nothing.

I've been lucky with that and unlucky with that. Growing up with my dad working in the foundry, I never thought I would work in the foundry, not for as long as I did. Never thought so. But I got hired in, and I just got content. That's it. Just got content. And the money was good. Right now, it's twenty-four, twenty-five dollars an hour. Which isn't a lot—at all. But when you look at the job market, everything else is nine bucks, ten bucks.

But we had to struggle with the economy as well. Had to take a lot of cuts, because had we not, I think they would have moved their company out of here just like everybody else did. They had threatened to do it several times, so we had to take some cuts—cost of living cuts, no raises. Before, every time the cost of living would go up, my check would go up. Well, now the company says, "We can't afford to keep going at this rate. We can't afford to keep giving you these raises, because if we do, we won't be able to stay competitive." So now you look at the company, worth a hundred and some billion—we've got parts on the space shuttle—and they still don't give anything back to the employees. We have to pay for our own insurance. You didn't have to before. The company used to pay for it—now you pay for it. That comes out of your check, so what you're making an hour ain't really twenty-five. You're not really making that. Really, it's not a good place to be right now—it's not good to be in that kind of work.

That's why most people are leaving Muskegon. It's going to be like a ghost town. It's going to be like a resort town. That's all you're going to see is resorts. Lakey's is gone. Campbell's is gone from Sanford Street. The paper mill is gone.

For a kid growing up around here now, at least in the city, it's tough. Everything outside the city is great—around the perimeter—but once you come inside, into the heart of it, it's tough. You've got to be tough in here. It's a tough place to be. You've got inner city kids that have nothing to do now. They can't go outside hardly because the crime is so high. You've got to keep them closed in all the time. I mean, you don't have to, but it's safer. When you go up to North Muskegon or in the Norton Shores area, everything looks nice, but once you come in from this little perimeter, it's a whole different ballgame. Especially for a kid.

When my kids were getting to the age where they were about to start high school, I sat down with a couple of administrators from the Heights who said, "We have to gear our curriculum towards the capacity of our students. You can't have a curriculum that's this high if there are only five kids who can really get it." So it became pretty obvious that at Heights the curriculum wasn't strong enough for my kids to go on to college if they chose to do so. They wouldn't have been prepared for college.

I also wanted Rod to be surrounded with a good set of guys, guys who weren't going to do anything too boneheaded. Young men are young men. Young men are going to make mistakes. But I thought it would be better for him if the guys around him weren't going to be saying, like, "Hey, let's go break into that guy's house and steal his stereo." I thought, "You know what? I've gotta make a decision here."

Which wasn't an easy decision. I thought about Muskegon Catholic Central, and that was about five grand to send them there. And then school of choice came up, but they only would take your child if they had room, and then you had to fill out an application. They had to check to make sure he wasn't a naughty child or a bad kid in school, and then they would let you know if they had the capacity to take them. That's when North Muskegon came up. That's how we ended up in North Muskegon, because we moved over there a couple of years after the kids started school. When I look at it, what it's done for the people we've met, the lives we've changed, the people who have touched us, it's pretty cool.

But I caught a lot of flak behind that. "Why would you do that? Why would you take your kid from here, from Muskegon Heights, and send him over there to North Muskegon? Why would you do that? This is where you went. This is where your roots are. This is where you went to school, and this is where he should go." I caught a lot of flak behind that, I really did. People did not like that. People did not like that at all. I caught a lot of flak behind that. I was a traitor. I was a traitor. Now, I was okay with that, because I felt that this had to happen, but it sure wasn't easy.

It wasn't easy. I looked at Rod when I let him out of that car for the first day of JV football practice, ninth grade, and I thought, "I can't let him go in there by himself. What kind of parent are you?" These are the things that were going through my head. "You're nuts. You're gonna let this kid walk in a school like that? There's something wrong with you." That's how bad I felt about it. I really felt bad. I parked out in front of the school and I said to him, "Would you like me to go in with you?" He goes, "That's not gonna happen, Dad." So I knew then he'd be fine. That right there, just that little bit right there, I said, "He can handle it himself. He can go in there and hold his own." I could see that when he said, "Dad, I'm good."

Because you think about how the kid's going to handle it. It's a lot that you're putting a child through. You know, a kid could come back and hate you for it. If it don't work out, you could be hated. Your child could hate you. I mean literally hate you. Because you see that, where some kids just literally hate their parents because of what their parents have done to them. So when you're making a big old choice like this, you hope that it works out and hope they like it. And Rod said, "Dad, it was the best thing you ever did." He said, "If I ever have kids, I wanna put them in a small school." It was good. We met some nice people. I mean, not everybody's going to be friendly everywhere you go, but if you are, that's what makes the difference.

So that decision was great for us all. I look at the people I met. I look at the lives that we touched and at the lives that touched our lives. And at the time I felt I was driving, that I was the pilot. But I really wasn't. I really wasn't. It was God that was driving, and I was sitting on the other seat, and He was growing us all for what Rod's doing now in his life down in Florida and for whoever else's lives that we changed. That was part of that big picture.

Look at North Muskegon now versus when my kids were there. When Rod went, in the whole high school, how many black girls were there? Melba—his sister. That was it. She was the only one in the whole high school. Not so now. There's quite a few now. We didn't know that we were opening doors—opportunities—for blacks at North Muskegon. We were just thinking, "Hey, let's take a chance." I think that worked out.

Now my grandkids—my older daughter's kids—they go to Mona Shores. Demari has got something like a 3.8 GPA. He's real smart. He's going to be an engineer or something like that someday. He's going to be something special. After football. Because he's a monster on the field. When he hits you, he just goes right through you. That's one of the reasons why Shores has seen some improvement on the field in recent years.

Because one thing you have to be in life is competitive. Not just in athletics. If you play athletics and your team's competitive and you win some and lose some, then you learn something. But if you lose all your ball games, I don't know that there's a lot of learning that goes on. And conversely, if you win all the time, then you don't know how to lose. It's important to learn how to do both, because in the workforce it's going to be the same thing. Might have some failures with this idea, the next one might be great. If you've got to work on an assembly line with a bunch of people, this guy might not be that fast, but if you can get a couple of pieces ahead to help this guy out, then that concept comes into play.

And I worry, because I think we're falling behind—the country as a whole. I think it's a great country to live in, don't get me wrong. I love my country. But I think we're falling behind.

I care how foolish we look as a country as a result of the leaders we have. To me, a leader's choice of words should be professional. If I'm going to speak to a country—or speak for a country—my words shouldn't sound like they came out of elementary school. I loved the way Obama talked. Loved the way Obama talked. And now, I mean, I listen to the way Trump talks, and I think, "That's our president? What school did you go to? It sure couldn't have been an Ivy League school." The way Trump talks, when I turn on the TV, I don't even want to hear him. That's my leader? I care about that.

And some of the things that he wanted to do as far as banning people from this country? You can't do that. This country is not built like that. This is not the way we built this country. You can't do that. Because if that were the case, then my son couldn't have went to North Muskegon. Okay? And I wouldn't have liked that. That's how I feel about everyone. Everyone deserves an opportunity to better themselves and their families, and they should have it. No one should have the right to say, "You can't have it just because you look like this or just because you came from there." This country wasn't built like that.

I'm old school. I believe everyone needs to be treated nice. I don't care if you've got one leg, two legs, one arm, one eye. Everybody needs to be treated nice. I don't care if there's two girls liking each other or two guys liking each other—everybody needs to be treated nicely. You cannot discriminate. When you're in a leadership position, you're the one everyone else is going to look up to. You. You're a leader. Kids are going to grow up thinking that what they see from you is normal—that's it's okay to talk about people this way. And the way Trump talks about people: it isn't okay.

If President Trump does something great for this country, I would be surprised. I would be surprised. I would be very surprised. I voted for Hillary. I did. And coming from a strong family of men—watching certain things that my grandfather handled, that my dad handled, and then watching my mother, watching other women, how they handled things differently—I would have never thought that a woman could handle that position. But we ain't had a whole lot of choices. It was either vote for Don, or vote for Hillary. And I know she had some issues going on too, but she was professional. She was smart. And I thought having her in there would give me four more years or eight more years with Obama's stuff. That's the reason why I voted for her.

I didn't think I would ever vote for a woman president. My brother-in-law said he wasn't voting for her. He said, "I ain't votin for no Hillary." When my brother-in-law got to Vegas, the first thing he sent me was a picture of the Trump Hotel. He sent it to me on my phone. Trump Hotel. Now, I don't know that he voted for Trump, but people in my family—they all said that they weren't going to vote for Hillary. That's how it goes. So I could see how this could happen.

But it was one of those situations when I thought, "Gotta get out and vote, gotta get out and vote." Because people fought and lost their lives for us to vote. Shame on you for not voting. Vote for something or stand for nothing. That's the way I feel. Vote for something or stand for nothing. And I didn't love Hillary, but I couldn't just sit there and do nothing. Because Trump, he's going to take care of his immediate family, and that's it.

Whereas our last president, I think he cared about our country. I mean, if you think about some of the stuff that Obama did, my brother says it didn't benefit him none—like the insurance; he didn't care for it because it doesn't help him. So there were some things Obama did as well that didn't help everybody, but he thought about the country as a whole. Not everybody is going to like all of the decisions, but he thought about the country as a whole. Obama—I think he cared about this country. And if he didn't, he sure fooled the crap out of me. Man, if he really didn't care about this country, then he sure did a good job of pretending that he did.

I never get into politics all that much, but if Obama hadn't have bailed out the automakers, that all would have gone under, and we'd be buying all our cars from everywhere else, and even more of the industry would have left Michigan. I think that was huge. That's what I wish we could have done in Muskegon when all that industry started to go. Because like I said, it's tough in here now. When it happened that you couldn't just go get a job that gave you a decent living, it got tough in Muskegon. North Muskegon, Norton Shores—those places are nice. But you get into the inner city, and life isn't easy. For a whole lot of people, life isn't easy.

TONY

"I, too, am America."

—*Langston Hughes*

Maintain, maintain. I just try to maintain. You know what I'm saying? Because things ain't going good for me. I worked at a couple factories and stuff like that, and it was okay. That's before I got in trouble. Once I got in trouble, it's really hard for me to get a job. On the application it's, "You got any felonies?" And you can't lie on there, because they're going to find out. Then once you say, "Yeah," then they don't call you or nothing like that. You call them and ask them what's going on—they just don't say nothing.

What kind of job would I want to have? I would just say a job. I always wanted to be a car salesman, but right now I just want a job. Because when a man get out of prison and they learned they lesson and want to come home and straighten out, and then they go try to get a job and they get denied just because of they history, well then maybe they say, "I'm gonna go rob a bank. I'm gonna go sell drugs. I'm gonna go do worse than that." In they mind it's just, "I can't get a job, so I gotta do somethin." You know what I mean? They deserve a fair chance. No question, you can't be a police with a felony or you can't be a firefighter, but I don't see nothing really wrong with a person with a felony. If they really want to work, let them work in factories, work somewhere like that. We all make mistakes. I don't care who you are—we all make mistakes. You shouldn't be held to that forever. They went to prison, they served they time, they came home. They paid they debt to society, now they should be able to come home and work. Because my most important job is to not be one of the bad guys, and that's tough when you can't get a job just because you was young and dumb back in the day.

I maintain that, man. I made a promise that I'm not going to go back to prison. I feel prison is no place for no one. We choose our decisions, our own destiny, so if you put yourself in that predicament, then that's the choice that you make. I made my mistake, and I realized that being locked up is not for me. I don't want nobody telling me where I can go, when I can wake up, when I can go eat. It got to the point where it was just, "I don't wanna be here." I seen so many friends that's doing life in prison—never coming home. Never coming home again to they little kid. They can't kiss they kid and say, "I love you." They got to say it through prison walls. So I don't do nothing to break the law no more. I've been out of trouble ever since oh-nine.

But like I said, man, it's hard, because things ain't going too good for me. I've been kind of like homeless a little bit. I lost my dad. My mom—she's real, real sick. I'm not really working now. I'm really house-to-house. Right now I'm at the room—Heights Hotel up there. That's the worst place you can be. They do all type of stuff up there, man. You really can't sleep. It's the cheapest hotel you will ever get. It's ghetto. And when I say it's cheap— thirty bucks a night. You can just imagine, you know what I'm saying?

And it's like, I been out of school for a minute now, but I had my education—my reading, my writing—but then I lost a lot of my memory. I graduated or whatever—Muskegon High School, class of '89—but now I have a problem even reading and writing. I'm not where I used to be, so things are a little hard for me.

To be honest with you, I was in a bad car accident. I really messed up my back and everything like that, and they didn't think I was going to walk again at first. It took me like three years of therapy and everything like that to get me back on track. I had a little, like, brain injury, so that kind of like messed me up a little bit. I couldn't hardly talk or nothing like that. My speech was messed up and they didn't think I was going to be able to talk, but I talk good now. That happened not too long after I got out of high school. That really messed me up a lot.

It messed with my mind. I had brain damage, you know what I'm saying? It was like, I wasn't the same after that. I felt it. I wasn't the same after that. I had the accident, and I couldn't focus like I focus before.

I got blessed by God to the point where I was able to talk again. It was a lot of prayer. I couldn't have did it by myself. It was God. I couldn't have did it by myself. He gave me the strength for it all, to be able to walk again and talk again. I had to go back and forth to therapy for like three years, off and on. Once I was able to walk just a little bit, then I was able to get on the cane, and I did the cane for a while. Then after so long, I got back strong to the point where I can walk on my own, and that was truly a blessing then.

They had gave me disability at one time. When I got locked up and went to prison, then they denied me. They keep denying me and denying me and denying me, even though it's no different than it was after I got into the accident. I can't collect disability no more.

I got to get off these streets, man, because I want to make a difference for Muskegon. Muskegon used to be the best place to stay to raise kids. I just want it to be that a way again. I don't think it's hard. It's not hard. But it's going to take effort. It's going to take effort from everybody that's concerned about Muskegon. I believe that we could all come together to bring Muskegon back. I think Muskegon can be a better place. And all the things that I been into, all the stuff that I did, those are all things that I can use to reach out and maybe help somebody someday. From a person who been there and done that, if you're talking to somebody, that's better than if you're somebody who never been there.

Out of fifty kids, if I can help one, I'll feel like I did something. I think I can be a good spokesman—let the kids know that if you don't focus now, the life that you're living is going to change, and it's not going to change for the best; it's going to change for the worse. If it doesn't end up in prison, it's going to end up in the grave. I don't want to try to really scare them, but just try to let them see that this is what can happen if you don't follow the right directions. I really feel that. Like I said, I really think that I can be a good spokesman. I really can talk to people. I really want to be able to talk to kids, let them know that, "This ain't what you really want, man. This ain't what you need. If somebody step on your shoe, that don't mean shoot em. If somebody talk to your girl, that don't mean shoot em." You know what I mean? You got to think about the big picture. What's going to happen to me if I get caught? Because eventually, if you keep doing it, you're going to get caught. Everybody make mistakes, but when you keep making the same mistakes, then that's when it's a problem.

We need more for the kids, man. We need more for the youth. More activity for them to go to. When I was coming up, we had open gym. You could go to the gym and ball. You had the skating rink. We had more stuff to do. Now I really don't see nothing for the youth to do. Everything they do, you have to pay for now.

Nowadays all the kids play video games and watch all the violence on the video games. Back when we was coming up, we had video games, but it was like Pac-Man, Centipede. It was simple games, and there wasn't no violence going on, but we loved it though. That's what the government needs to do: they need to ban all these violent activities like on the games, because it's to the point where kids watching it so much, they believe they can actually do that. They doing it on the video game, so they feel they can go out on the street and do that.

Kids now ain't like they was back then, just due to the fact that all the violence and stuff going on. It's more violent. A lot more killings and stuff going on. So many murders going on around here. And it's mostly just about bragging rights. It's about respect. It's crazy. I mean, it really is not necessary for all this killing going on around Muskegon. Back when I was growing up, you got into it with a person, it might be just a little fistfight or something like that, then that was that. It wasn't all about the violence and the gangs and the guns.

I don't feel like the parents nowadays teaching them right. Nowadays, if a parent say something to a kid, the kid is ready cuss them out. When I was coming up, if my parents say something, you know to do just what they say. And you didn't just listen to your own parents. Back in my day, if you get into trouble or something like that and another parent see you, they always spoke out—and you listened to them. The majority of parents back then was more strict, but they showed more love. My dad was in the Marines, and when he say you couldn't go nowhere—that you was on punishment—that's what it meant: you wasn't going nowhere. Tough love. At the time, we might didn't like it, but overall it all made sense.

And it wasn't just at home. At elementary school, Angell School, we had a principal named Mr. Scott. They don't do this today, but he had a big paddle, right? And if you didn't do what you supposed to do, you went to the principal's, and he would whoop you with that paddle. When he would do it, he would call your parents and let them know—they wouldn't say nothing. You know what I mean? Back then, you didn't want to get into trouble at school with Mr. Scott, because he didn't play. Everybody who went to Angell School, if you mention Mr. Scott, they will say "paddle." That's how it was, man. I mean, I didn't like the paddle back then, but I think if we had that more now, things would be different.

I'm not saying there wasn't nothing wrong back then. Robberies, stuff like that: it happened, but it wasn't to the point that it is today. A long time ago, you never heard about all these murders and all this unsolved this and this and this and this. You know? It's a problem. It's a problem, I think. We need to come together, united, and come up with a solution to the problem. I don't think we doing a good enough job coming up with a solution to the problem.

I think things can get better here in due time. I do. I'm praying and I'm hoping it does, but I think the community of Muskegon needs to do more than what they doing. Instead of sitting here, worrying about what the police is going to do to solve this murder, it's about what are *you* going to do to make the community more safer—neighborhood watches and stuff like that. It don't always have to be on the police to clean things up. They got places to be, people to see. They got a job to do. They can't be in every place at one time. So if the community come together and not be scared to say what they seen about what's going on, it'd be better. I hear people saying all the time, "I don't like the police." I say, "Why?" They say, "Because they don't do they job. They got all these unsolved mysteries, murders around here, and they not tryin to solve none." I say, "Wait a minute now, what have you done to help them?"

A lot of people say that talking to police, that's called "snitching." But it's not snitching when you try to get your community together. That's not "snitching." To me, that's trying to get the bad people off the streets to keep the good people on the streets. Like, if you see somebody kill somebody and you report it to the police, that's not snitching. I don't call that snitching. You might have saved some other person's life from getting killed—you understand?—by telling the police about what you saw so they can get the bad people off the streets instead of letting it keep going on and on and on. It shouldn't have to hit your home directly before you step up and act. It's already hit home when it happened to somebody in your community.

Because there got to be a solution to the problem. And maybe it all starts with the president, but there's so much stuff that we need to just do here ourselves. I voted for Hillary, and I'll tell you, the only reason I didn't vote for Donald Trump is because I think he just wants power. Maybe Trump could make a difference, but I just don't see it. His main thing now is to get rid of Obamacare. I mean, there's way bigger things than Obamacare. He should be focused on more jobs, you know what I'm saying? Helping America. I believe he could, but he's got to focus on that. We need factories here. We used to have factories in Muskegon. Put more jobs here.

I just hope we get it together, man, in Muskegon. I just want it to go back to a good place for the kids to be brought up in. Muskegon. Let's bring Muskegon back. There's always a solution to a problem. You might not know it right now, but eventually, if we all put our heads together, I think we can come up with something.

ASALINE

*"The elation that comes of great hopes
and changes...had turned into this?"*
—*Eudora Welty*

I was just like any other kid: I was in band; I was president of our Spanish club; I was in French club. I got to go to Europe—they would select two students from our school to go on an exchange program, and I was one of them. I stayed with a family in Bremen, Germany, and we were able to visit the Berlin Wall. I still have the pictures. When I came back, I was homecoming queen. But I never thought that I was a popular kid or anything like that. I always felt that I was on the outside, and so I identify with kids that have that kind of feeling. A lot of kids do—even ones that may seem like they've got it going on and they're on top of the world and they're the jock and go to all the parties and all that. We all have insecurities. Growing up, I never thought I was good enough.

I graduated somewhere in the top ten of my class, and I got a full-ride scholarship to the University of Michigan, but I got pregnant. At that time, you didn't go to college pregnant. Just last week, I was cleaning out some things and I came across the letter—my acceptance letter and a copy of my response—and I realized that I never mentioned to them that I was pregnant. I had just told them, "I'm going to be getting married, so I won't be able to accept the scholarship this year." Well, I never did go to college until later on.

My husband and I didn't get married right away, but we were both working, and shortly after I graduated high school we moved into the city of Muskegon. We were trying to find a home, and there was an ad in the *Chronicle* about this two-apartment house on Pine Street. The upstairs apartment was for rent, and so I called, and the lady I spoke with on the phone was telling me how nice the neighborhood was and how nice the apartment was and all of that, and then she added, "You don't have to worry. There aren't many blacks in this area. We don't rent to blacks." There was this long pause, and I said, "Ma'am, I hate to tell you this—no, I really don't hate to tell you this: I'm black." Then she hung up on me. It was funny. I was incensed, but you have to have a sense of humor. You do have to have a sense of humor, because otherwise it just bugs you.

In 1971, we bought a little two-bedroom home just south of Apple Avenue on the west side of the highway. Then we moved to Norton Shores in 1981, and I'm still in that same house off of Lake Harbor Road. So I don't know exactly when things started to change in Muskegon Heights, because I wasn't there, but when I go by our old house where I grew up, everything is in disrepair.

I grew up in the '50s and '60s, and The Heights was a wonderful place at that time. During the War and after the War, the factories needed workers, and where else would they get cheap labor? Down South. So a lot of people migrated up from the bottoms because there were jobs in the factories and the foundries. A lot of the people who came ended up living in the old Army barracks and in East Park Manor—the projects. That was where a lot of people coming up had to stay, because there wasn't anywhere else for them to live.

My dad was one of the first African Americans in the county to own a home, and it wasn't easy for him to get a loan—not because of his credit, but because it was very rare for banks to lend to minorities. My dad would always say, "Credit is everything, because credit is your word. It is your integrity." He always had very good credit—"A-1 credit" is what he called it—but he was denied three or four times before he finally found a bank that would lend to him—Lumbermen's Bank—and he stayed loyal to them the rest of his life.

Our neighborhood was almost all African-American. Most of the families who lived there were renters, but they took pride in the place. The yards were all neat. Almost everyone lived in a two-parent home—moms and dads with kids. Families knew each other. We were all friends. We played in the streets. We were always within shouting distance of home, so we didn't have to worry about curfews. The families took care of one another—helped out. If we were outdoors playing and somebody got angry and had a fight or an argument, one of the neighborhood parents would come out there to settle it—separate the kids that were beefing, talk it out, that sort of thing. It was the kind of place where everybody cared about each other. Everyone pitched in and helped each other. That's what neighbors do.

Our family had the most kids out of anyone in the neighborhood, but almost all the other families still had at least four. Nobody was particularly well-off, but everyone worked hard. The fathers were blue-collar workers. The mothers were either stay-at-home moms or worked as nurses' aides at Hackley Hospital. The men worked hard and took care of their families, and the females were very strong—the motherly type—just like my mom.

When I was in fourth grade, my mom and my biological father divorced. My mother had six children at the time, and my dad—who I call my dad, who essentially raised us—he had no children. He married my mother, and then they had four additional children, but growing up there were no "half-"sisters or "half-"brothers. We were just brothers and sisters. And we still are.

My mom was—and still is—a seamstress. She was a stay-at-home mom for the most part, but she took in sewing—wedding ensembles, bridal dresses, curtains, men's suits, coats. You name it, my mother could make it. She made sure we were well-clothed. Once, she had applied to the school for free-and-reduced lunch, because we didn't have a lot of money—my dad didn't bring in a lot of money. The high school principal sent home a note with us denying her application. The note said something like: "Mrs. Davis, are you kidding? Your kids are the best-dressed kids in school. You don't need free-and-reduced lunch." People thought we had a lot of money, because we were able to come to school looking really nice, but we could only do that because my mother had a flair for fashion and could make this stuff for little to nothing.

I can recall being embarrassed because we couldn't afford nice shoes—that's one thing she couldn't make. She would buy those really sturdy, saddle-bag looking shoes—really thick soles. I was so embarrassed. And unless your shoes wore out, you didn't get a new pair. So, when I was in junior high, I figured out a way that I might be able to get a new pair of shoes: I took my shoes down to the basement, and I just kept rubbing the heels on the cement wall until I'd whittled them down to almost nothing. They were all lopsided and everything, and of course they looked even worse than before. Well, when my mother found out what I'd done, she made me wear those shoes anyway. I was so angry. I was embarrassed.

We were poor, but we never felt poor—we never realized we were poor. We lived in this little two-bedroom, one-bathroom house. But my dad was very handy. He made a bedroom or two in the basement, and we had a makeshift bedroom on the front porch, and so there was plenty of room for everybody to sleep.

My dad is an interesting character. He worked at Campbell — Wyant & Cannon, on Sanford Street, and he was in the same boat as many men: he was doing that dirty, nasty work. My dad was the best welder in the foundry, but they wouldn't promote him to welder, because that particular job was reserved only for white men. My dad was doing the work, but other people were taking the credit for the work that he was doing. He was performing the duties of a welder, and he wasn't getting paid for it. But he was a rabble rouser. He actually got into fistfights twice with his superiors, and he was fired—twice. But they had to bring him back, because he was good. And eventually he got that promotion—eventually he became a welder. But that was just the way it was. He was friends with these people he was working with, but they didn't see anything wrong with taking home a higher wage when my dad was doing the most highly-skilled part of the job for them. It really wasn't fair: At the end of the day, my dad was taking home a lot less money than these guys who couldn't do the job as well as he could do it. But like I said, eventually he did get that promotion.

My dad was very smart—very worldly. He had been in the military during World War II—T/3 Sergeant, Engineering Light Platoon Company. He was also a combat infantry Ranger, and towards the end of the war he served in General Patton's Army. They had a mission in France, and the Army wasn't integrated at the time, so he was assigned to a black platoon. Well, they were going out with some of the French girls, but that kind of stopped after a few of the white soldiers told the French girls not to date the black soldiers—these white soldiers had told the French girls that the black soldiers had tails. That's hilarious, and it's sad. It's ludicrous when you think about it.

My dad was an artist, he was very well-read, and he made sure that we got to do cultural things. We were always in band in school, and we also went to all sorts of concerts. We would go to the symphony and to orchestra performances, but we would also go to other events. When I was just a little girl, my dad took us to see James Brown. Another time, The Ink Spots were playing in Grand Rapids, and I remember getting an autographed picture. I remember that the first play he took us to was at Cherry County Playhouse, which at that time was on Sanford Street. We went to see Peter Pan, and I was just mesmerized to see Peter Pan flying across the stage. We would also go to basketball games—wherever the Heights Tigers were playing, we would all pile in the car and go watch them play.

On Sundays, if there was nothing else to do, we went down to the lake and had a picnic. It was just wonderful growing up.

We would also all pile in the car and go to Detroit, or we'd go to Chicago. But we never stayed in a motel; we always stayed with friends or relatives. We took vacations all over, but it was only to where our relatives might be. At that time, we could not stay in a hotel—especially if we were travelling in the South. If we were going South, we pretty much drove straight through. We would always pack a huge lunch and big gallons of water, because we couldn't just go into a restaurant. There were certain bathrooms that we either had to use or could not use. I remember, one time, travelling to Mississippi—where I and my older sister were born—we were out of water. And I remember: my dad parked the car—took a chance—took the big water jugs, and walked across a field to a farmhouse to get water. We were really kind of concerned—worried—"Is something going to happen to him?" He came back just fine, but we had to be worried in that type of situation.

I remember the story of Emmett Till. I remember being young at the time, and of course, when that happened I was petrified. I was angry, but I was really, really scared. My dad explained to us what had happened. There were pictures in the magazines. Emmett Till had an open casket—that was another thing that stuck with me as I grew up. This isn't ancient history. Emmett Till was not much older than I was, and he was lynched while visiting his relatives in Mississippi.

I graduated high school in 1968 and got my first real job with the help of the Urban League. They would find out what jobs were available, then they would call young people in and prep them. They trained you on how to fill out an application, how to carry yourself in an interview, how to interact with customers, and then they would send you over to the company. That's how I got started as a teller at Muskegon Federal Savings & Loan.

Then, somehow, I got stuck. After a few years, I was training people to do the job of assistant branch manager or department head. I was doing the training for these people—mostly men—that they'd hired to do these jobs. And my husband would tell me, "That's just not right." And I knew it wasn't right. It would make me angry. He would say, "You should do something about that. You shouldn't sit still." So, with his prodding, I just kind of put my foot down. I said, "If I'm good enough to train people for these jobs, I'm good enough to get a promotion." So that's when my promotions started happening. It was after I had just had to put my foot down and say, "This is not right." Then I got one advancement after another.

My husband, John, was one of the most influential people I've known—one of the most respected people—because he went through some really tough times, and he stood firm. He came out alive. He was bloodied, but he came out alive. A lot of what I learned, I learned from watching him. Not just watching him, but being with him—going through some of the things that he went through.

He had gone to Nebraska on a football scholarship, but he suffered a severe knee injury that wrapped up his football career, and after surgery and all that he went to work at CWC. He was always very community oriented, and so even when he was working and going to college, he did volunteer work. There was a set of after school programs in Muskegon Heights, and he would go and play basketball and volleyball with the kids, and then he'd go to work at the foundry.

After a couple of years, John decided that he didn't want to work in a foundry anymore. He wanted to do something better and bring himself up in terms of job opportunities, and that's when he decided to go back to school. He finished his education here in Muskegon—first he went to MCC, then he went on and commuted to Grand Valley and got his undergraduate degree in Police Administration and Sociology.

He also applied for a position as a policeman, which is kind of funny, because in an African-American community especially—even back then—a lot of people didn't trust the police. Before John became an officer, I remember, he had a '64 GTO, and he would be doing things he shouldn't—like racing in the street. One time one of the sergeants pulled him over, and they knew him because he was the one who was always in this fancy car speeding, and John had to get out of the car. So John is standing next to the car and he asks, "Well, what are you pulling me over for?" And the officer said, "You got a busted tail light." John looked at it and said, "No, I don't." So the policeman takes his nightstick—boom. "You do now." I laugh about it, but he was upset. Of course he was upset. But that didn't make him not want to be a policeman. He still respected the police. So he became a police officer, and he served on the force for seventeen years.

He bucked the system when he was a policeman. He was always going to stand up for what was right. Sometimes it's easier to just be quiet, but he couldn't do that. He was loud and indignant whenever there was unrighteous stuff going on, and that got him in trouble. At the time, there were far more white patrolmen than there were African Americans, and if maybe there was prejudice—or plain racism—in the way that they handled people, or if someone filed a report that wasn't quite accurate, John would always speak up. Whenever he encountered something that he didn't think was right, he would say something about it, and that sometimes got him into trouble. He was let go more than one time, but they always had to reinstate him. He always got back in, because he always was on the right side. Even after all the struggles he had with the administration, people just loved him.

He was a patrolman for a few years, and then he became a detective. He worked with Central Narcotics. And therein lies the rub.

They used "snitches," for want of a better word. And I won't give a name, but I'll never forget his name. He was John's snitch, and somehow or other, someone got to this guy, and he manufactured a lie and said that John had sold him some narcotics. They never found anything. Anybody that knew John and knew how smart he was knew that he would have never done that. That was just not him. But nevertheless, he had to go to court, and of course, his reputation was severely tarnished. It took all of our savings—not just our savings; we had to borrow so much money. Our attorney really took a chance, because we didn't have a lot. We were a new family with young kids, and John was suspended from his job, so he wasn't earning any money, and I'm working at the bank for not much money either, so it was really hard. We didn't know if John was going to go to prison or what was going to happen.

It was horrible—me going to court with him every day with his family. His mother, everybody just terrified thinking, "Wow, they're gonna put him in prison. He didn't do it, but they're gonna put him in prison." He had to go to federal court in Grand Rapids. Judge Fox was the judge, and Judge Fox was incensed, to put it mildly. The charges were trumped up, he felt. There was no credibility with the witness, and Judge Fox really berated the prosecution team. He threw out two cases, and then John was acquitted on the one count they did try.

We celebrated, but then there was the appeals process, and that's how the case ended up at the United States Supreme Court. In the end he was acquitted, but it was a long process, and it was hard. John weathered the storm, but I think that does a lot to a person's spirit. He didn't let us see it so much, but that either will make you or break you, and in his case, he was determined that it wasn't going to break him. He rose just like a phoenix out of the ashes.

But that thing will still follow you. It doesn't matter that you were found Not Guilty. It doesn't matter that the Supreme Court felt there was no case there. Every time John would get a promotion, there was always that question. But people in our community loved him. They knew that he had a real heart for the community.

John continued on and got his master's degree in Public Administration from Western Michigan University. I was mostly helping with finances. I had a full-time job, and then: the kids. So I didn't have time to go to college. Both of us couldn't go at the same time. But after he finished, he said, "Now it's your turn." That's when I went to college, was as an adult.

I went to MCC, then Grand Valley, where I got a degree in Finance. I'm really proud of the fact that I was Outstanding Person in finance based on my GPA when I graduated. Then, from there, I went to Western and got an MBA with a focus on diversity, inclusion, and organizational change. So I struggled to go to college, but fortunately, I was still able to go on scholarships, and I had my husband there to help me with the kids. I was working full-time, he was working full-time, but we still made it happen. I always look back at that. I know a lot of women struggle to get an education at that stage in life, because they have to do everything. Well, my husband wasn't much of a cook, and he never would clean the house or anything like that, but he would take everybody to dinner, or he'd bring the dinner in. If I was trying to study, he would make sure that the kids had something to do—he would take them away and play with them in the park, go bicycling with them. He was very helpful. So I was delayed in terms of earning my college degree, but it can be done.

After that, I worked for several different banks, and because of the frequency of mergers and acquisitions, sometimes the bank changed on me—Huntington Bank, Ameribank, Fifth Third Bank, Wells Fargo. In the early '80s, I was the assistant manager at a bank over on Henry Street. I would do CDs and savings accounts and mortgage loans and car loans—all this stuff. One of our customers—he was a much older man; he's gone now—everybody knew that he didn't want me to wait on him. This went on for about a year: he would come in, and after a few visits, everybody just knew that he was not going to be directed to take care of his business with me. Well, the receptionist who worked at our branch had a mother who would clean house for this older gentleman. The receptionist and I were really good friends, and I also knew her mother a little bit. I called her mother Aunt Bertha. (She was a white lady, but her name was Bertha.) One day, this gentleman came into the office, and everybody was really busy, so the receptionist told him, "Mr. Such-and-such, you're just going to have to wait a few minutes. Asaline is the only one who's available right now, but we won't make you see her. You can just have a seat and wait." He said, "Oh, no. I don't mind seeing Asaline. She's Bertha's friend." After that, whenever he would come in, he would insist on waiting for me. It was kind of cute.

It makes you understand that until people know somebody, it's easy to stereotype and think that this person isn't as good, or this person isn't as smart, or this person is shiftless or lazy or violent. When you don't know the person, you maybe believe the stereotype of what you might have seen on the evening news. But when you know people—when you get to know people, or when you get to know people who know that person—you give yourself a chance to open up.

Anyway, I worked at a lot of different banks, and I did a lot of different things: mortgages, managing, training. I've done development of online programs for mortgage applications. I've done a lot of stuff. But now I'm happily retired.

Stepping back again—in 1988, John had had enough of being a police officer. He had been fighting long enough. He said, "I'm done with this. I'm going to go do something else." So he took a job with Muskegon County as a Substance Abuse Coordinator. He did that job for a couple years, and then there was an opening to be Emergency Management Director; when he took that job, he was the first African-American director in Muskegon County. Then, when the Public Health Director left, he went into that position, so his last job was as Muskegon County Director of Public Health.

He passed away in '99 of—of all things—colon cancer. That's one of the cancers they say you should never die from. People think, "Geeze, how come he didn't go to the doctor?" Well, he did go to the doctor—for a year and a half he was going to the doctor, and he was misdiagnosed. At age fifty, you should have a colonoscopy, but instead of a colonoscopy, his doctor suggested a sigmoidoscopy, which only goes half way up the colon. His cancer was in the upper colon and never could have been detected with a sigmoidoscopy. We all knew John was sick, but his doctor was treating him with antibiotics for what he thought was a severe sinus infection that had spread throughout John's whole system. He never checked John thoroughly enough. After about a year of going back-and-forth, back-and-forth, we were on our way up north for a conference, and I felt that John had a fever, so we stopped at Mercy Hospital on the way, and the ER doctors did some work and said, "I think you need to turn around and go home. Go see your doctor first thing on Monday."

That's when they finally got it figured out and we could finally start to treat the cancer. John underwent extensive surgery, he was undergoing chemotherapy at UofM, and for a little while he felt well enough to go back to work full-time. He was golfing—travelling. But then he just got sicker and sicker, and he died at age fifty-three. If you go into the Health Department, they have his picture up in there, and the building is named after him. After his death, I can't tell you how many people would come up to me and tell me what he had done for their family, how he—quietly, behind the scenes—had helped them get out of the trouble they were in, or how he'd gone to bat for them through the court system, or how he bought a bicycle for kids whose parents couldn't afford it, or how he would deliver groceries to people in need. He died too soon, but he left a legacy.

I have five children. Actually, altogether, I have seven children—because I have two sons who are as much mine as the kids
that I've birthed. One of them is in the military, in Stuttgart; he
has four children. Then I have another son who is with Muskegon
Public Schools; he has four children. Then I have my oldest daughter, who is a special-ed teacher in Lansing; she and her husband
have four children. My next daughter is an attorney here in town;
she's only got one child. I have another daughter who is a manager
at Spectrum Health in Grand Rapids; she doesn't have any children.
There's my son Jon, who also lives in Muskegon; he has two children.
And then Jer—my youngest. Jeremy has been gone since 2009; he
left two little girls.

Sometimes it seems like it was just yesterday, and then other
times it seems like, "Wow, that must have been years and
years ago."

I had been at work all day. Then, after work, I was visiting
my mom, and my mother had asked me, "What are you having
for dinner?" I said, "Well, Jer's home. More than likely he'll do
roasted vegetables in the oven, and then we'll figure out what to
do for meat." That was around eight o'clock in the evening. When
I drove home, I was taking the route near Lincoln Park Elementary
School—going the back route—and I heard the sirens, but of course
I didn't think anything of it. I got home, and Jer wasn't there, and
I still didn't think anything of it. That morning, on the table, he had
left me a donut and a note. It said, "Have a donut on me. I love you."

Like I said, I didn't think anything was amiss. Then the officer
came to my home with Jer's backpack and his bicycle and his basketball, and I can't even recall exactly what he said. I thought maybe
Jer had gotten into an accident or something. I asked, "Was it a car
accident?" The officer said, "No, but I think you need to get over to
the hospital." Something in the back of my mind wouldn't let me
face reality—that something is wrong here; something is despe-

rately wrong. I had on my pajamas, and the officer is saying, "I think you need to go to the hospital. He's over at Mercy Hospital." I'm thinking, "Oh Lord, did he get hurt playing basketball? Is he going to have to have surgery?" I thought maybe he fell or something like that. Looking back on it, I don't know that this policeman actually knew that Jer had died.

I changed my clothes, got in the car, and then it hit me. I called my daughter when I got out on Seaway Drive, and she became alarmed. She asked me, "Well, did you ask the officer what happened?" I said, "No. He just told me to go to the hospital." Then I called my mother and said, "Something happened to Jer. Please pray."

When I got to the hospital, I had started to become alarmed, but it really didn't sink in until they asked me to go into the room where the doctors talk to the family. I went in there, and my daughter called me again, and I said, "Well, I'm in this room. I'm waiting for the doctor to come in." And she said, "I'm on my way." Then I knew something was wrong. So I came back out, and they said, "Mrs. Scott, just have a seat. The doctor will be in." I said, "No. I'm going in right now. I want to see my son." I pushed past and went through the doors.

The funniest thing was, when I got into the room, he just looked like he was sleeping. They had the respirator on him, but he just looked so peaceful. Then that's when they told me everything that had happened. It didn't make any sense. I fainted, practically. I fainted. It just didn't make any sense.

He had played pickup basketball with some friends, and my son Jon had gotten there after the game and said, "Do you want a ride home." Jer had said, "No." And Jon told me—he said, "Mom, when I shook his hand, his hand was cold." But Jer didn't want a ride home, because he was on Jon's bike, and he didn't know how he would get the bike home. So he pedaled, cutting through the elementary school, and that's when he became distressed. That's when he had the heart attack. A woman with her children was there, and she thought his behavior was odd. I'm sure she thought, "This guy must be drunk or on drugs," because she said that he kind of sort of laid his bike down, and then he sat down, and then he lay down on his bike. Then she really became alarmed that something was odd, so she called her cousin, who was a maintenance guy at the school, and he came out and saw and said that he thought Jer was having a seizure. He asked him his name, and Jer was able to say his name, and that was it. There was a video from the surveillance camera, and I didn't see it. Two of my children saw the video, but that's something I would never want to see.

It still doesn't make any sense. That's what they said at the hospital. They said, "We don't see any signs of drugs or alcohol in his system. This just doesn't make sense. This guy is really in good shape—muscular, ripped. You can tell that this guy is really in good shape. He doesn't look like he's abused himself. That's why we have to have an autopsy." The autopsy took about a month. There were no drugs, thankfully. There was no alcohol, thankfully. We kept in touch with the coroner out of Lansing. He was so kind. He knew that we wanted answers, and he performed over one hundred tests. In the end, he found atherosclerosis, which is a narrowing of the artery—one of Jer's arteries was narrowed by eighty to ninety percent, and another by fifty percent. Jer had an enlarged heart, and his heart was working very hard.

I am a product of everything I've experienced, as most of us are. Now, as I go through life, I'm a lot older, and a lot wiser. I have a better understanding about how some people are going through some things, and all I can really say is: we should all be more loving of one another. We should take better care of one another than we do. And I'm not just saying that because I'm wonderful or anything, but I think that when you've experienced some losses, it kind of opens up your understanding. It can be so harmful if you let it be, and that's the hard part—to push forward having experienced more than one loss. I always say that when my husband died, it broke my heart; but when my son died, my heart shattered. That's something that most parents, hopefully, will never experience. They shouldn't have to. It's so foreign. It makes no sense.

A lot of times, people will try to be friendly and they'll say, "Well, you'll understand it one of these days," or, "God doesn't make any mistakes," or those trite sayings. All I can say is: I still don't understand it. I really don't. I don't know what good comes of losing people, especially at an early age. But I do know that it will either make you or it will break you, and you have to find a way to cope. That can make you a stronger person. It can make you a more understanding and giving and kind person. But there are other ways to do that. There are many other ways to do that. There are far easier ways to do that.

Still, my life is so full. I have seventeen grandchildren and four great-grandchildren. I really am thankful.

Like I said, I am happily retired, but I stay plenty busy. I have always been a community volunteer. Right now, I'm vice-chair of the Community Foundation of Muskegon County. I'm on the boards at the Department of Health and Human Services and at Brookhaven Medical Facility. I'm a Rotarian. I have community service at heart.

I am also the president of the Muskegon Covenant Academy, which is a charter school. What we do is, we take kids from age sixteen to twenty-two who have either failed or dropped out or maybe couldn't make it in mainstream schools, and we give them the chance to earn an actual diploma—not a GED. We've only been in operation for two years, and in June we will have graduated fifty-four kids. It's awesome. And we're going to have a housing component of that now, called Covenant Hall. This June, I hope we'll be completely finished with the renovations in the old Child Haven location on Terrace Street, so that will become a dormitory for our students who don't have a home, because a lot of the kids who attend Covenant Academy are either couch-surfing, or they're completely homeless. Now those kids will have a place to call home. That's important to me—the way that we look out for one another.

A lot of people in this community are struggling, and they have been for too long now. The jobs aren't here like they were back in the heyday. We used to have Lakey Foundry, Brunswick, LiftTech, the paper mill—all kinds of factories and foundries. Anyone could get a job. Whether you had a college degree or not, you could walk in and you had a job just like that.

When those places closed, it really devastated the community. When Lakey closed, they didn't honor your pension. People lost everything: their retirement, their healthcare, everything. Back then, there was no safety net for people in that type of situation. There's more of a safety net now, but nowadays it's just more difficult to find the kind of job that pays enough to really support a family.

Now you've got lots of underemployment. The unemployment rate may not be as high as it was a few years ago, but I'm concerned about people who have got no insurance because all they can find is this little rinky-dink fifteen-hour-a-week job, or people who are working two or three jobs but still have no benefits.

There are not a lot of educational opportunities for a lot of people. Schools are still segregated—in some cases more segregated than when I was growing up. One of the saddest things is, when kids go to college, they typically don't come back to Muskegon. Sadder still, when kids don't go to college, it can be really tough for them to build a decent life. I can't tell you how many people I know—particularly African-American young men—who have gotten caught up in the justice system for something petty and have just had it follow them around. There are a lot of people who are disenfranchised, and I just don't know that we have the will to come up with solutions that will benefit everybody.

I'm so afraid. I'm afraid not for me, but for my children—for my grandchildren more so. I don't like the direction that we have travelled—us. It isn't whether you're a Republican or not, or whether you're a conservative or a liberal or a Democrat or a libertarian or whatever you might be. I'm a human being, I'm a civil person, and I'm a kind person. Those are things that I don't think we want to lose in our country. So when I look at someone being accepted—becoming mainstream—who is able to spout bigotry and hatred towards any group—I don't care if it's against African Americans or if it's Hispanics and The Wall or if it's Muslims—if you're in a leadership position and you can't be kind and civil to people, in my opinion, you give license to other people to behave that same way. I'm not saying that the current president manufactured this—he certainly didn't. But he gave a voice and he gave a legitimacy to people to say and do some truly awful things. It's perpetrated by fear. Violence is actually perpetrated by fear. If I know you, I'm not going to fear you; but if I don't know you, then I'm going to believe the stereotypes, because that's all I know. Donald Trump, in his campaign and in his presidency, has done much more to reinforce those divisive stereotypes than he has done to break them down.

I voted for Hillary Clinton, and I don't mind saying that. There are things in the Democratic platform that I don't agree with, and there were a lot of things I didn't like about Hillary, but I felt that she was the more competent candidate. With all the rhetoric that Donald Trump was spewing—all that right-wing stuff—there was no way I could identify with him. So when people would say to me, "I'm not gonna vote. I'm not gonna vote, because both of them are horrible," I would say, "Well, you know what? You have to look at them, and then select what you think is the lesser of two evils. You can't just stay home." But I think a lot of people did just stay home, and that's a real shame after what so many other people sacrificed just so we could have the right to vote.

My mother grew up on a cotton farm in Brookhaven, Mississippi. My grandfather owned some land there—twenty acres or thereabouts. They had been sharecroppers at one point and, obviously, being in the South, they weren't always able to vote. In Mississippi, they wouldn't even let you register. Legally you could register, but in practice you had to know the whole Constitution—you had to answer all of these questions. Then you had to pay some kind of a tax, and not very many people could afford to pay that tax. That's how they kept blacks from voting. But in 1955, there was a mass effort on the part of African Americans to get people mobilized to vote, and it was spearheaded by a man named Lamar Smith, who was African-American and who also happened to be a good friend of my grandfather's. My grandfather was a landowner, and he was also biracial, so he had a lot of white friends, and at the time when Lamar Smith was getting people registered to vote, my grandfather's white friends told him, "Don't do it. Don't do it. There's a lot of talk that if you go down to the courthouse, there's gonna be trouble. You need to stay home." My grandfather and Lamar Smith decided that they were going to go downtown and register to vote anyway, and when they got down there, some of my grandfather's friends again told him, "Don't go to the courthouse. Do not do it." My grandfather didn't. He went there, but he didn't go up the stairs to the courthouse. Lamar Smith did, and was murdered in cold blood on the courthouse steps. He was shot. There were plenty of witnesses, but no one was ever charged or tried. I'd have to ask my mother about this, but I think the first time anyone in my family voted would have been after we moved North.

I think of how much we struggled. And we got so far. People thought that when Obama got into office we could all sing kumbaya, but I've always said this: "You can legislate how people must act and what they must do, but this legislation will not change what's in someone's heart." At your core, if your values are opposed to something, it doesn't matter what the law says; you will still believe what you believe, and you will still feel what you feel. That's why we are where we are: because we haven't come that far. We've come a long way, but we haven't come nearly far enough in our hearts.

It just pains me, because you can hide behind a mantle and say, "I'm not racist. Oh, I'm not racist." But then it comes down to your actions. One of my friends is definitely struggling with this, because he's a good person at heart, and he tries to find the good in Donald Trump. We've had so many discussions. He says, "Well, give the man a chance. They're just not giving him a chance." I say, "He's telling you who he is. Why are you not believing him? Why are you not believing him? He's telling you what he's all about. He's been telling you what he's all about for thirty years."

The Central Park Five: In the 1980s, Donald Trump took out this huge ad—I think it cost him like $85,000—because he was a proponent of bringing back the death penalty to be used against this group of minority young men who were accused of raping and murdering a jogger in Central Park. That's a horrible crime, but the thing was, even after this group of kids was exonerated by DNA evidence, Donald Trump never took back what he had said about them. He didn't apologize. The man doesn't apologize—for anything. The man is who he is. I don't think he's ever going to be any different.

Birtherism: Don't let me get going on that one. Trump wasn't the one who started that, but he seized the moment. The man is smart. He knew it was a lie, but he hammered on that time and time and time again and kept that thing going. Still today, there are people who don't think that Barack Obama is a U.S. Citizen. They think Obama pulled the wool over people's eyes.

It's just funny. If you tell a ridiculous lie—it can be as crazy as all get out—but if you tell that lie time after time after time, people start to believe it. It's a lie, but they will begin to believe that lie. And I dare say, even the people who are espousing that lie—if they say it often enough, some part of them begins to believe in what they're saying.

Thank God we have a free media, because right now, what he's doing is, he's trying to marginalize them. It's a form of brainwashing—drip, drip, drip, fake news, fake news. I fear that we're ambling towards a place we don't want to be—a place I don't want us to be.

So when this friend says, "Give him a chance. He could change"—Donald Trump is not going to change. He is who he is. And maybe he is a billionaire. Maybe he is a smart man when it comes to making real estate deals. But he is not the man for this job.

Right now, we're at a crossroads. We have to decide: Do we want to continually improve, or do we want to go backwards? I think it's up to all of us to decide that question. We all need to do the little things we can do. That starts at home with your kids, with your neighborhood, with your school, your church, your job. There's a lot of work to be done. I still love this place, but there's a lot of work to be done.

WILLIAM

"People know what they do; frequently they know why they do what they do; but what they don't know is what what they do does."

—*Michel Foucault*

The big turning point in Muskegon was right about the time that I came here. That was in the mid-1970s. What happened was, there was a proposal to put a steel mill—it was called North Star Steel, I believe—on Muskegon Lake. It was going to be a state-of-the-art steel mill. They were going to use electric furnaces as opposed to coal-fired. It was going to be state-of-the-art.

Lakey Foundry had just closed down, Campbell — Wyant & Cannon was winding down, and North Star came over here to Muskegon and dangled a steel mill in front of us? That's a real temptation—"Holy crap, all these people who got laid off from all these foundries, we can put them back to work."

But there was a group led by a guy who was actually the chairman of the board of County Commissioners, and they organized. They took a lot of grief, but they opposed bringing that steel mill in here and putting it on the lake. They said, "This lake is not going to be an industrial dump. We are going to make this lake the centerpiece of the community in terms of attracting tourism." And they successfully blocked it. North Star ended up going up to Duluth, Minnesota. That was the turning point. That's when we turned away from being an industrial town.

I've seen us transform from a smokestack community into a more blended economic base and seen us become more of a tourist destination, taking advantage of the water resources. When I came here, if you went outside the courthouse and looked down Terrace Street—where there's all that open waterfront land—that was a huge, smoke-belching foundry down there. That was Lakey Foundry. Then, next to it, there was a large industrial complex called Teledyne. You couldn't see the lake. All of that down there, where now you've got the PNC Bank and the old Sealed Power headquarters across from the farmer's market—all that down there had big chain-link fence around it. Dirty. Smokestacks spewing out smoke. You could see it settling over the lake. It was like Allentown. That's what it looked like down there.

On the other hand, it employed thousands of people, and when they shut down, those people never went back to work. They either were able to get workman's comp—having worked in a foundry environment, a lot of them qualified for worker's comp benefits because of silicosis and other stuff associated with foundry work—or they went on welfare. People never went back to work. It really hit hard in the African-American community, because the migration from the South up here was because of the work in the foundries. Those jobs disappeared.

Muskegon Lake is beautiful to look at now, but it's not doing anything for the economy. Again, I didn't grow up here, but I've seen that transformation.

Why did I come here? Alright. I grew up in a small town called Three Rivers, not too far from Kalamazoo. When I finished law school—I went to Georgetown, in Washington, D.C.—I had a number of opportunities to take the associates route at a big law firm. One of the firms that I was really interested in was called Fried, Harris, Shriver & Campbell. Key name in there for me was Shriver. Sargent Shriver, who was President Kennedy's brother-in-law, was in that firm. Eunice Kennedy was Sergeant Shriver's wife, and my wife was Eunice Kennedy's private secretary for many years while we were in Washington. I seriously considered going that route.

The office I wanted to get into was in the Watergate. We loved Washington, D.C. We wanted to stay there. But you don't just get to go to the Watergate; that was the premier office. Before you got to go to the Watergate office, you had to go to New York—Broad Street— that's where the main office was for the firm. So we went up to New York with Shrivers one weekend. It was awesome. Had a great time. If I could have lived like that in New York, I would have gone to New York in a minute. But I was realistic enough to know that I wasn't going to live like the Shrivers or the Kennedys in New York. We wanted a family. I wanted children, and I just didn't want to raise them in that kind of environment. I was from a small town, and I wanted my kids to have that experience. I toyed around with the idea of kind of a compromise, which would have been to come back to Michigan, be closer to my hometown, but still be with a big law firm. I interviewed with Dickinson Wright, a big law firm in Detroit. I interviewed with Clark Hill. I got offered. I really thought seriously about that.

But I also was interested in politics and public service, and I just didn't see a path if I went the associate, big law firm, big salary route. I didn't see a path to accommodate everything I wanted, which was: a good place for my family, plus public service. I just didn't see the path there.

Well, I knew a fellah here in Muskegon whose name was John Boeschenstein. John had been chairman of the Democratic Party here for many years. He was very well connected politically. He was a very close associate of a guy named G. Mennen Williams, who was the governor of this state for many years before a guy named George Romney came onto on the scene. John had a lot of political connections, and I talked to him about coming back here and practicing law with him, and he invited me to do that. So I saw this as an opportunity to hit on all those objectives: find a good place to raise my family; have a path to maybe some political activity or public service; and practice law, even if it wasn't on the level that I would have been on had I been in Washington, D.C. That's what led me here.

I came to Muskegon, but I did not join John Boeschenstein's firm right away. I decided that if I wanted to be in the legal practice, I wanted to be a trial lawyer, and so the prosecutor's office was the best place for me to get thrown into the fray and get some real experience trying cases. It didn't pay much, but it was a good place to get the experience. I was in the prosecutor's office for maybe a year.

Then I decided I wanted to go into private practice, and that's when I joined John Boeschenstein. My work was predominately criminal, but I did a lot of stuff. I represented a lot of labor unions in this area—the county employees, various fire departments, a handful police departments. I battled mightily with Harry Knudsen. Harry was corporate counsel for Muskegon County, so any time there were any issues with regard to management/union questions with County employees, it was Harry and I doing battle. It was all over nothing of any serious, dramatic consequence—just people being disciplined or discharged. We'd have to litigate whether or not there was good cause for discharging them or disciplining them, because if an employee is disciplined, they have a right to have a hearing on that before an arbitrator to determine whether or not there was good cause for their discharge. It was pretty mundane stuff. Still, some of my most exhilarating moments in practice were battling with Harry. I loved to battle with Harry. Loved it. It was a battle, and I loved it. In addition to that, I did everything from misdemeanors to homicides.

Probably the case that I have the fondest memories of—the case that really caused me to leave private practice—is

United States, Petitioner v. John Arthur Scott. That's the case I litigated in front of the U.S. Supreme Court.

Back in those days, we did not have WEMET, but we had basically the precursor. It was an amalgamation of different police departments, and they would do what was called "loan an officer" to what we called Central Narcotics. Norton Shores would contribute one or two officers, Muskegon would contribute maybe three or four, the Sheriff's Department would contribute maybe three or four people, the Heights would contribute a couple. All of these guys were undercover guys. They wore plain clothes. They had beards, earrings, the whole shooting match to fit into the drug culture.

John Scott was one of the detectives assigned from Muskegon Heights. Well, there was a guy that had been an informant for them, and this informant eventually went to prison himself. When this informant got down to prison, he was none too pleased about it. He thought he had been dissed by the local police, so he called the DEA—called up one of their investigators—and he said he had some information on corruption within the Central Narcotics Unit. The DEA—amazingly—went down and listened to this fellah, and he basically gave them a statement that John Scott was dirty, that he was dealing drugs himself—heroin and marijuana. I still, to this day, having been a prosecutor and a defense attorney, do not understand why the DEA ever tried to take down a police officer with somebody who that officer had sent to prison. I mean, the incredibility of the motive to testify—it was a defense attorney's dream to have somebody like that be your accuser. But they did it. They charged him with three counts of delivery. And we went to trial on it.

The U.S. Attorney tried it on the prosecution side, but before we went to trial, I filed some motions to dismiss the case preliminary, and Judge Fox—who was a good friend of John Boeschenstein's—he was the federal judge in Grand Rapids. He granted my motions as to two counts—he dismissed the charges. That left us with one count, which was the heroin count, and we did go to trial on that.

It was a long trial. Lot of publicity, obviously. It was a very long case, and the ultimate verdict was Not Guilty. We celebrated our victory, came home, and I was shocked a month later when I got notification from the Solicitor General of The United States indicating that they were going to file an appeal in the Sixth Circuit Court of Appeals appealing the decision of Judge Fox to dismiss the charges on the other two counts.

Now the issue became double jeopardy. In other words, could Scott be tried on those charges that had been dismissed by Judge Fox? Could he be retried on those? He clearly could not be retried on the charge that the jury had acquitted him on, but the other two charges had not gone to a jury, because they had been dismissed before trial by a judge. So the question became: "Did jeopardy attach?" That's the legal vernacular for what happened. Had jeopardy attached on a motion to dismiss before he went to trial? That was really the kernel of the issue that was litigated. So we went to the Sixth Circuit in Cincinnati. We argued the case before a three-judge panel, and we prevailed.

Again, big celebration. Excited. Happy. So happy that it was over for John, because it's getting expensive. I was taking a reduced fee for this because, frankly, it was pretty exciting to get to litigate a case this far—I just hated to do it at John's expense; I wanted it to be over. So we celebrated, and then I just about dropped out of my chair. I can still remember sitting in the office when we got notification that the Solicitor General was going to file for a writ of certiorarI with the United States Supreme Court.

Then it's a whole different ballgame. The way the case has to be prepared changes. You have to be admitted to the Supreme Court Bar, and you have to have somebody that's a member of the Supreme Court Bar admit you. I found a gentleman around here by the name of Alex Rogaski. He was quite a ways up there in years, but decades earlier he had gotten admitted to the Supreme Court Bar, and so I got in touch with him and got him to sponsor me to go in. That's no big deal. I mean, as long as you've got a sponsor and you're in good standing with your state bar, anybody can be admitted to the U.S. Supreme Court Bar.

So I got admitted to that. We went down. I was, what, twenty-nine? Twenty-eight? Went down and argued the case in front of the U.S. Supreme Court, and I was really intimidated by it, because the Chief Justice at that time was a fellah named Warren Burger. If you've ever seen a picture of him, he looks like God. I mean, he looks like he should be on the ceiling of the Sistine Chapel—he had that demeanor about him. He was very authoritarian. Pretty intimidating. And he had just delivered an address to the American Bar Association in which he was complaining about what he called "piper cub pilots flying 707s." (707 was the big jet back then—this was before there were 747s.) In other words: kids in the court room. Kids coming out of law school. Well, here I am, twenty-eight, twenty-nine years old, litigating a case against the Solicitor General of the United States in the U.S. Supreme Court. I thought: "Exhibit A: here I am. The piper cub pilot. I'm flying the 707."

So anyway, I went down, litigated it. My wife was there; she flew out with me to do it. And it was just really ironic, because when I was at Georgetown, I was right there in close proximity to the Supreme Court, and I could remember going over there only just five years before as a student and looking at all this and thinking, "Wow, wouldn't that be something someday, when I've got gray hair—or no hair—to be able to come out here and do this?"

It was probably the most intellectually stimulating thing I've ever done in my life. At one point, I got into a full-blown dialogue with Justice Byron White, who they used to call "Whizzer" White, because he had been an All-American running back at the University of Colorado. He was considered at that time to be the intellectual giant of the Supreme Court, and I went toe-to-toe with him for what seemed like an hour. It was an extended dialogue, and I held my own. I was so energized by that, I didn't want to stop. It was just so stimulating intellectually. I honestly don't remember exactly what it was about. It was all about the double jeopardy issue. We were just going over interpretation of cases, and I'm giving him my interpretation of cases he authored the opinions on—so I'm treading on sacred ground here—but we just went back and forth, and I held my own. I felt like when I was done, I had gotten my point across. At that point I was like, "Bring it on. Who's next?" You know? I was really feeling pretty good about it. Quite an experience.

The Supreme Court voted 5-4 to remand the case to the Sixth Circuit for what they call an *en banc* hearing. They have a nine-judge panel then. So now I've got to go back and re-litigate the case in front of a nine-judge panel in Cincinnati. I went back there, and they sustained my position on it. That was the end of it.

At that point, I started looking for something else to do. I had other cases after that, but I was starting to lose the enthusiasm for trial work. It was kind of like, "Been there, done that."

I never got to see the kids at all. The only time I got to see my two oldest daughters when they were babies was on the weekends when I'd be writing a brief. When I was writing a brief, I'd hold them on my lap. That was it. Never around. Just always working. All of a sudden it was like, "God, I've gone to the U.S. Supreme Court. What else am I gonna do?" I'd done everything that I'd thought I might have a chance to do in the big law firm, and I'd done it from here. Now I just wanted to see my kids. I wanted a life.

Well, a position on the District Court opened up. The problem was: this was a vacancy—not an election—so the Governor is going to make the appointment, and the Governor was a Republican. His name was William Milliken. Very popular. He was the last three-term governor we had. He was a moderate Republican, but he was nevertheless a Republican. He had been the lieutenant governor for a guy named George Romney. And all the lines that I had laid in the water were on the Democratic side. But you know, I connected up with some people who had some Republican ties, and I put in for it, and I like to think that I ran on my merits, not on my political connections. I got the appointment. I got the appointment. I had to run for election then in two years, and I was re-elected. So that's how I started on the bench.

After that, when I left the courthouse at five o'clock every evening, it was over. No more phone calls at all hours of the night and weekends. That was over. My third daughter was born right around then, so I finally got to find out what a baby's all about. Then Nick came along. It was great. I had a life. Like I said, I went home at five o'clock and had dinner with the kids. I was able to go to their plays and sports and everything like that. It was great.

Later on, when I got my current position on the Circuit bench, I was opposed by the chairman of the state Republican Party. By then the Governor was Engler, who was also a Republican, and I can remember the editorial in the *Muskegon Chronicle* (that's back when we had an actual paper). There was a big editorial that was very kind to me saying, "He's eminently qualified, he'd be a great judge, but he does not have a snowball's chance in hell of being appointed to that position, because of his political affiliations." Well, I got that job too.

So, for the past few decades, I've been looking at Muskegon largely through the prism of a judge, and due to that, the people that I see with any degree of regularity are not our best side—it's not the profile that we want to project. What have I seen happen to the city? In other words, what have I seen happen to the environment that I'm in? The transformation that I see is something that I think is in no way unique to Muskegon: a lot more violence. Now, again, I don't feel that this is unique to this community. It's in Kalamazoo. It's in Grand Rapids. It's in Holland—people don't realize how much violence there is in Holland as a result of the gangs down there; they have a big problem with Hispanic gangs in Holland. This isn't anything that's unique to Muskegon, but we've experienced it along with everyone else.

The young people just are desensitized to violence. They just seem to be desensitized to violence. What do you attribute that to? I'm not sure. I used to think a lot of it was video games—the influence of that. I can tell you anecdotally that I've had cases where I know that the violence in video games had driven kids to violence. But that's anecdotal; it's not empirical. It's nothing that I'm about to develop a theory about. I don't know. But there's been a transformation in terms of younger people being desensitized to violence. I see more violent crime involving younger people who don't think anything about shooting somebody over the most trivial thing— over "disrespect." I've got to be honest about this. This is not a racial comment, I just take the facts as they come in front of me: it is particularly concentrated in the African-American community. Young, male, blacks. Lots of violence. Lots of firearm activity. I'm not saying it's their race; it's the environment they're in. Most of them who come through my courtroom come from an impoverished environment, and that leads to frustrations—and a lot of gang activity.

It's just like—look—this heroin thing: it's a white, middle-aged woman thing. These heroin users are mostly white, and a whole lot of them are women in their thirties. Those are the facts that come in front of me. I think a lot of these women get started on prescription drugs for one reason or another, and if they have an opioid base in them, then they get addicted and move on to heroin once they can't get the prescription drugs anymore. Again, that's anecdotal.

I also think marijuana is a gateway. I sentence fifteen-to-twenty people a week, and every time I see a drug problem—every time I see it—it starts out with marijuana in high school, then it moves on to prescription drugs or cocaine, and then it moves on to methodone, and then it moves on to heroin—sometimes meth, but meth is basically restricted to the white community. Those are just the facts that come in front of me.

So, through the prism of a judge, I've seen this community become more drug-addicted, and I've seen this community become more violent. We've become more violent. Younger criminals—hardened kids. My theory there: no male role models, particularly, again, in the African-American community. That is documented—the absence of African-American fathers. They're just not there in an increasing number of cases. When I first came here, that was something you'd see, but back then there were grandparents. The grandparents filled the breach. There was always a good grandpa and a good grandma who had been working in the foundries here all their lives, who had made a good living, and who had been contributing members of our community. If their kids went astray and had kids who they couldn't support, the grandparents would step in and make sure that those kids had a chance to get on the right track. Well, those grandparents are increasingly rare nowadays. The grandparents now are those kids who got off track, and there isn't that solid older generation to fill the breach. As a result, there's just an impoverished community from the standpoint of having male role models. That's problem number one. I just read yesterday: for two-thirds of the babies that are born in this county, the mother is on Medicaid. Two-thirds of them. I was shocked when I saw that. It hasn't always been that way, and I've seen that transformation.

Now, there are also a lot of other things going on in this community. If I'm looking at this not through the prism of a judge, but as a regular citizen, on the good side I see us going more in the direction of a Traverse City—more of a tourism and recreation economy than a foundry and factory town. This place is pretty lively in the summer. You can't get a hotel room. Everything is booked. I think they're starting to bring it back. My son-in-law's company put in a lot of those big box stores down around the Lakes Mall, but now they've gotten together with some of the big rollers in town to put up a six-story building right there where they had the sand volleyball tournaments downtown. That's just Phase I—they're planning to build two more after that. These are going to be nice looking buildings, and that's really starting to fill in that gap down there on Western Avenue and Clay Street that was left when they tore down the old mall.

The paper mill—when I first came to town, there were maybe eleven hundred people working there, and those were high-paying jobs. These guys were making sixty, seventy thousand bucks a year, and these were the guys working out in the shop. That sucked a huge amount of cash flow out of the community when the paper mill shut down. But it was inevitable, I think. Now the paper mill site is headed in the direction of non-industrial development, and the nice thing about it is: the people who are in charge of that whole thing are people who have lived here their whole lives, so they want that done right. It isn't an outside corporation that's looking to get the biggest bang for their buck.

So yeah, I've seen that transformation too. When I got here, the old downtown was still here. It looked like an old-time downtown. Then they came in and put in that mall, and we were really excited when that mall went in. It kept the downtown alive for a long time. I hated to see them put the Lakes Mall out there off the highway in Fruitport Township, because I knew it was just going to put the downtown under. Now it's coming back, we hope.

I've seen that transformation in the city, and I've seen that transformation in myself. I think people, as they get older, tend to become more conservative, because they like things the way they were. I took the natural route that I think most people do as they age—they become more conservative. Everything was better when they were kids, that sort of attitude.

Obviously, I'm not in the Republican Party mainstream at this point. I'm just not. Trump scares the hell out of me. I'm just not comfortable with him. We have what, almost three hundred and twenty million people in this country, and the best we could come up with was Hillary Clinton and Donald Trump to be our president?

I mean, out of three hundred and twenty million people, you've got to believe that there are at least a couple out there who I could vote for. Actually, there were. You know who I would have liked to have seen was John Kasich. I just think he was spot on. After Trump became the nominee, I was convinced Hillary was going to win, and so I was raging at the Republicans, saying, "Kasich could win this. He could win. You fools!" I never thought in a million years Trump could win. But I voted for Trump, and I voted for Trump for one reason and one reason only: The Supreme Court. Trump's going to be here for four years. Maybe eight, but I think more likely four. Either way, this president is probably going to have three appointments to the Supreme Court. I knew these appointments were coming up, and I knew he'd make the right appointments. And he is. Those guys and gals are going to be around a whole lot longer than Trump will be. Those are the people who are going to decide things for my grandkids. They're going to be around for a lot longer than I am. Trump isn't. I don't see a Trump administration making much difference one way or the other as far as this place is concerned.

SUZY

Why can't we do something with this incredible place? Muskegon is one of the most ecologically unique areas on the planet, and we can't seem to figure out what to do with it. The lake—the lake is the emotional center. When I've lived elsewhere, it was almost like a grief not to have it. You can almost feel it calling you. It has a power over you—it's physical. You go out there, and even if you're only out there for ten minutes, you come back and you have a whole different perspective.

We have the potential to draw people and tourism. In the '20s, the film industry made their vacation place in Muskegon. The silent movie stars would come here to Buster Keaton's artist colony right on Pigeon Hill, but that all crashed, and in the '30s they sold the whole thing to Nugent Sand. Nugent Sand leveled it—mined the sand and shipped it away to foundries and factories. Pigeon Hill just disappeared, and the resort went with it. That was part of that dichotomy between, "Do we use our resources to attract visitors, or do we use them to feed furnaces?"

We have a history of just kind of blundering. I was a child—a preschooler—when they tore down the old courthouse. When they did that, I cried my eyes out for a long time. Every time the bus would go past there and I would see that gaping hole, I cried my eyes out. And that blue monstrosity they built in its place? I would shed tears. I would say to my mother, "How could they do that? How could they tear down that beautiful old stone building with the clock tower and put that ugly thing in its place?"

Downtown should have been left as downtown. I was adamantly opposed to them building the mall. By then I was a teenager. Everybody else was saying, "Oh a mall, that would be so cool." No. To do that, you have to destroy downtown. I always felt that downtown should have been better preserved and utilized, not razed. And today they're trying to rebuild it. Who's going to come? There's no reason to come. It's not beyond repair, but it's close. I was only a kid, but I just had that feeling that we did not know how to take care of what we had.

Or use our resources. We had the right idea to clean up the lakeshore, but when Lakey foundry left, I remember it was devastating to the community. People who lived in my neighborhood lost their jobs and never fully recovered. They were laid off and couldn't find work. We just have never found the balance in Muskegon between manufacturing and protecting the physical environment. That's the piece we never quite get right.

There was a time in the late '70s and early '80s when there were some very serious environmental threats, and it took a lot of citizen involvement to protect the area. I was very involved with that in the '80s. In my basement, in a filing cabinet, I actually have the physical memos of the cheats at Ott/Story who were pumping all of the horrible pollutants into the ground that destroyed Bear Creek and the Bear Lake watershed. I have the memos where they talk about what they're doing and how they're going to get away with it and not get caught. You know, "The Department of Natural Resources people are coming on this day, so shut this down and cover this up." I have all that. And the only reason I have it is because no one wants it. I don't know what to do with it.

Marathon Oil polluted the groundwater severely. Residents on the north side of town—their drinking water was brown and vile. There was a major lawsuit filed against Marathon Oil to restore the groundwater. Harry Knudsen was the lawyer for the County at that time, and he was arguing the case on the plaintiffs' side. Well, the company denied any responsibility. They said, "We didn't pollute your groundwater." But when it came time to cross-examine the company official who insisted that the water was perfectly safe and that they had done nothing to the water, Harry went around, and he collected samples from the residents' wells. He put them in a nice, big, clear glass jar, and after the official had made his statement that there was nothing wrong with the water, Harry poured out a glass of it, told him what it was, and said, "Now you drink it." The man refused to drink it. Despite the fact that he had just said that it was perfectly safe, he would not drink it. Harry won the case, and there have been several significant environmental cleanup efforts made in the area since.

But before it was the chemical industry, it was the manufacturing. When my parents moved into their brand-new house in the Heights in 1952, my mother thought that the contractors had walled up a raccoon or something, because she would smell this vile smell. She said, "It smelled like rotting flesh." It was horrible. Until one day she had the neighbor in. My mother said, "Smell this, smell this. It's in my house." The neighbor said, "That's just the paper mill. It will be better in winter when the house is closed up."

The paper mill released a cloud of sulfur-smelling gas that you had to go ten miles to escape. Then again, it was the paper mill that allowed my dad to buy a house and escape poverty. Then again, the paper mill polluted Muskegon Lake to the point that you couldn't even swim in it. Then again, the sawmills polluted it plenty before that. And then again, without the sawmills, there would have been no Muskegon.

Our family got here after the lumber boom. No one knows exactly when. It can be pieced together. When you look at ship records and things it gets really confusing, but before World War I, my grandfather—"Pa"—came. He left the music school. He had gotten a scholarship to go to this elite music school and be trained as a professional, but he was so emotional, homesick, shy, whatever, that he just couldn't take it. He walked away and left and gave it all up and went back to the village. He was too young to leave home. Then, by the time he was a young man, there was nothing to do. Poland was not even a country. It had been partitioned between the Austrians and the Germans and the Russians in the 1700s, and Pa was from the Russian part—the most economically depressed part. There was no job, just extreme poverty. So he put together enough money to get passage. He married Babka, then promptly left her and came to America. He came here to make money. He came to Muskegon.

Now, why he came to Muskegon? No one knows why here, except: there were jobs here, and there was a Polish community here. Somebody else from the village probably was here. So he ended up in Muskegon, and he worked for Brunswick. Then, when World War I broke out, he went and enlisted. That was like the win, win, win situation for him: he had a paycheck, so he could continue to send money home; he got his citizenship, which was what he really wanted; and he got to fight for Poland to have a chance at becoming a recognized country again, which it did at the end of the war. It was huge.

After the War, he went back to Poland to get Babka, and there was Mietek—my dad. It took a while to get the family's paperwork together. The new Polish government did not want to grant Mietek a visa, because he was considered a future conscriptee. Helen was born while they were still there cutting through all of the red tape, and in the meantime, Mietek turned five, and the fare changed. Up until five years old, there was no charge, but at five years old, you were considered a regular passenger and had to pay full fare.

The family had to leave him behind. There was no way to earn enough money to bring him. They had to leave him behind with aunts.

So Pa, Babka, and Helen came here to Muskegon. They lived in a flat above Felix's Pool Hall. They had an extra room in the flat—they had two rooms—and the bed I have upstairs now, they owned that as an extra bed. They rented that out to two men who worked opposite shifts. One slept all day and went to work at night, and the other slept all night and went to work during the day. Babka cooked and did their laundry. That's how you survived.

Babka scrubbed floors for people—she was a cleaning woman for the doctors who lived in the mansions on Sanford Street, just south of Muskegon High school. Pa was trying to find work wherever he could—sometimes at the Brunswick plant, sometimes odd jobs or playing music. He was considered disabled after the war because he had been gassed with mustard gas, but he was earning money. They were sending everything they could spare to Poland for Mietek's support.

It was the 1920s, so Prohibition was the law of the land, and it's rumored that one of the ways they made the money to bring Mietek here was that Babka made bootleg—bathtub liquor—but I don't have any way to verify that story.

All I'm sure of is: In 1929, Mietek left Poland. The aunt took him to a shirt maker and had a sailor outfit made for him, then they bought a ticket and put him on a boat across the Baltic from Warsaw to Liverpool. There were porters who were responsible for making sure he got on the right ship in Liverpool, and he sailed from there across the Atlantic to New York on the SS *Leviathan*, which was the largest passenger vessel in the world ever to sail. From Ellis Island, he was taken to the mainland and put on a train. On the train, the conductors fed him a banana, and he thought,

"You crazy Americans"—he had never seen a banana before, and he didn't know you had to peel it. He got to Muskegon on New Year's Day, and when he came into the station, Babka and Pa and Helen were all there waiting for him.

He went to private school at St. Mike's, just off Sixth Street. Everybody went to private school. It didn't matter how poor you were. In that immigrant community, you went to private school through the eighth grade, and they found a way to pay for it. They were living hand-to-mouth, but they paid that tuition. St. Mike's was the center of everything, along with the Falcon Hall. They always lived within walking distance of those. That's where all the Polish people lived. You worked, you went to St. Mike's, and you did Falcons. You didn't mix with "the natives."

After eighth grade, my dad went to Muskegon High School, and he really struggled. He was looked down on because he was an immigrant. In class, he was always seated in the back of the room, and everything was written on the chalkboard in the front of the room. He never said a word to anyone about the fact that he couldn't see well enough to read what was on the board, so even though he had a keen intellect, his grades were terrible. Later on, he got glasses and his grades magically changed, but his social circle remained exclusively Polish.

After graduation, he did one summer in the Civilian Conservation Corps. He would go up to Oceana County planting trees—hard, filthy, dirty work. The living conditions were just totally rough. I don't even know if there was running water. He was hot and sweaty and he hated it. He did it with Pete.

Pete was his best friend. He was always together with Pete, and on the morning of September 4th, 1939, Pete came to my dad's house early—before breakfast—and he said, "Come on. We're going to go to the paper mill and apply for a job." While they were walking to the paper mill, they passed an old man. They walked to the mill, and on the outside there was some little booth with a guard who took the job applications. They talked to the guy in the booth, and they were hired—the two of them. They took the last two jobs. My dad said he always felt sorry, because as they were walking out, the old man was just getting there, and my dad knew there was no job left for him.

The paper mill was my dad's first "man" job. And because he had money coming in, he said to his sister, "You should go to college. I'm gonna send you to college." But she was working too, and she didn't want to quit, so he went to college. While he worked at the paper mill, he went to evening classes at MCC.

This was 1939, and the college put together some forums about the war in Europe. My dad was invited to speak from his point of view as a Polish immigrant about what was happening. Hitler had invaded Poland from the west on September 1st, and then the Soviet Union had invaded from the east not too long after that, and there were Polish people in town who were ready to go over there and fight. Most Americans had no interest in being in the war at that point, but a number of people from the Polish community actually went to France and joined the army there to fight Hitler.

Well, as time went on, my dad and Helen pooled their money and bought a two-story, barn-roofed house on Sixth Street. That house had been built by a Dutch family named Weebee in 1903. They had daughters who worked for the Amazon Knitting Mill, but the daughters were grown women now and so the family sold the house. (That dry sink in my dining room was theirs; they left it there.) It tells you something about the history in 1903—there weren't that many Poles back then next to St. Mike's. The big influx didn't come until later. That sounds so crazy in our time, but really, people pretty much stuck to their ethnic communities.

They bought the house in early 1941. My dad is working at the paper mill—he's still going to school. Helen is working at the drugstore downtown. Things are going pretty well. And then, of course—December 7th. They hear something on the radio, and the first thing they do is go downtown to the drugstore, because they know that's where everybody will be. And sure enough, there are people all over downtown talking about what it all meant. You can just imagine. My dad said, "Forgive me, but the very first thought I had when I heard about Pearl Harbor was not about the destruction and the devastation and the horror, it was, 'Oh my god, I have a mortgage, and I'm going to war. What's going to happen to my family?' " Then he learned later that one of his good friends went down on the *Arizona*—and he's still there. The body was never recovered.

My dad was drafted. He was able to finish the winter semester, and then he was called up and had to report sometime in the spring. Helen quit her job at the drugstore and went to work for Continental Motors—in the factory. Right over on Getty Street. She was a Rosy the Riveter, making parts and engines for tanks and planes.

My dad's unit went overseas to Europe, but shortly before they were scheduled to go, he was called out to type. One morning, just as his unit was getting ready to ship out, they were lined up for roll call, and the commanding officer shouted, "Any of you idiots type?" Everybody else just stood there; my dad raised his hand— "You! Out! To the hospital!" They needed an admitting clerk. So he started typing, and he spent the rest of the war stateside while his unit fought their way through Italy and France.

When he was stationed in Chicago, the nice thing was Ravinia. He got to hear all kinds of wonderful orchestral performances—things that he wouldn't have had an opportunity to hear in Muskegon.

He could also get a weekend pass, and he would come home to Muskegon on the train. If you were a soldier and you had a pass and you were going home, they would let you ride for free, so he would do that. During the time that he was company clerk and wrote out all the passes, whenever he figured it was time to go home, he would just write himself a pass signed by Captain Nemo Ludwig. He would show his pass, he'd get on the train, he'd come home, then he'd head back. And he never was caught. Nemo Ludwig? He just figured that name was so strange that no one would ever think you'd make it up, that they'd never question it. And they never did.

Later on, he was an MP. He guarded POWs—in Iowa—and he had great POW stories. The Italian prisoners he particularly enjoyed, because most of them were more kind of *c'est la vie*. They weren't rigid like the German POWs. The Germans were much more rigid. The Italians, they were Italians. Even if they were fascists, they were still Italians. And he would bring them things: like, he caught a cormorant, and he didn't know what it was, so he brought it to these Italians, and they told him what kind of bird it was, and then they cooked it and ate it. It was injured beyond care, and he knew they would cook it. He liked the Italians.

But the Germans, when they spoke to him, he would say, "It was never a conversation; it was an order." It was usually just the commanding officer who spoke for everyone else. Just, the way he would phrase things: "Music! We must have music." This was the order. "Bring me a Victrola. We must have music." And then: "We must have girls. We must dance. You must bring girls." Everything was an order: "We must! You must!" Maybe it was just the language barrier, but my dad found it fascinating that someone would be in that situation and try to order him around with no deference. Just the arrogance of it.

But still not as arrogant as Mussolini's nephew. My dad left his gun outside and locked himself in a cell with Mussolini's nephew. Mussolini's nephew was a POW, and in the middle of the night, my dad let himself into the cell— which was strictly forbidden—and he had a conversation all about the war and fascism and everything else. Mussolini's nephew did not speak English—he spoke Italian and German—but my dad was good with languages and could figure it out and they carried on this conversation. He said that of all the people he ever met in his life, this guy was probably the most arrogant person who ever drew breath. He was just so arrogant about fascism and how superior it was and how superior the Italians and Germans were to anything American. He was complete rhetoric— filled beyond belief with propaganda. But my dad just couldn't resist that opportunity. "How am I going to go away and say I never spoke to Mussolini's nephew?" They could have court-martialed him.

But Army life was hard on him too, because he was a very private individual. He was reading a book of poetry one night in the barracks, on his own time, and the officer—a lieutenant or a captain or whatever he was—came in and said, "What are you reading?" My dad said, "A book." The officer told him, "I wanna know what book it is." My dad put it away. "This is not your business. It's not your business what I'm reading. This is my own time." The officer insisted. My dad wouldn't tell, so the officer made him scrub the latrine with a toothbrush. The whole thing. The toilets, the floor— the whole thing. He had to clean the whole barracks latrine with a toothbrush. But he wasn't going to tell them that he was reading Walt Whitman.

He did not take well to the social mentality in the Army either. He said that the guys, every weekend what they would do was, as soon as they got paid and were on leave, they would go to town and they would get drunk—chase girls. That was it. He said that was not for him. It just was not for him. He couldn't see the fun in that, and so he would stay behind. There was one other guy who would stay behind too, and his name was Giles Wheeler. Giles would stay behind because he was a Mormon, and he wasn't going drinking and carousing and chasing girls. He had a wife at home.

So he and Giles became really good friends—very close, best friends. When they were transferred out to different places, they continued to correspond—every day. They played checkers, and they continued to play checkers by mail throughout the duration of the war. One day you make your move, and then you mail it.

But before they were separated, Giles challenged my dad to write to this girl he knew, who was a friend of his wife's. She was the roommate—Lucy. When Lucy left home and moved to Independence, Missouri to work for the government, she roomed with Daisy Wheeler, who was Giles's wife. So my dad wrote this funny letter to her, and she quipped right back with an equally funny letter, and it started a correspondence. Then, at the end of the war, before he was released and came home, he went to meet her, and they met and got married. Right then. He didn't even tell his parents. When he brought her home, it was a surprise. That was the outcome of his lack of participation in the Army social life.

They moved to Ann Arbor under the GI Bill, and he went to the University of Michigan. They had my brother there, and they wanted to stay. They did not want to come back to Muskegon. Helen had moved there at the same time—gotten a job, gotten married. Pa was dead by now. But Babka would not leave Muskegon. She refused. They begged—they pleaded for her to come to Ann Arbor—and she would not go. So my dad figured that he had to come back here. He couldn't leave his mother here alone, so they moved back to Muskegon. They bought a house on Glendale in the Heights before they came back—one of those little GI houses, built by Mazurek, another Polish guy.

They moved to the Heights, and he went to work teaching school at Orchard View. He took the bus to work. The thing about Muskegon in those days was, you didn't need to own a car. Even living in the Heights, you didn't need to own a car, because three steps out your door, the city bus went by, and it would take you right downtown, where you could do anything you wanted or catch a bus to go anywhere else. It was just that different way of life. He saved money not having a car, and he paid that house off within a couple of years. He was only making two, three thousand dollars a year, but they saved like crazy. My mother always said that if she ever saw another can of Spam in her life, she'd throw it—that's what they ate for protein.

My dad worked the summers at Keene Lumber, and the rest of the year he taught at the school with what he called "all the old biddies," who thought that he was very avant-garde and modern because he played classical music and had his students do creative writing assignments. But in 1955, the year I was born, Keene offered him to come work full time, and they doubled his salary.

He went, but he didn't really go for the money. He went because he said he would be old and fat from stress teaching in school. It wasn't from the students he was stressed, it was from the structure—the administrative side telling you what you should do and shouldn't do and looking askance at you. He was interested in the students and enjoyed that part of it. He was a popular teacher, and he had former students who still were coming back to see him through the '70s and '80s when he was working at the lumberyard, but he said, "I will be healthier and financially much better off if I do physical, manual labor." Keene's was closer to where we lived, and my dad rode his bike to work at the lumberyard every day. He rode his bike in any kind of weather—rain, snow, sleet. Only a blizzard made him walk. Otherwise, he rode through the snow with his skinny-tired English bike. He did that until he was in his eighties.

There was such a difference in the community generationally that I don't think you see today. We lived in that little house in the Heights, and next door to us, in another Mazurek house exactly like our house, was a set of retired people—the Andersons. Anderson had retired from Norge four or five years earlier, and I was friends with his grandchildren. All of his kids lived a few blocks away—within walking distance—and they had their families. Families stayed closer together. Different generations were living in the same neighborhoods. You could just go around the block, and there's grandma and grandpa Bartells', and then a block away is the next generation of Bartells all raising a family. That continuity made for a very nice community. That's how the Polish community had been, but now it wasn't a Polish community anymore. The war changed things. All these GIs coming home needed housing for starting families, and as they spread out into suburbia, the ethnic makeup changed. It wasn't ethnicity that bound you together now, now it was locale.

Still, the Falcons continued to play a major role in our family's life. My dad's friend through the Falcons was "Walter Kurdziel"— Vladić Kulje. He came here as a teenager with nothing, and his English never was good like my dad's, but he started the Kurdziel Iron Works up in Rothbury, and he became a millionaire. He always drove a big Cadillac. He had big rings on his fingers; he smoked a cigar constantly. He was a big wheeler and dealer. He was the president of the Falcon Hall for many years, and my dad was the recording secretary, so they went a lot of places together. And very often, I went along—or, sometimes, the whole family went along. We would go all kinds of places in the back of his big Cadillac, and he would roll down the window to ash the cigar out every now and then. We certainly weren't millionaires, but we would go places with millionaires. And nobody thought a thing about it.

Which was another interesting part of the neighborhood: While you had all these foundry workers, kitty corner from us was Harry Knudsen, who was the lawyer who argued the case against Marathon Oil (my brother ended up becoming his law partner later on). Two blocks away, there was a doctor. There were some business people mixed in. My dad had come into the neighborhood as a teacher. You don't usually think of doctors and lawyers mixed in that kind of blue-collar neighborhood, but there were.

At that time, Muskegon really was a factory town. If the wind shifted and came from the north, you'd get a layer of soot from CWC covering everything. You couldn't get on the roads at three o'clock. Five was okay, but at three o'clock there were traffic jams. First shift ran seven-to-three, so that was when you had all the men coming out of the factories, and the roads would be just packed with cars.

And not everyone drove. In those days, a lot of people lived near the plants, and lots of them walked to work. My neighbor next door worked for Sealed Power, which was right there by the railroad tracks that separated Muskegon from Muskegon Heights; he rode his bike to the factory every day. Another neighbor walked to CWC, and it was like clockwork: every afternoon at 3:20, Mr. Van Wyke came walking past carrying his metal lunch pail.

CWC covered two big city blocks. Sanford Street ran right down through the middle of the factory, so when I was a kid walking to junior high, we would walk right through there, and you could look inside and see all these men all black. Not that they were African Americans—they were just covered in residue. Their bodies, their clothes, everything would just be covered in black dust. You could look in and you'd see the fires: blue fire, orange fire, yellow fire—lots of sparks. I remember thinking that that must be what Hell looked like. We would walk through there, and we would cover our faces, because it just spewed out brown smoke.

There were people all over town who worked at Lakey's, and when Lakey's went under in 1972, it was huge. It was this huge economic loss. Suddenly, all of these people had no jobs—no pensions. When the company went bankrupt, they did not honor your pension. Any medical benefits were all gone.

There was a family that lived down the street from us, and they never recovered. Mr. Healey had been at Lakey's probably ever since he got out of the military. He had been in the Navy, and it was his job to clean up the bodies after Pearl Harbor. Then he was deployed to the South Pacific for the duration of the war, and he never spoke a word to anybody about what happened there. He couldn't do it. All anybody knew about was that first assignment—cleaning up the dead bodies. He just couldn't speak of whatever happened next. He was a very gentle, soft-spoken, tender-hearted man. There was nothing rough-and-tumble about Merle. But whatever he did was so awful that he could never say a word of it to anyone. That was the guy who came back and worked at Lakey's for thirty years and lost close to everything.

After he lost his job, he was not sitting home all day; he was out doing whatever things he could. The mother went to work washing dishes at a diner in Muskegon Heights, but they really struggled. He wiped out all his savings to keep his house payments going, so they paid for their house. He kept old cars together. No one thought they were poor. But it was tough for them. They had a lot of kids.

He eventually got hired in at CWC, but not right away. He started over—at the bottom of the pay scale—and he never did make up a pension. He died young—he had a heart attack—so his wife was left with nothing but part of his Social Security and a house that you couldn't sell, because the house in the Heights, by the time she was ready to get out of there, wasn't worth anything. $13,000 for this big, old, two-story house with five bedrooms and a huge formal dining room? They never recovered from that foundry closing.

That's something that really started to change when I was a kid. For example, Norge was a national brand name industry—refrigerators—and they left in 1960 and went south. I was in kindergarten when they left, and the reason I remember when Norge left is: Stephanie was one of my friends in kindergarten, and she had to leave in the middle of the year and move to Arkansas. I remember as a child being devastated at that thought: "You could have to pick up, and your whole family would have to move, and you would have to go someplace way south that you'd never heard of?" Emotionally, I didn't like that idea. I felt so sorry for her. It broke my heart that she had to leave.

The Heights was a really nice community, and it was not just a white community. During the War, there was a large influx of African Americans who came from the South and settled in the Heights—and it worked. Now, I don't know from an African-American perspective if it worked, but from my perspective, growing up in that fifty-fifty community, it worked very well. In my neighborhood, there was one black family within a couple block range, and I never thought a thing about it. I never knew anybody who thought a thing about it. They were the only black family in the elementary school—the Kelly family. And they were perfectly lovely, respectable. I never encountered any prejudice or heard anybody speak disparagingly of them or call them names or call them out or even really talk about them like they were any different just because they were a different color. Now, maybe people did, but that didn't happen in my part of the world.

When I was in fourth grade, in my class we got two other African-American kids. I remember the day they came—you know, new kids. I didn't think anything of it. Then, a year later, we went to visit Central Elementary—we walked over to play soccer or something—and Sharon Howell says, "Oh look, there's my house right there!" I'm thinking, "You live three houses away from Central? I wonder why you bother to walk to Glendale." I was a pretty sharp cookie—I was sharp enough to know there was something strange in that. But it never occurred to me why. Well, now I realize: they were trying to integrate the schools a little better. There was only one black family at Glendale school, so they sent two more—Howells and Sanders came.

No one's mother looked like Mrs. Sanders. Mrs. Sanders was just truly beautiful. She was tall, and she was willowy, and she had beautiful, long, thick, perfectly-coiffed hair. She dressed very tastefully. She was very soft spoken, very genteel, very much a lady. She was just beautiful. When she came to a function at the school for the first time, one of my friends was so mesmerized by her that she said, "Oh, I wish she could be my mom." I don't remember what Mr. Sanders did, but they were definitely professional.

In the mid-'60s started the "white flight." But it wasn't just "white" flight—a lot of the professional people, white and black, started to move out of the Heights. The professional class left. There weren't doctors and lawyers in the neighborhood anymore, because they didn't want their kids in the school system. Sanders and Howells both moved to Norton Shores. Their parents did not want them going to Heights High School.

By the time I got to junior high, the school was probably about seventy-thirty black, and I started to experience prejudice the other way. I was targeted. Looking back now, I kind of know why, but back then I didn't have a clue. I was tall, I was mature, and I definitely was a pacifist. I was always the person who stopped the fights and tried to keep everybody happy. Plus, I was a lowly seventh grader, and so I was targeted by these eighth graders.

You couldn't see them coming. You didn't know who they were. But they would come by and run past and shove me down. One time, they tried to push me down the stairs, and I fell. These were stone steps. I grabbed ahold of the handrail, and I didn't tumble—I was just a little bit scraped up. I let it go. I never said anything.

Then, when I got to high school, I was actually beaten up—on my birthday. I was jumped in the hallway by a group of upper-classmen girls. The mob formed, a male teacher saw it—he knew what was coming—and this teacher just locked his door and let it happen. My brother went down to the school afterwards, and the principal wouldn't even deal with it. He knew better. The vice principal just said, "It was her fault. She must have been intimidating these eleventh graders." I hadn't even spoken to them. I'd dared to walk into the bathroom—that was my crime. White kids were not supposed to go into the bathroom. And you didn't. Not unless you were going to smoke. There were a few tough white kids who'd go in to smoke; otherwise, you did not use the bathroom at school. That's what I had done. I'd gone into the bathroom. You just didn't, because you were white. You were a white honky. I had several experiences where my life was in danger for no other reason than that I was white.

Marching band practice was usually right after school. One afternoon, something had happened to the band instructor—Mr. Marklevitz—and practice was cancelled. All the other classes were notified, but ours wasn't. There were six people in our class who were in band—three of us white, and three of us black. So, after the last class of the day, Finnis Cochrane, Charles Booker, DonDon Marshall, Connie Christie, Barb Healey, and myself all went upstairs to go to band practice. The band room was on the second floor on the far side of the building, and while we're walking up there, we can hear some things—like there's this whole group of students just assembling behind us. By the time we realize that the big double doors to the band room are locked, there was what looked like two hundred people lining the halls. I don't know exactly how many there were, but the hall was completely filled, and those were wide halls. This mob announced that the white honkeys were not going to get out of there alive. We were there, we were trapped, we were stuck, and we white honkeys were not going to get out of there alive. That's when DonDon spoke to the crowd. He and Booker and Finnis linked arms with us—with them on the outside and DonDon right in the middle—and his exact words were, "Fine. You come and get em, but you have to go through us first." And the crowd parted. We walked out of there, we walked all the way out of the building, and we took off and ran home.

There was nobody in that mob that I could recognize. I never knew any of those people. They were not people in my class.

I still meet people from my class. Last week, I ran into somebody I hadn't seen since high school. She ran up to me at the grocery store and threw her arms around me and said, "I'm so glad to see you. It made my day. You should come to the reunion thing." It wasn't the people who were physically in class with us who did it. It wasn't the people who we knew and who knew us. It was all upperclassmen.

I got a pretty good idea of what it must have felt like to be an African American in a white school in the South. I don't mean exactly, but in that environment, that was kind of what it must have been like. You were afraid for your life.

It changes your perspective about a lot of things, but as a result of that, I have never felt any inclination towards that kind of prejudice. I mean, maybe we're all prejudiced, but I never felt a need to retaliate. To me, it was all just mystifying, like, "Why would people act this way?" I still don't get it. I still don't get what the excuse is for anger and violence and retaliation. I didn't get it then, and I don't get it now. This was hatred.

Summer came around. We didn't go on vacation, except to Falcon things. My dad just didn't take vacations unless it was an obligation. And back then, kids didn't really get jobs in the summer, but you did something. Some kids picked berries, some kids had a paper route—I babysat, and I had a really nice arrangement. I had started babysitting for this family when I was about thirteen. They had two kids, and the father worked for the City of Muskegon Heights and had four weeks of paid vacation every year. They were going to California, and they had a pop-up camper with enough room for six people, and so the summer I was sixteen, I got to go with them to Disneyland. When I got home from that trip, my mother said to me, "How would you like to not go back to high school?"

All of these friends of mine had figured out how to go somewhere else. Some were moving out of the district. A bunch of people were going to Catholic Central. A bunch were going to Christian. I had actually applied to Christian, and just before I left for vacation, we had gotten a letter from the school saying that they would not accept me as a student because—and this is the way they worded it—"You would not feel comfortable in a Christian environment." They left it at that, and that was it.

So when my mother asked me how I would like it not going back to high school, I said, "I have no desire to go back to high school." She said, "I've got it arranged that if you wanted to do this, you could go to Muskegon Community College." My response was, "Fine. Good. Nobody's going back to school anyway. I'm sick of high school." I never learned anything in high school; we'll put it that way.

I don't know how she pulled it off, but she had talked to Wayne Reed, who was a counselor at MCC (and was still a counselor when I was teaching there). He had said, "Well, you can come to MCC if you have a GED, but you can't take a GED test until you're eighteen—unless you get some kind of written permission from the superintendent of schools." So my mother went to John Sydnor, who was the superintendent of schools, and said, "Lookit. You know my kid. Why should she waste her time in high school?" He signed that paper. Snap. Boom. Like nothing.

I went and took those tests, and I was amazed. I thought they were the easiest things. I hadn't had most of the courses, but after I took the test, the people in the office talked to my mother and she told me, "These people are all amazed. They've never had anyone ever score that high on the test. You're in the top one percent nationally."

But I have no high school diploma. It's been kind of interesting through the years, because people ask, "Where did you graduate from high school? When did you graduate?" I just say, "I didn't," and I leave it at that. There was a doctor at the Mayo Clinic when I was a patient there. We had been chatting, and he asked me what year

I graduated from high school. I said, "Well, I didn't." His response was, "But, but...you're so articulate!" And then he caught himself, "I mean, I mean, not that a high school diploma makes a person articulate, but..." But I've kind of had fun with that through the years. I just say, "I'm not a high school graduate," and I don't clarify it unless I'm really asked to.

I started at MCC the same year all of my friends were starting their junior year of high school. I had enough credits to transfer after two years, but that's right when my mom died—colon cancer that metastasized—and I just wasn't ready to leave home. I ended up doing three years at MCC and then two at Michigan State.

When I went to Michigan State, I got a scholarship—an academic scholarship that paid for half of my tuition. Now, do you want to know what the scholarship amount was? That paid half of my tuition per term? One hundred dollars. My tuition at Michigan State University in the '70s—this is not the '60s, this is the '70s—was two hundred dollars a term. You could afford to go to college.

I graduated in 1977 from Michigan State, and there were no jobs for teachers. There were no jobs for anything. One of my best friends graduated with a double major in computer science and accounting, and it took her three years to find a job. The economy was horrific. It was the worst time to graduate.

But I still had connections in the Heights. Melva Parks was an older woman. She was a widow, I believe. She had been a teacher for years, and then she became the principal at Lindbergh Elementary School. She just was a character. She got whatever she wanted. She made things happen. Some people didn't like the way she made things happen—it depended on which side of the argument you were on. But she loved her "babies." She called all of the students her "babies." "These are my babies." She was a strict disciplinarian, but all of these elementary school students were her babies, and she always made sure that her babies got the best of everything.

She had her hand in politics all the time—local politics. She courted the school board and the city council. She had her finger in every pie. In October, she got a grant to develop the school library, and I got the job to do the development. I put in so much sweat and tears trying to make a library out of the thousands of books that were just thrown in there with no system. I worked like a dog. And in addition to that, I would also see classes. The teachers got prep time for forty-five minutes twice a week, and I got their classes during that time. I was told, "Do something constructive with them. We don't care what." It was a bit stressful, but I loved it.

I guess Melva took a liking to me. At the end of every year, she had to do an evaluation on each of the teachers. There were check boxes: "Satisfactory," "Excellent," that sort of thing. I got top marks in every box. I didn't think anything about it, but then, later, one of the teachers who had been around a while said, "She never does that. She just doesn't. She just doesn't rate people that way." That teacher was shocked when she saw my evaluation.

The grant expired, and I went back to subbing all over the place, but I made sure that I always had one day a week when I didn't work so that I could go in and finish the library project—volunteer work.

Then Melva created an opening for me. She just called me in one day in the middle of the year and she said to me, "I'm gonna open a preschool. I've worked it out. I've got the money, and you're gonna come and teach it." I said, "Okay. What about the seniority issue?" I was not next in the seniority line. There were many people in the district above me. She said, "Those people aren't gonna want that job. Trust me. They're not gonna want that job." I said, "Alright." I don't know what she did to make them not want that job, but I knew lots of people who wanted to work with those little ones.

She would send us out into the community to go door to door—talking to parents and people about the importance of education and having their kids in school. That school covered the projects in the Heights, and we went all through that community, knocking on doors. I went with the kindergarten teacher, and mostly I let her do the talking. I thought it took a little bit of bravery to just go out and start knocking on doors and then go inside and sit in people's living rooms and start talking. I thought that took a lot of bravery, but she didn't act like there was any bravery at all involved. To her, it was just a piece of cake. I don't know if it really was, but that's how she made it seem. It turned out to be a really good experience—educational.

I taught preschool in '80, '81, and '82. After that, there was a round of layoffs, and I got laid off. But in the meantime, I had gotten sick working in that building. It was the old Lindbergh School with the mold, the dust, the chemicals that they'd spray. Also, Stan and I had gotten married in 1980, and we moved into an old remodeled house in Lakeside that turned out to have hidden mold, and all of that just took its toll on my immune system. When the school called me back in 1985, I knew I just couldn't do it physically, so I went to work at MCC part time and was there for fifteen years, and I was also involved with Little Learners Preschool up until 2016.

We would have been better off economically with two full-time incomes, but personally we were better off with one full-time and one part-time earner. Stan never had a high-paying job. The lowest-paying professional job you can get—worse than teachers—were journalists. But he liked it, and it was fairly secure, and we did okay. We were okay economically until 2008, when journalism died and Stan lost his job. Boom. At age fifty-six, we weren't anywhere near ready for retirement. We weren't prepared. I mean, we had been socking some things away, but we needed that extra ten or fifteen years to continue accruing retirement savings.

Especially since we'd had so many expensive medical things with our kids. If you've got to drop ten grand there, fifteen grand there, and twenty here, suddenly your retirement doesn't look like you want it to look. But we were very frugal and we lived very frugally, so we were okay.

We survived without any job at all for several years. Stan just did whatever he could get here and there part-time. He went to work at Walmart, but nowhere where you make real money anymore. The real money jobs aren't there. He got an offer to come in and interview for a job where you work from home for a company in Grand Rapids. It was like a dream job. It would have been a hard job for somebody who doesn't have his really unique skill set—you had to have the PR background, the writing ability, editing ability, and research experience, plus all the technical and computer skills. "Well," I thought, "that's Stan. There aren't too many of those guys out there." Then we looked at the pay scale, and he didn't even bother to respond. It was a joke. Just a joke. He was going to work like that full-time for twelve dollars an hour? You're not going to respond to that.

But that's all that's out there now. That's what is there all over. There's not much out there with what I would call "real money." Twelve bucks an hour is not real money for a professional skill set. Manufacturing jobs are actually doing better now, but he's not going to go for a manufacturing job at sixty-five years old.

One of the things that hurt us the most was Obamacare. We were not making it well, but we were okay with limited income—until Obamacare. It hit us hard. We still had insurance from the *Chronicle* when Stan left. That was a promise. We were insured under the company, and that was a pretty good deal. He lost all these years, but he would be able to draw his pension, and he would be able to keep his insurance—and they committed to keep the kids on the insurance as long as they were living with us and had issues. That was part of the severance. But Obamacare changed all that. It changed the rules that the company was bound by.

We lost our insurance and had to go on the Obamacare exchange. Well, the Obama exchange wouldn't even take our older son. Our younger son could only stay on our insurance for one more year under for the rules, but for just the three of us, it cost sixteen hundred dollars a month. That's Stan's whole pension. What do you live on? Your whole pension goes to Obamacare. That became a little mind-boggling. And the insurance that we got from it is useless. It has a $28,000 family deductible—per year. The paperwork and the red tape make you think of Russian bureaucracy—it's worse probably.

That was our destruction. That really changed everything for us in terms of worry and concern. It changed our attitude about whether you're poor, impoverished, or okay. Obamacare was basically what did that to us. I know there were people it helped, but unfortunately, we're not the only people this happened to.

So how are we? We're good. We're blessed. We make every day. We always have what we need. But it's a tenuous existence. We just qualify as middle class according to the federal government's definition, and the only reason we do is because Stan is able to have a pension and work a $34,000 a year job.

This so-called retirement is not what we planned for. I thought I would work when my children were done with school, but because of our sons' medical disabilities, that just wasn't possible. One of us has to be home at all times, and so what do you do, hire somebody? That would cost as much as I could make by being out of the house.

This is not at all what we expected. It wasn't the economic level we thought we'd be at. But I would never complain either. We're so fortunate. We're very fortunate. We never expected to be at a high-income level, because we had two low-paying professions and we made the choice to really be a one-income family, and that turned out to be absolutely necessary. We didn't know it would still be necessary now, but we really do feel fortunate every day.

We will see what happens. In 2008, when I watched the changes in the world of journalism unfold, I worried and I mourned. I felt like we were losing something important, and the last nine years have been a manifestation of that. Every now and then, I listen to the mainstream media just a little bit—just enough to go "*hfffffmp.* This is not the truth." But people don't know that. The way things are portrayed, if you don't know any better—if you don't do something to educate yourself outside of mainstream media—you don't have a clue what's really going on or what's happening. And maybe I don't really have a clue either, but when I listen to the media, I feel like it's hopeless—that we're just going to spiral down until there's no personal freedom left, and we won't know what hit us. Everywhere I turn, I see free speech in peril in favor of political correctness.

Ten years ago, if anyone had told me that I'd be excited about Donald Trump, I would have told them that they were being idiotic, but just the fact that Donald Trump—being who he is—got elected, means that the people spoke. I didn't think that was possible anymore. I still have a little bit of optimism. There's always some hope. I'm kind of an eternal optimist and a total pessimist at the same time, but I'm not worried that Donald Trump is a fascist. I don't see that. I see that as a media portrayal that is baseless. But when you really develop an understanding of what is going on, it's obvious that something has happened in our country that doesn't make any sense. Something is amiss.

HAROLD

"It is painful to be conscious of two worlds."
—*Eva Hoffman*

I was in Kuala Lumpur, Malaysia. We've been through there several times. They consider themselves to be a developing country—they have billboards in KL that say, "Fully Developed By 2020!" But the airport is superb. They have high-speed monorail service from the airport to downtown—inexpensive, fast, beautiful, quiet. The city is about thirty miles away, and you can be there in twenty minutes.

Back here, I was on the Amtrak down to Chicago to see *Hamilton*—which was fantastic, just like everybody says. To get to the train, you have to drive an hour to Holland. Then, on the train, they had wi-fi. Well, it was so slow I could hardly get my email. I had to use my hotspot.

In Kuala Lumpur, it's all high speed—high speed train, high speed internet. Same thing in Hong Kong. We were there in November—fantastic. In Bangkok's new airport, they have high-speed service from the airport into the center of town—cheap, clean, efficient. We don't have that here. It's crazy. Here you have to come out of an airport, flag down a taxi, pay a hundred bucks to go somewhere? It's ridiculous.

Technologically, we're easily fifteen, twenty years behind developing countries in Southeast Asia. The last time I was in

Thailand—2015—I was in a village outside of Chiang Mai. I was in a rural area, and I noticed some of the debris in the garbage cans—wire. I look at it: it's fiber-optic cable. They're installing fiber-optic communications house-to-house outside of Chiang Mai. We don't have it here. It's ridiculous. They have cell phone service that's cheaper and more reliable than ours. Here I max out at 25 or 30 megabytes per second. Something isn't right.

1951 is when I was born. Right here in Muskegon. Mercy Hospital. Dad was forty-one. My mom was forty-two. I came along later in life for them. At that time, Dad owned a tavern called the Sepia Cafe, and the focus of the family really was the Sepia Cafe. The earliest things that I remember are my mom and Dad taking me there on weekends. They would have entertainment—musicians primarily—sometimes local, sometimes nationally-known entertainers of the time who were doing the African-American circuit. When it would get time for me to go to bed, I would be taken to Dad's office behind the bandstand and put to sleep in his chair. There was a stripper from Detroit that he would hire to come in, and I remember that on those nights, I would have to go into his office very early in the evening. Satin Doll was her name. She appeared all over the place, and Dad was one of the nightclub owners who would hire her.

We were all kind of expected to participate in working in the family business. It wasn't that we were forced to; we just kind of did it. I would pick up glasses from the night before; I would empty ashtrays. It was nothing really heavy duty, but we were all involved in doing that. Dad had a pool table there, and I was allowed to use that in the daytime when he was setting up. I could have anything that I wanted, so I could have unlimited Squirts. I remember that. I would drink so many I thought I was going to explode.

It was great for my mom. She would help out with the tavern—she would make posters for the events, and she would count the money at home. The cafe was very successful and by then Dad was very successful, so she was basically a stay-at-home mom. In the evenings, she had a table at the stage with her best friends and relatives and she would hold court, so that was fun for her.

Sepia Cafe was a centerpiece of Muskegon, and it was certainly the centerpiece of our family when I was growing up. Dad hired his relatives, so a number of my uncles worked there doing various things, and a number of my aunts too worked as waitresses.

Dad had a lot of ambition—I think more so than any member of his family. He was smart—driven.

He came from a poor family in Washington, Missouri. His mother was partially German. His dad was Indian/African-American. My grandpa had a good deal of technical know-how—he was a blacksmith—and there were a number of Germans who emigrated into that area, including members of the Busch family. One of the Busch brothers started a brewery there that had the name Busch Brewing Company, and Dad's dad worked for them repairing the equipment in the brewery—at night. That's how he made a living. Well, when Prohibition came along, they didn't brew beer anymore, so my grandfather was out of a job. That was the motivation for moving up North.

Dad was the first black graduate of Muskegon Heights High School—in 1929. Dad learned a great deal. He was capable of doing a great deal. His older brother—Uncle Page—had promised him that when he graduated from high school, he would send him to college, and then to medical school, because they wanted Dad to be a doctor. Well, Uncle Page was heavy into the stock market and lost his money in the crash. He couldn't finance Dad.

So Dad worked during The Depression in the foundry. I think it was Lakey's, but he always just referred to it as "The Foundry." Forty cents an hour. His focus was on working hard, working smart, saving money, listening, and taking opportunities when they were available, and he was very successful in doing that. He saved his money, and he saved up enough to buy the house they lived in for cash—five hundred dollars; this was in 1935. Shortly thereafter, he started a business in downtown Muskegon called Central Storage. The business parked cars and washed cars, and he got a contract with the Postal Service to wash and store their vehicles as well. That was big: a Government contract.

Then World War II came along and Dad took a job as a driver—a chauffeur—for the president of Continental Motors, which was headquartered in Muskegon. They were building the engines for airplanes and tanks, and so Dad would drive him to Detroit, because there were meetings with the other executives from Ford and General Motors, and then to Washington, D.C. They had some high-level meetings and things, and Dad was there. Dad was really smart, but he was African American, so they felt that they can talk and he doesn't know anything—Dad knows everything. When he would hear various discussions, he filled in his boss on what they said. He served drinks, ran errands, did whatever else, but in addition to that, he'd keep his ear to the ground. So Dad says that he was treated very, very well—paid very, very well during the War—and he saved all his money.

During the War, Dad was also appointed to the housing board in this area. The powers that be had brought up a lot of men from the South—blacks primarily—to work in the foundries, but the problem was: they had no place to live. Men were sleeping on the streets; they were in these flophouses; they were sleeping on grassy areas and in parks. It was really awful. And so Dad wrote this pretty detailed article in the *Chronicle* about how this had to be attended to, that, essentially, people weren't animals—that they had to have appropriate living conditions, appropriate sanitation, and that there had to be accommodations not just for the workers, but for their families. He gave some recommendations as to what should be done, because there had been a very significant riot in Detroit due to similar conditions, and not just the National Guard, but Army troops—with tanks—were brought in to put it down. Dad said, "If you don't fix it, the same thing is going to happen here. Get it done." That led to the construction of the so-called "projects" in Muskegon Heights. In my opinion, an African-American person writing in a mainstream newspaper and calling people out? In 1943? That's a pretty big deal. And he was listened to.

Anyway, the war ended, and Dad had some money saved up, so around 1947 or so, when the opportunity came up to buy the tavern, he and a friend went in as partners and bought it. Shortly thereafter, Dad bought him out.

D ad would have these dinners at Sepia with hundreds of people, and he would film them—people having fun with each other, conversing at the tables, drinking. Then, in the future, he would show these videos on the screen, and people loved that—seeing themselves. I was fascinated by that stuff. Unbelievable. It was fantastic.

One of the great things is: Dad trusted me. He treated me not as a kid, but almost as an equal. Before I was three, he taught me how to run his movie projectors—thread them, rewind them, care for them. One of the things that fascinated me the most was: Dad would have live radio broadcasts from the cafe. He had that audio equipment—amplifiers, microphones, speakers, all of that stuff— and Dad would always involve me in that. I thought that was so cool.

The tavern had one of the first television sets in Muskegon County—with a very tall antenna—and Dad would bring in the fights from Chicago. There weren't TV stations yet in Grand Rapids or Kalamazoo, but Dad had the idea that if you show fights, you can bring in a crowd on Friday nights. And it worked well. That was a huge draw for people.

Well, of course, if he had one at the tavern, he had to have one at home, so by the time I was born, TV was an appliance that was there. When I was a little kid, I didn't realize that I had neighbors who didn't have TVs yet. I thought that was kind of odd, because that was the norm for me.

We lived right in the shadow of Nelson School. I would walk up from my house to Third Street, which was the business district, and it was one great little store after another—car dealers, an A&P, Cole's Bakery. It was really great.

I can't recall anything as being run down or in poor condition, or violence or gangs or anything like that. It was different. You go through there now, and the houses pretty much are the same, but the condition was much nicer when I was growing up— nice lawns, well kept, lots of activity going on. It was a very nice, stable neighborhood. And safe, too. But when I go up and down Monroe Street or Mason Street now? It's the same old houses, but oh my god, they've fallen apart—boarded windows, glass broken out, lawns which are bald but for weeds and bottles. It's just so different. So different. At that time, it was a thriving, safe, middle-class neighborhood.

Anyway, my mom and Dad had prepared me educationally— intellectually. My mom was very focused on providing resources early in life and taught me how to read by the time I was two. Dad bought a set of the Encyclopedia Britannicas, and I loved poring through those, looking at pictures of the cities—New York, Detroit, Chicago. It was fascinating, looking at skyscrapers and imagining what it would be like to be in those buildings.

I went to elementary school at Nelson, and I did very well. I was able to run movie projectors from the time I was two, and so when teachers had to show films and they didn't know how to thread the projector, I would do it for them.

I did extremely well in school. School was easy. Whatever I had to do, I wanted it to be as perfect as possible. I got a lot of satisfaction out of getting good grades. I loved science and mathematics.

Then something very unusual happened in junior high—seventh grade. They divided kids up based upon their performance on standardized tests. We had six or seven different classrooms—groups of twenty-five or thirty kids. I didn't know it at the time, but it's obvious now what they did: they would tailor the curriculum to the kids all the way down to the lowest performers.

In my group, the curriculum was really challenging and fascinating. There were experimental books from Yale University called SMSG—School Mathematics Study Group—the so-called New Math. It was absolutely wonderful. I loved it. But an interesting thing happened: from that point on, there were no other minority kids that I ever saw. None. Except at an assembly where you had all the groups together. For whatever reason—zero. That became the norm, so I didn't think anything of it at all.

In ninth grade, we went to Muskegon High School, and it was the same thing. Now we were bringing in kids from the other junior highs from around the area, and I was in the group which—and I didn't make up the term—some of the other kids would refer to as "The Elite." Interesting group of kids. Very competitive.

When we moved on to the tenth grade, they had a replicated college environment for about one hundred twenty-five of us. The whole tenth grade class was about six fifty, but only that smaller number of us was in this special group, and we rarely got to see the other kids in school. We even passed through the hallways at different times. We wouldn't even see each other.

A number of the texts that we used were college-level texts. We had lectures in a lecture hall. We learned how to take notes. We listened to speakers, then we would have breakout sessions where we would have smaller groups. I didn't know until later: this was just like college. It was really wonderful, because when you got to college it was like, "Wow, this is no different." We were prepared.

One of the teachers I had in high school, my speech teacher—Mr. Poling—had been a radio announcer in the '30s. Mr. Poling inspired a number of well-known local broadcast personalities—including televangelist Jim Bakker—and he recruited me to take his radio class. I really enjoyed it, so that led to some other things.

I would do the announcements in high school, and when you have a school that's twenty-two hundred kids, that's a pretty big audience. I'd do them every day, so all the kids knew who I was—I was that voice on the PA system every morning. I also did MC work for a number of the events at school. Then, in twelfth grade, somebody called Mr. Poling to see if he had anybody who could work at the radio station in Whitehall, and he sent me up. My mom or Dad would pick me up at lunch hour and I'd go work a shift and then come back to school. I did weekend work there too. That's how I got into radio.

After I graduated, one of my friends was working at WMUS, and they needed somebody there, so he recommended me to the program director, and they hired me. By then I was going to Muskegon Community College, so I worked the morning show Monday through Friday on WMUS from five thirty until ten o'clock, then I'd go to college and do my activities there. It was great fun. Wonderful experience.

We did so many innovative things on the air at that time. We were really entrenched in the community, in providing service in the form of letting people know about road conditions and weather alerts. That was new. We would have that information from the various agencies in town. For example, Central Police Dispatch would provide updates on areas that people should avoid due to traffic accidents or other incidents. The blizzards of '77 and '78 shut the town down, but we were on the air for twenty-four hours a day; we slept at the radio station, and we had people on the whole time talking about what factories were closed or what shifts would come in. That was wonderful—the fun that we had in addition to just providing a real, professional service.

During the time that I was working at WMUS, academically I moved on to Grand Valley, and there I did what was called "pre-professional studies." In my case, the focus was on science, so I had my basic pre-med curriculum plus a good amount of mathematics and computer science. I had learned how to program in Fortran, and then I took a class in statistics where I had a professor who taught us how to use a new language called BASIC. This was in 1973—way back—using the mainframes. I would take the formulas—the concepts that we learned in the statistics classes—and I would write programs to solve those. You know, "Why should I be doing this by hand?" Anyway, I convinced the statistics instructor that if I understood the rationale for the formulas and I could write the programs, why couldn't I use the computer? Because, essentially, it's my logic that's in there. He said, "Fine." So on the final exam, I took all the problems, punched in all the numbers, and had the whole printout in fifteen minutes. The other students were still sweating over it with their slide rules and calculators. I was the only one who had gone through and converted all of the algorithms into computer language and tested them. And it worked.

After Grand Valley, I was accepted to a number of medical schools and finally decided to go to Washington University in St. Louis. I went for two years and then left, so I've got a lot of useless information that sometimes becomes valuable—trivia night or something like that.

After I left medical school, there were several things that kind of converged, and those are: my knowledge of radio and my educational background, my love of electronic devices, and a need at the radio station for producing what's called a radio station log—a log of all of the events that were heard during the day. It's called "traffic." It's an FCC requirement.

Now, a log generally is a list of things that have occurred, but in radio, that's not necessarily the case. In radio, it's a list of something that is going to occur. You verify it, and then it acts as the document that you provide to the FCC in order to inform them of what was done on the air. In practice, the salespeople would sell their contracts for advertising—typically they would sell a package of five hundred thirty-second spots that were going to run for the next three weeks at various times in the day—and then every day the secretaries would have to go through all of those contracts and determine, "Oh, today they're running ten spots. Let's see. We're gonna put one here, here, here, here." They would go through all of the advertising contracts and all of the public service announcements and news and other events and then type up the schedule on a typewriter. Creating that thing was an all-day job.

My idea was: Why couldn't a computer do that? This was '78, and at that point in time some microcomputers had come onto the market. Apple had been out since '75, and there were a few others prior to that.

I convinced the ownership of WMUS to do the following: I said, "Here's what I'll do: I will buy the computer"—which cost about ten thousand dollars at the time—"and I will write all the programs. I will test it. And in thirty minutes, I can produce a complete, typed log of all of the events, which now takes two of your people eight hours a day to do. If it works, I want you guys to pay me a fee. If it doesn't, you don't lose anything." They agreed to it, and I spent—oh, god—I think I slept maybe three, four hours a night for six months. I wrote the first draft of this program, and I took it in to WMUS. I trained one of the secretaries there how to use it, and it worked. It was—to the best of our knowledge—the first microcomputer-based system in the country for generating "traffic." It was great.

Then we put it in at a station up in Petosky. Went up to Duluth: another station. In Wisconsin: another station. Then WKBZ bought it. WGHN in Grand Haven bought it. Then the people who owned WMUS said, "Well, we'd like to go into business with you and sell it across the country," and we sold—geeze—about a hundred across the eastern part of the US.

That took me fifteen years or so, up to '92, when I sold the rights to it. That's when we moved to Thailand for the first time. We've been back and forth ever since.

When I come back here now, in certain respects, it feels like stepping back into the Dark Ages. I'm extremely disappointed in what's happened to Muskegon. Extremely disappointed. There was so much potential, and we are falling into an abyss— if we're not already there. I remember the thriving downtown. I remember the thriving Muskegon Heights' downtown. Now I'm afraid to drive a car through certain areas of Muskegon Heights. Isn't that awful? That's terrible to feel that way.

You really have to walk through an area, I think, to get a feeling for it. Well, in 2012, after coming back from another year in Thailand, my sister and I went out door-to-door campaigning for Obama—get the vote out. We were walking door-to-door in the Heights, and I read that in that same street, there were several murders that went on. That's pretty scary stuff. I mean, there's still pride, and there are a few islands—beautiful, well-cared-for homes with manicured lawns. And then: desolation.

My sister used to teach in the Heights, and she would take her young kids—third and fourth graders—on field trips to Lake Michigan. They had never seen Lake Michigan. They had never seen it in person. Can you believe that? We're five miles away from this gigantic body of water. It's like an ocean. And they've never seen it. It tells you something.

So, what do I think about this community? The only thing that is going to make Muskegon resurrect itself would be a massive number of high-paying jobs, and there are so many things that have to be done with the infrastructure around here to provide that—not just locally, but nationally.

As an example, I was at LaGuardia with my oldest son a few years back. We got off the plane and we had to walk out of the airport and down a city street to the Subway. Is that insane? That's insane. That's what Trump was talking about. We need to change that. We need to invest in our infrastructure to approach what other parts of the world have as standards. I've listened to Trump talk about infrastructure—he hit a nerve. My sister and I went to several of his rallies; we followed everything that he did. He talked so much about airports in our country being Third World. I'm like, "You better believe it."

So I supported him. I did. I think primarily because I brought my daughter-in-law into the country, and all of the battles I fought getting her here legally—and the money I paid, and the efforts with immigration and with the State Department and with the consular division at the U.S. Embassy in Bangkok and the consulate in her home city—these were battles, all of them. That was just to get her in.

I filled out all the paperwork: the forms are ambiguous. They're outdated. I mean, questions about "Were you a member of the NazI atrocities during World War II" still being on the forms for a woman who's twenty-five years old from Thailand? And you have to answer it and not laugh? It's crazy. What a waste of time. Then the consular office in Bangkok lost her paperwork. First, they said it never arrived. Then, when we showed them that they had signed for it, that there was a signature, that they did get it, that they'd had it—that's when they told us that it was incomplete. That would have delayed Chad's wedding by three months, because it would have put her at the back of the line. I wrote this tirade and I said, "You will not delay her by three months. You will grant her an interview immediately, and if you do not, I will be on a plane. I will be in your office, in Bangkok, demanding that you tell me to my face what you did with her papers. Fix it." That didn't seem to move anything forward. Then we got Congressman Hoekstra's office involved—he was the Chairman of the House Intelligence Committee—and the consulate changed their tune.

I think that our whole immigration system needs to be better in assisting foreigners in how to navigate that path, because it sure isn't easy. Help them out a little bit. I'm all for that. But after going through that process, when people are here illegally we're supposed to look the other way? I'm incensed.

So what do I think of the president? My wife said something a year and a half ago: "He's going to blow up the system." He's unpredictable, he's completely different, and if you want the place turned upside down, he's the one to do it. It may not be an easy ride, but he will do it.

JONATHAN

*"Politics should bore people, because
the work of government is boring."*
—David Masciotra

I ended up working for Congressman Pieter Hoekstra for five
years, even though my politics totally don't line up over there.
(I voted for Hillary. I was just so shocked by what I was seeing on
the other side, it wasn't something that in good conscience I could
really support.) Anyway, when I graduated from high school, I had
decided that I wanted to be a journalist. I wanted to be a producer
on television—not on screen or anything like that, but behind the
scenes, managing things. I went to Central Michigan University,
and when I graduated, I started working in radio in Mount Pleasant.
After a couple of months of that, I ended up getting a job in Lansing
in the State House doing communications. A lot of small radio stations in rural Michigan don't have a budget for news staff, so I was
kind of like a stringer. I was a quote-unquote "reporter," but it was
more like just letting the reps talk, and then we would do the editing
and send it out to their local radio stations. While I was in Lansing,
I made a few connections and eventually went to work on the political side.

In Pete's office, I was a case worker. I was based in the district—so I was right here in West Michigan—and mainly I helped
people who were having issues with federal agencies: it would

usually be someone who was on disability, either through the VA or Social Security, and they'd be having issues either with getting their disability payments, or they were getting cut off and they were trying to figure out why. Obviously, if somebody's on disability, they don't have a lot of resources, so I would sort of work through all their issues and get their files from the agencies and try to figure out what was wrong and figure out how to get it back on track.

The office was pretty focused on special cases of individual constituents. Most Congressional offices have between five and seven staff members who are dedicated to casework, because it's a tangible way that constituents can see that their member of Congress is working for them. It's not necessarily a way to get votes, but it's a way to make sure that you're not losing votes, because the good stuff that happens doesn't get a lot of publicity, but if something gets screwed up, that does get a lot of publicity. The fact that Members hire staff just to work on that kind of thing tells you that it's pretty important, and for the individuals who are having problems, having that extra avenue is often a really big help. a lot of times you think of the government as this big, ugly thing that people can't figure out how to work through, so if you can talk to someone who is in your community or is a county or two away as opposed to someone in an office in D.C. or in Lansing or wherever, it just makes it a lot easier to handle problems.

Like I said, I did that for five years, and then Pete announced that he was leaving office at the end of the term, so I was trying to figure out what I wanted to do. I had never intended to be involved in government—by no means was that what I had originally planned to do when I went to college. I just kind of stumbled into it. But I have this knack. I'm not sure this is a good knack, but I have this knack to be able to explain complex governmental issues in a way that people can understand. I can—I don't want to say "dumb it down," but I can say it in English as opposed to Governmentese.

And it was actually kind of fun. So I was like, "Okay, what other things can I do with this?"

Well, I knew I didn't want to be a congressional staffer anymore—I was kind of done with that—and one of my friends from college worked in Cheyenne, and she was like, "You should come out here, this is cool, blah-blah-blah." So I moved to Cheyanne for a year and worked in administration at a college. I thought, "My grandparents lived in Colorado. Cheyanne is only seven miles over the border, so it can't be that different." No, it's different. Beautiful state. Odd state. But I knew, kind of, "Wyoming's not my place." A gay guy living in Cheyanne is not the best thing to be. I was there for a little while, and then once again I was trying to figure out where to go.

An economic development job at a non-profit here in Muskegon opened up. I knew that that was a good path into city management, and economic development was an obvious transition spot for me because I was familiar with the tools from my time in Pete's office, so when that position opened up, I worked really hard to get that, and I did get it. I became the Downtown Director—that job was really all about promoting individual business development.

Unruly Brewing opened up while I was in that position. A lot of the work was done before I got there, but overall it took a coordination of some state tax incentives combined with a pretty big grant from Consumers Energy to re-do the space. There were also investors, and they all kind of worked together to try to get something going in that building again.

It's in one of only three original buildings left on that section of Western Avenue. In the mid-1970s, Muskegon tore down over a hundred buildings and displaced around one hundred and twenty businesses to make way for the mall. As the Downtown Director, the consequences of that was the most painful thing, because we had this huge shell downtown that had been created for "progress," and then that shell was torn down and we were left with a sand-pit. There was so much that needed to be done with the leftover infrastructure before any sort of development could really even get started, and that only got more difficult after they outlawed Congressional earmarks.

I had some experience with this as a staffer—Congressman Hoekstra only did earmarks for projects that built things. Basically, Pete said, "If we're gonna do earmarks, it's gonna be for projects that have impact and bring value to the community." It wasn't funding for, like, The Pickle Museum or whatever joke gets made about pork barrel spending and waste. In Pete's office, it was about: "What can we build, and what can we do to better the communities that we're working in?" Shoreline Drive here in Muskegon—that was done with some earmarks. Rebuilding Western Avenue and a lot of the cross streets that had been removed because of the old mall—that was done partially through a Congressional earmark. The underground infrastructure that had to go back in: sewer, water, electric—all that kind of stuff that the city wasn't able to do on their own was at least partially paid for with federal money. But that tool went away, and so— particularly for local governments—trying to work federal dollars into projects became more complicated. It kind of changed the metrics for locals, because a half-a-million-dollar project for a city is a lot—to Congress, it's a rounding error. But that tool's not there anymore.

There were a lot of fits and starts in downtown. Everything was raring to go, then 2008 happened and there wasn't a lot of economic incentive to do anything, so a lot of buildings just sat undone for a long time until there started to be some outside money coming in. As far as our work was concerned, it was also just a lot of helping the City and the Economic Development Agency to get out of the way and let the people with the vision to open these businesses do what they wanted to do. A lot of what I did as Downtown Director was working with businesses just to say, "Okay, in terms of regulations and building codes, this is what you absolutely have to do; there's absolutely no bending on these rules. But we have some flexibility over here." Then we'd work with the City and/or the County to say, "Okay, can we do this? Can we be flexible here? Here's what the businesses are running up against. How do we help them so that the thing doesn't fall apart?" The goal at that point was to get the buildings that existed filled. It's like, why are you going to build something new when there's a building across the street that's just sitting vacant? It doesn't make sense. So we were really trying to get to the tipping point where we were using all of the existing buildings, and we did get there.

The downtown footprint in Muskegon is over thirty square blocks. For a city of forty thousand with around a hundred and twenty thousand in the surrounding area, that's massive. As far as the geographic area is concerned, our footprint of downtown is comparable to what Grand Rapids' is. That's a massive downtown. If you think about Holland, that's four blocks. That's it. And it's nice. But when you look at our actual business count in downtown Muskegon, we have more businesses than they have in downtown Holland—ours are just spread out. So the job was really trying to figure out, "how do you fill it in?"

Well, there was something between twenty and twenty-five new buildings that were constructed in downtown Muskegon between 2005 and 2015. You had the Chamber of Commerce building, the Sidock building across the street where the *Chronicle* is, and then you had the Culinary Institute of Michigan. There were more than forty buildings that were renovated—places like Unruly, Pigeon Hill, 18th Amendment (the distillery in the old State Bank building). As of the end of 2015, I think it was all but two of the original downtown buildings on Western that had some type of activity in them.

There are over twenty restaurants. There are over forty retail shops. There's stuff to do, you just have to be able to get between them. That was another challenge that we were facing—first just getting people to come down here, then getting them to walk instead of parking behind, driving to the next place, parking behind. It was that kind of stuff.

I think Muskegon is finally about to turn the corner. We're at the point where we've got the critical mass downtown. People want to be here. They're not afraid to be here.

I think you're going to start seeing new buildings go up to do some infill. You'll start to see more people living down here. There are townhomes that have gone in, and those cost between two and three hundred thousand dollars, so you're getting folks of different income levels coming in. Traditionally, downtown has been a very depressed area. The folks who lived down here really didn't have disposable income, and there really wasn't much for them to walk to, which was bad, because if you don't have a lot of means, you probably don't have a car. You want to be able to walk to a store and get healthy food, you want to be able to walk and hang out someplace where they're not going to charge you to get in, but not a lot of those places are going to open up unless you have some people with more disposable income. You need that balance, and we're starting to get that balance. Once that income level starts to go up a little more, I think you'll start to see more stores open up, and that will allow folks to not have to leave downtown just to get a loaf of bread or a gallon of milk, which they have to do right now.

I think that twenty years from now, you'll probably see six to ten big new buildings down here. I think you'll see a lot more people living down here. I think the look of the downtown will be a lot different just because you'll have more density, and once that density happens, people just feel more comfortable walking around.

Because people don't like walking by empty spaces. It feels unsafe. My office was on the second floor in the new Chamber of Commerce building, and I looked out on Western Avenue. If people were on the south side of the street, they'd cross to walk on the north side, because there are buildings there. In the summer, the vacant lot on the south side of the street actually turned into a volleyball court—there's sand there and they bring in a couple of volleyball nets—but other times of the year, people would cross the street to avoid the empty space. I don't think they did it consciously, but when they were walking up to it, they'd cross the street so that they could walk in front of the buildings—which is great, because there are businesses there and they could see what was going on.

It's important for people to be able to see that activity. One of the things I've learned is that engineers and architects like to put mirrored glass on buildings because it's slightly more energy efficient, but clear glass is infinitely more important for a business, because you want someone to be able to walk by and see what's going on inside. For example, Subway downtown has mirrored glass, and they couldn't figure out why on the weekends they didn't get any customers. Well, it was because no one could see inside during the day—especially when the sun was hitting the windows, it would all reflect back, so it looked like they were closed. So we started giving grants to the businesses to change out their windows. If they were going into a space that had mirrored glass, we would give them half the money to help them change out their windows, and we would explain why they should do it for business development reasons—that way it became a business decision and not just an aesthetic decision, and those businesses that did it see much better foot traffic.

The farmers market was another huge change. That has ten thousand people a week coming downtown, and it's bringing people downtown who hadn't been downtown since the mall was still here—people who previously might have thought that this was an unsafe place. Matt hates going to the farmers market with me because I end up talking to all these people and he ends up just standing there. It's a social place. People hang out there. There are picnic tables. It's a nice place to eat. You can see the lake.

I think that developers and potential business owners are coming into town and seeing that. I mean, at Unruly, the cheapest beer is five bucks. The Cheese Lady down the street—that's not really cheap. There's a really good Indian restaurant up on Third Street. You can have a higher-end product down here and it will work, and that was always a big concern for a long time—"The type of business I wanna open up isn't going to work downtown, so I'm gonna go put it in a strip mall down by the new mall." Fine, but then, you know, what kind of experience do you want your customers to have? What kind of experience do you want to have as a business? I think you'll start to see a lot more activity and a lot more people living down here.

Because there is that demand. Right now, over seventy-five percent of the housing downtown is income-based, so if you make any money at all, it's hard to find an apartment. If you get a market-rate one, great—people don't leave those, because the market-rate ones are so cool. The Amazon building is a cool building. It's in an old textile factory that had just been sitting empty for decades. It's got lake views and all that kind of stuff. Well, I think twelve of their units are market-rate. The rest are all income-based.

The challenge is kind of a chicken-and-egg problem: Can you get a developer to come in who's willing to take the risk to do market rate? There are huge subsidies for income-based housing from the Department of Housing and Urban Development. Developers know that if they put in income-based housing, they're going to get money from Section 8; they know they're going to get money from HUD or from the state housing authority. For a developer, the return on investment on income-based units might be lower, but there's not as much risk. The problem for the city is: income-based housing really doesn't do anything to increase the economic mix downtown, so you end up not having that balance that you need for commercial development. There's also an issue of financing. Because there are so many income-based units downtown, it's tough to get financing for market-rate projects—the median rent is artificially depressed, and so no out-of-town bank is going to look at the numbers and decide that a market-rate project is going to be profitable here.

That being said, you've got Watermark Lofts in the old Shaw Walker plant—that will eventually be 128 market-rate units. Terrace Point Landing is going in next to The Lake House—that will have sixty or seventy condos that start at two-fifty and go up from there. At Terrace Plaza—the old Sealed Power headquarters—they're converting the top two floors into market-rate apartments starting at around a thousand bucks a month. Once those are successful, that will make it easier for other developers to get banks to lend. But for now, it's mainly projects like the Heritage Square townhouses across from where the old parking garage on Clay used to be. With Heritage Square, the developer said, "I'm from Muskegon. I want to make the investment. I'm gonna take the risk and do it." We're starting to have those dominoes fall.

But that doesn't mean it's a straight linear process. That was one of the big things we had to combat when I was the Downtown Director: business longevity. Like most things in life, a business—especially a sole proprietorship or a small business—can't self-perpetuate forever. Because people become so accustomed to big box store franchises where once they're open they're open forever and if they close it's because there's something wrong, when we would have business turnover, people would freak out and be like, "Downtown's dying! It's an awful place! No one can keep a business open!" So a large part of what we did was to try to educate people about that. As an example, there used to be a really good farm-to-table restaurant that ended up closing because the owners wanted to do something different. If you looked inside, every day at lunch there was a wait. It wasn't like they weren't making money. But they did decide to close up shop, and so I'm trying to explain to members of the public, "Mia & Grace was open for ten years. That's a pretty good run. If you're the owner and you're also the one who does all the cooking and you've got a kid and you're getting up at four in the morning because you do everything fresh every day, that's pretty tiring. They just wanted to do something different." But people would still get really negative on downtown. It's just much more complicated than I think a lot of people realize it is.

DEREK

I hate all politicians. I hate them all. They're fake. To go to D.C., for me, I think would be hell—to be around most of those people. There's very few that I would work for, and even then, I probably wouldn't last very long in D.C. I don't think I would enjoy it.

You know, the problem with dealing with these politicians is, you tell him your opinion, but then you have some lobbyist walk in in a five-thousand-dollar suit, and whatever that guy says automatically has more weight than what any of their constituents says. The lobbyist is viewed as smarter. That's why I didn't go to Washington.

I grew up in North Muskegon but then moved to Marquette, Michigan, then to Colorado Springs, then went to Calgary, Canada, and then back here. I was a short track speed skater, and they have an Olympic training centers in all these places. (The one in Calgary accepts international athletes.)

When I was living in Canada, one of my hobbies was writing political editorials. I would send them to the *Chronicle* and other places, and one of the guys that read what I would write, he did some research and was like, "This guy is living in Canada, he's an athlete, and he's sending stuff in to his home paper? That's weird." He was a guy that agreed with what I wrote, so he asked me to stop by his office building when I was in town next. He's kind of a well-known businessman around here, and he was planning to run for Congress.

Pete Hoekstra had announced that he was retiring, so this businessman was running, and it kind of morphed into me being his campaign manager. I started off as a nobody on his staff, but positions changed, and I ended up being the top guy by the end of the primary.

Well, my guy lost the primary. Then, going into the general, it's a safe Republican district, so there's no question that Bill Huizenga, who won the Republican primary, was going to win the general election—he probably went on a cruise and didn't even campaign after that. But there were a few people afterwards who wanted me to do something for them, and the new Congressman, he contacted the guy I worked for during the primary and said, "Is there anyone on your staff that you would suggest I hire or possibly bring to D.C.?" Basically, he was talking about me without using my name. And I told my guy to tell Bill Huizenga that I said, "Go fuck yourself." I shut that door. I don't have time to work for someone I don't believe in.

After that primary campaign, I started volunteering for a group called Campaign For Liberty. I actually ended up being the Muskegon County head of Campaign For Liberty. It was a lot of organizing—organizing people to write to their representatives or to call them or to go to an event.

An interesting thing about the group is: they attack more Republicans than they do Democrats, because I know the Democrat's going to vote the way I don't want him to no matter what, so the people I'm more worried about are the weak Republicans. Unfortunately, if you ask a politician, "Do you mind voting correctly on this bill about raising my taxes?"—that doesn't really work. Most politicians kind of rely on most of their constituents not really knowing how they voted, you know? If you pass a few bad votes, no one's really going to pay attention. That's why the approval rating of Congress is like six percent, but like ninety-nine percent of them get re-elected every time. Everyone hates them, but no one knows why. So, if all of a sudden people are bringing up their bad votes, that does make a difference.

There's three-day-long classes on this, but basically, all politicians have two things in common: they're all very nice, and they all hate negative press. Even if you say to them, "I disagree with you on this," they're going to be very friendly and nice to you, because they don't want any confrontation, so you have to be strategic about it. Like, if a politician was having dinner in a restaurant, and you told everyone there that he raised their taxes—if you went around the room and now he looks like an asshole and everyone's staring at him—that works better. For us, interestingly enough, Campaign For Liberty and Saul Alinsky use a lot of the same tactics.

I think it is quite effective, but I'm not as involved anymore. For the right candidate, I probably would get back into it, but it's all about principle for me. There's nobody locally who I could really enthusiastically support, and with a full-time job and a kid and all of that, I'm plenty busy.

I work in sales for a manufacturing company. The company has a whole bunch of lasers. Really, anything you can make out of metal, we do. We laser cut, we bend the metal, we weld it. We do some automotive, some office furniture, some health care products—really everything.

Muskegon kind of had a lot of the industry leave, but there's some of it left. Most of our customers are in Grand Rapids or Holland—the big office furniture guys: Steelcase, Haworth. I have a big customer that makes handicap minivans. What they do is: they buy a brand-new minivan, cut the center right out of it, cut the floor right out of it, and we make a new floor for them. We make all sorts of parts, and they end up putting a wheelchair ramp and everything in.

With manufacturing in the United States, it's obvious that a lot of that has left. The political climate has encouraged business—by their regulations, their taxes, their everything else—to send jobs elsewhere. And in return, our government pays people to do nothing. Overall now, we've had in some areas three or four generations that have no will to take care of themselves, and once you take away the work ethic—once you take away the self-sufficiency—really it becomes a moral problem. It becomes something bigger than just, you know, "Oh, we need a jobs program." It's so much bigger than that. The fix isn't just some stimulus bill, and it also isn't just bringing jobs back to the United States. You've got people that can't and don't want to do a lot of the jobs that are open here right now. I joked the other day that if Trump really did bring all the old factory jobs back, he'd go down as the worst president in the history of the country, because there's nobody left who wants to work.

When I thought that Trump had a chance of winning, the primaries hadn't even started yet. I was visiting a customer, and they were having some work done on the front of their facility—on their offices—so I had to park back by all the shop employees. I counted nine Trump stickers in the parking lot. You know damn well most shop employees in the past twenty years haven't voted for hardly anyone Republican, so I thought, "Wow, you're seeing this, and the primaries haven't even started?" I don't put a bumper sticker on my car anymore, because working in sales, you don't want to have a customer who doesn't agree with you get in your car—that's not a good thing for business. So that number, to me, was big. There was no other sticker in the parking lot other than those Trump ones, so I said, "Holy crap. Ten percent of the people in this parking lot are putting stickers on their car? That's crazy." It made me think, "He's got a shot."

Now, I think I'm going to be disappointed in Trump. He wasn't the one that I was supporting. I don't think he understands the

Constitution like I wish he would. His opinion on—what's it called, like, if the government wanted to put a highway through some-body's property? That's blatantly unconstitutional, but Trump supports it. If we declare another unconstitutional war, I'm going to be disappointed. Will the average supporter be disappointed? The average Bush/Obama supporter would not be, so I don't know.

There's a lot of things where, I used to fit in the Republican tent on most issues, but Trump wasn't talking to me in his speeches. He was only really talking to a small segment of people, and a lot of these people have been affected by past policies of both parties. The story everyone tells about how their grandpa worked in a factory in Muskegon and lived a good life, owned a nice home—everyone's looking at that and saying, "That doesn't exist anymore." If Trump brings some of that back—all joking aside—I think his supporters might not be disappointed.

One of Trump's biggest strengths: he's had a real job. Most politicians have never had a real job in their lives. In the last elec-tion, there was exactly four: Donald Trump, Carly Fiorina, Ben Carson, and Rand Paul are the only people that have had jobs in their lives. The rest of them have worked for the government. And not that that isn't a job—not that you don't have to be smart to do that—but to me, you're unqualified to be President. It's been thirty years now at least, and we've just now finally started to realize that these career politicians have screwed it up so bad that we should look at it like, "Anyone except someone who's been in the govern-ment their whole life." In reality, I think everyone probably should be happier with Trump winning than with anyone in the last forty years, because he's the only one that wasn't "one of the boys" or "one of the girls" in the club.

Probably the best thing I can say about Trump is: all the right people hate him—on both sides of the aisle. I think there's a huge problem in this country with the fact that guys have a six percent approval rating and you can't vote them out. I think it's conceivable that it's rigged. I mean, I'm told that D.C. isn't rigged, and it went ninety-eight percent for Clinton or whatever it was. I heard—and this is totally hearsay—I heard that there was one Romney vote in all of Muskegon Heights. One. There's places in The United States where you have more than one hundred percent turnout. How can that happen?

But Trump still won. Will Trump do a great job? That remains to be seen. Will he be corrupted like so many people are as soon as they go in? Maybe. But how many of his supporters will even notice? You look at the average American—people aren't willing to educate themselves. And they're not going to get the truth from the media.

Kind of a hot-button thing is fake news right now, but the mainstream media—Fox included—is fake news. Like, literally, I don't know of a single cable channel or news station that you can watch and not get fake news. I think that they're so far gone. When eighty-five or ninety percent of the coverage was negative on Trump, you can talk about Russia influencing the election, but there *were* people trying to influence the election, and it was the people in our media that hated Trump.

I think a lot of the things that people don't like about Trump— most of that hasn't been even reported quite factually in my opinion. For instance, the whole "he doesn't like Mexicans because he said Mexico sends their rapists" thing. What was reported was that he had said, "T-H-E-Y-apostrophe-R-E." The media all said that he said, "They are rapists, murderers, whatever." But what Trump really said was, "Mexico has sent their rapists and murderers." That's a statement. If it happened one time, then that's a factual statement. And yet, what was reported was that he had said, "They are all rapists, murderers, blah-blah-blah-blah." That's just another example of the media being so bad.

I would have never voted for Trump had Gary Johnson not smoked himself completely stupid. A lot of people who share my particular thinking were kind of left without a home, because usually I vote for the Libertarian, but it was like, "The Libertarian candidate is no good. What the hell am I going to do now?" I'm sure it wasn't a large percentage of people like me, but it wasn't a large percentage of people that swayed the election. Who knows?

I think the hugest part of it is just that Trump had never been in government, and I think that everyone didn't realize how mad people are. People are pissed. Most of them aren't even sure why they're pissed—they're just pissed. They see: "You're successful because you're working in government, and I don't have my job I had because you've advanced and I haven't."

How many people do you know that can live comfortably off of one income now, you know? Things are a lot more expensive, and that is a direct result of voting for the same sort of people over and over again. Jobs are leaving. Everything's getting more expensive. We're further in debt. The dollar's worth less and less. It's based on nothing. I think eventually we will have a currency crisis in The United States. The things we're doing with our dollar—printing money—it eventually is going to come to it. I'm not yelling and screaming that it's going to happen tomorrow. There's a heck of a lot of wealth in this country. A can can be kicked down a long freaking road in The United States. But eventually, I think that it's inevitable if we don't change course.

I think there's a divide in The United States that can't be fixed. I think, honestly, that in The United States, we probably need an orderly dissolution into two parts—into two countries. It's getting worse every day, and hopefully it doesn't get bloody.

But you know what? I have a fifteen-month-old. I'm taking care of her, raising her in what I view is the right way—just being as involved as I can with her. Work is going well. The economy is coming back around. For us right now, it's going really well, and we've personally had a bunch of good years in a row.

JEFF

*"I wish we lived in a place more like the
America of yesteryear that only exists in
the brains of us Republicans."*

—*Ned Flanders*

As soon as I found out that my wife was pregnant and Donald Trump got elected, the first thing I thought was, "Jesus Christ, we're gonna have a civil war." Like, "I'm gonna have to physically kill people to protect my family." That's how it felt. That was immediately where my head went—that we were going devolve into a war of some kind, that it was going to be chaos: Armageddon.

It was like everything had fallen apart. I mean, I purposely waited until I was making enough money to afford the kid and give it the right life. During my twenties, it was just not a great time in Muskegon. The recession hit us a couple of years before it hit the rest of the country. Unemployment was always over ten percent around here. It was kind of a darker time. Even if you had a college education, there weren't that many good jobs to get. Most of the manufacturing had left. And yeah, without that, you got stuck in a crappy retail job like I had.

I was wasting my life away working at Sears—hating it, getting treated like garbage by a large corporation that didn't care about me. Also working at Lowes—also a large corporation that just didn't care. Scraping by. I was on food stamps for a bit because I was making $7.40 an hour, working fifty hours a week and still not able to make it.

I was a backroom associate—a "BRA." I unloaded the semis. I loaded people's products into their car. I was a handyman; I did some repairs. I just worked myself to death. I would gain typically ten pounds of muscle during November—that's the heavy shopping season. It was like football again.

I was in New Zealand for a couple years. My brother was living over there, and the country is beautiful, but I was basically just doing the same kind of work over there that I was doing here, and so I moved back.

Then I came into the electrical thing. I read about this class they were doing at Grand Rapids Community College. It was an eighteen-week class where you went four times a week for seven hours a day, and it was basically the first two years of apprenticeship school. I said, "What the heck. Why not give it a shot?" I went and got the government assistance to do it and I just really excelled at it. It was about five thousand dollars, and I'm still paying it off now, but it was totally worth it.

That program gave me enough knowledge that I was able to get an interview at a company called Van Herron Electric, in Grand Rapids. I got hired and went to work wiring apartments and hospitals.

After three years, I wasn't super happy with where Van Herron was going. The way they treated and paid their employees—basically, if you weren't really, really conservative and from a certain part of Grand Rapids, you were kind of on the outside, and they let you know it. They'd be pushing you, "Why aren't you doing this faster?" It was always, "faster, faster, do it faster," even though I was one of the faster ones out there. They would make you think that your job wasn't that secure.

They would also listen to Rush Limbaugh at lunch and try to strike up conversations, and I think that was to my demise, because I told them that he was a bigot and a loudmouth and a sensationalist. A week later, my supervisor told me that I was one of the worst workers they had.

So I started looking into union. Actually, the organizer hunted me down. He stalked me on Facebook and made contact with me and I ended up meeting him. I talked to him, and I quit Van Herron and joined the union. Went to work right away.

Now I'm a third-year apprentice electrician. I'm building a power plant for MJ Electric in Holland. It's a gas power plant that uses steam to turn a turbine and then cycles the condensate through a network of pipes under the streets and sidewalks of the city to melt the snow. I get teamed up with a journeyman typically, and we do whatever task the management tells us to do. It started out with us doing five and a half miles of underground pipe, which was months and months and months. They would dig a trench, then we'd get these hundred-pound sticks of four-inch conduit lowered down, and we'd screw them together (or glue them together if it was PVC). You'd have to get satellite points of where to bring them up to where the building was going be, because there was no building. That's called duck bank. We did five and a half miles of duck bank. And while we were doing that, the building basically went up around us. As it started to get more complete, we started to pull the wire. We pulled all of the high voltage cable that would go up in the switch yard to the switch gear in the plant, and then we pulled the cable that went from each turbine generator to the switch gear.

I'll be working on this power plant project for another couple of weeks to a couple months. They're very cagey about saying when the project will be over. Because it's union, a lot of these guys travel all over the country. If you tell them, "Yeah, we've got a clear end date in one week," then they're going to leave right now, because they want to find the next two-year project and get on it. They don't want to wait one week, two weeks, three weeks, and then be laid off and not be able to get on that project. If a new project is starting, there's a call, and that call will be done by the time this project they're on is finished. That's just how it works.

There's a certain amount of work in West Michigan, and the union gets about five percent of it—we're so outnumbered by the non-union because they do it cheaper, because they don't pay their guys enough. Our contractors have to bid projects just like anybody else: different construction going up, different line changes at plants, things like that. The contractors bid that and then, if we get it, they call the hall saying, "Hey, I need this many journeymen, and whatever apprentices you can send," and the hall says, "Okay, we've got this many guys out of work, we've got this many travelers."

If you want to work, you can work, but you might have to travel. A lot of guys keep working all year round because they're willing to leave their family behind for a few months—go work in Gary where BP is, or in Wisconsin or Chicago, or all the way out to California, where the scale is twice what we make here because the cost of living is higher. Usually you can just get online or you can call different halls saying, "Hey, how many are on the books? What projects do you have coming up?" Their dispatcher will tell you, then you drive in and sign the books. A lot of guys get in the camper, do a big tour, and they sign all these different halls; then, when they catch a call, they call their other halls and say, "Hey, take me off the books." That's pretty much how it works. Or, if you don't want to leave your family, you take unemployment until work comes up. Unemployment is significantly less than what we make, but you budget for that.

I'm hoping that I can primarily work in and around Muskegon. It seems like there's enough work here, it's just whether or not we get it. Like, Mercy Hospital is putting up a new two-hundred-million-dollar project off of Sherman Boulevard, but our contractors didn't even bid it, and so I'm probably going to have to waste an hour and a half driving to and from work every day to work on something in Grand Rapids. If I have to travel once in a while, I will. But I prefer not to.

I plan on living here. Me and Jen talked about it recently, because there was a very good chance she could have moved to Chicago for work. Her company still wants her to work in Chicago, but we made a conscious decision to be here, because this is where we want to raise a family. It's not perfect—she wants our kid to speak several languages, and I'm not sure how much opportunity there is here for that. (She went to French immersion school until fourth grade and lived in France, and that's very important to her, so since we can't really find immersion schools here, she's kind of scrambling, like, "How can we teach this kid languages?") But still, we want to raise a family here, because we know it's a good place.

I liked growing up here. We were really privileged. As a kid, it was great. I had a lot of freedom. I would basically get up and either go to school or, if it was summer, get on my bike and go to Kirk's house, and we'd spend the whole day outside either playing baseball or football or building forts or whatever—shooting pellet guns, lighting off fire crackers, getting in trouble. I want my kids to have something similar to that.

That said, a lot of friends moved away. And a lot of the people who are still around, I just don't see them anymore. People here—I think with the rest of the country—they just got so politically divided that it's hard to see eye to eye, even with people you considered to be like best friends. The guys I grew up with, the people around here—they're good people, but there's some insidious ideas that kind of leak into them. I see things that friends post on Facebook—little comments—and they don't realize that they're being so hateful.

I'll just put this out there: people don't realize that they're racist. It's like they feel victimized somehow, even though they've never been victimized. I think they think they deserve more—and it's hard not to agree with that. Everyone thinks they deserve more. You're selling your life to this company, you know? That's what you're doing: you're selling hours of your life; you deserve to be compensated adequately. And people around here are still strug-gling. They're not struggling because Mexicans are taking our jobs, but I think that Trump kind of gave people permission to believe whatever they wanted to believe, and a lot of people listen to the conservative news media and they believe everything that they hear wholeheartedly—I think because they want to.

This part of the country's core beliefs are very strong right now, and it's taking us backwards. Trump's whole campaign legitimized all of the things that I fought really hard throughout my life to be like, "No, this is the wrong kind of thinking." Make America Great Again means Make America White Again. It's like people want it to be the '50s again. It's never going be the '50s. The '50s weren't even as good as people make them sound. How many people got lynched in the '50s? Maybe if you were white and middle class and could buy everything you needed, then the '50s were alright. But when I talked to my grandparents—who were adults in the '50s—they talked about how they were just struggling to raise my parents. All my grandparents ever talked about was that, back then, they saved everything that they could possibly reuse. My mother had seven brothers and sisters. They were scraping by. But: Golden Age. It's this golden-tinted fairy tale.

That's part of the problem with a small town—there's one overwhelming belief system that people adhere to, and it's difficult to even get a different perspective. If you get out and go to college or see the world, then you realize what it really means to be a good person and care about people.

With the kid coming soon, that's what I'm focused on more than anything. I'm hoping to emulate my dad and mom and just teach the kid to be a good person. That was the one message that got through: it doesn't really matter what you do, just be good. Treat people well, and things will work out for you. You can make opportunities for yourself nowadays.

Melissa

*"In the long run, there's still time to change
the road you're on."*

—*Led Zeppelin*

My best friend started working at Wilbrandt Farms, and she was like, "Come on, we'll get you in here." I needed a job to help buy a car—hitting high school and all that good stuff. I was already babysitting for everybody around, but I was still like, "Alright, I'll go down, fill out an app."

They hired me. I learned how to drive a tractor that summer— one of those humongous souped-up tractors. I had to back it into the garage, and I took out the garage door casing. Took it out. Gone. Caused a lot of damage. They let me drive it again, though. They just wouldn't let me back it in. I was fifteen.

We would go down in the field and plant celery, and after the day's work, we had to go back through and move the irrigation pipes. They would already be running for four hours, and we'd have to go out there and unclip the pipe and then lug it across the field to where we had just planted. You'd get out there and you'd sink to your knees in this muck of black dirt and fertilizer—smells like fish guts. By the time it was time to go home, you were pitch black dirty. When I'd get home, my dad wouldn't even let me come in the house. I had to go out back and hose down. I did that for four summers—May through August. When there wasn't anything for us to do outside, I would work inside with Mrs. Wilbrandt and sell flowers. It was a lot of fun.

I was working at Little Caesars once I hit sixteen. I worked at Little Caesars in North Muskegon through high school. Graduated and—enough is enough—so I started working at Chili's on Henry Street. While I was working there, I bartended and trained people on serving, but I also got another job at Herman Miller, working third shift at their Hickory plant. I started there working through Adecco—the temp agency—because I needed something with insurance, and I wanted more hours.

At Herman Miller, I was putting together the fabric tiles for cubicles. You had to do a tuck with needle-nosed pliers and scissors to keep the material on the frame so that when you looked at it it was nice and pretty and flat and flush, and we had to do it differently depending on the type of piece, so I learned the difference between a military fold and a hospital fold, and I learned how to use a sewing machine. It was sewing, wrapping, doing the corners—then you would put it through this other little machine that would put it in a bag and seal it, then you'd look at the invoice and get however many you needed and put them over on this bander; it would band them together, and you would put them on a skid. Once you had that completed, you took this huge rubber band that was probably an inch-and-a-half to two inches wide, and you had to wrap this whole thing and then get a hi-lo driver. Well, they would never see me wave my hand. I'm short, you know? So I'd go out and I'd grab that frickin rubber band and I'd pull it out like six feet—"PAH! BAH-BAM!" Then the hi-lo driver would know to come and get it. Well, then I got in trouble, because the big-wigs were in. Usually they're not in on third shift; they're only in on first. But there was one day they were there—"We can't have you doing that. That's a safety violation. What if the rubber band breaks?" "You're absolutely right. I am so sorry. Done. Done." So I couldn't do that anymore.

I would get paid Thursday night. We would get out of work Friday morning, and Getty Street Grille opened up by six, so we would leave Herman Miller at five-thirty and go eat breakfast. Then we'd leave there and we'd go to Dog House Saloon for six, seven, eight hours, then walk out into the sunshine—blinded by the light—go home, four-hour nap, get ready, and go out Friday and Saturday.

I used to follow Two Headed Chan—used to follow them hardcore. I would go to Battle Creek, I would go to Flint, I would go to Detroit, to Ohio. This guy who I've known from church since we were kids played the bass, and so that was really neat to see him again, reconnect. I would go everywhere—all of the Battle of the Bands. That's how I got to see Dope and Mushroomhead and Motorgrater. It would get crazy at those shows, but I just stuck to my beer. Nothing else. That would be our Friday and Saturday, and then sleep all day Sunday to get up to go back to work Sunday night.

For about five months, I did both: Chili's and third shift at Herman Miller. Chili's would constantly schedule me to open the bar, so I'm getting out of work at six in the morning, going home, winding down to take an hour-and-a-half nap to get up to work from ten thirty to five to go home to take a three-hour nap to get up to go back to work. I did it for five months. Finally, this one day, these customers were in—left me a forty-five-cent tip. He said, "You know, nothing was wrong..." I'm just standing there. I'm like, "I hate this job. I hate my life here. I'm done." I had already counted all my money down; I was done for the day, and I went into the office and I told them, "I'm done." They were like, "Yeah, you're done. You're going home for the day." I'm like, "No, I'm done. You need to find somebody else please to cover my shifts for the rest of this week, and I'm gone. Goodbye." "Well, we won't hire you back." "I won't be back here asking for a job. You have my word on this." And I left.

Well, in the process of all of this, I met my kids's dad. At a wedding. Mutual friends. He asked me to come down for a visit. To Florida. He asked me, "Do you like Nascar?" That's how he got me: "Do you like Nascar?" I was like, "Well yeah, these are my racers. What about you?" He said, "Yeah, well, yeah. I'm Tony Stewart." I'm like, "Yeah, cool beans." He's like, "I've got an extra ticket to the Pepsi 400 in Daytona"—the race of the year—"All you need to do is get here. To Florida. That's all you have to do. Everything else, don't worry about it. Just get here." Alright.

Well, I may or may not have had a boyfriend at the time, and he may or may not have been in Georgia at that moment—basic training. May or may not have. So I made the decision. My mom was like, "You know, I don't want you to be married fifteen years from now and look back and be like, 'Damn. What if? What if I just would've went?' You know?" I told her, "Right. Absolutely right. Done. Gone. I'm doin it." So I took a week, and Fourth of July weekend I was down there. We went to the race—Pepsi 400, blah-blah-blah. Three days in he asked me to move down. I was like, "Aaaaah. Let me think on it. Cool?" At the end of the trip it had progressed to, "Okay, I'll move down, but you gotta let me have six months in." I had just gotten hired in at Herman Miller. So I got back to Muskegon in August and I started as hired in, then I stayed until February, and on February 10th of oh-six I moved down to Florida.

Once I got to Florida, I needed a job, obviously. I started working at Chili's University, and I did that for around three months. Then a girl who I met down there called me, and her and her boyfriend were sitting at this bar called The Brass Mug, and they said, "Hey, they need a bartender here." Okay. They put a guy on the phone—Rick. Rick gets on the phone, and he says, "Hey, when would you be available?" I say, "You know, whenever. Why don't you let me know when you want me to come in for an interview?" He's like, "Well why don't you come in today at three-thirty?" So I got out of work at Chili's, went home, changed, went to The Mug, had my interview with Rick. He says, "I'll let you know." I'm like,

"Alright, cool. Thanks. It was great to meet you guys. I'll see you later." Whatever. I leave there and I go over and I'm having a couple shots of whiskey, couple beers with my boyfriend at this other bar. It's six o'clock, and I get a phone call. From Rick: "Hey, can you start tonight? Seven thirty?" "Gimmee water! Gimmee water!" I'm downing pitchers of water. We leave there. I get Dan home. I turn around and go back to the bar.

That night, The Mug was supposed to have a bunch of bands. They had all been cancelled, but people didn't know that they had been cancelled. I ended up doing a twenty-five-hundred-dollar night behind the bar. My first night there. By myself. Rick walks in at two thirty, and I've still got over half the bar full. He comes behind the bar and he's like, "What happened?" I tell him, "I don't know, but I just know that I've been rocking it. That's all I can tell you." So I ended up quitting Chili's and working there five days a week. Days, nights, whatever. The Brass Mug.

Then, stuff happens in life, and my ex-at-this-point ended up getting a DUI. I was up here in Muskegon for my little brother's twenty-first birthday. I'm getting ready to go to an arena football game at L.C. Walker, and it's five, five-thirty in the afternoon on a Friday—Friday the 13th—and I'm talking to Florida like, "Hey, I'm heading to Mom's now. We're gonna get ready. We gotta be here for dinner at this time, and then the game starts at this time. I'll call you when we're done. Are you gonna go home?" He goes, "Yeah, I'm gonna finish this beer, go home, hang out with the dog, let him out, make some dinner." I'm like, "Alright, awesome."

He called me at twenty after ten: "Baby." "Yeah?" "Baby, I just got pulled over." "For what?" "Drinking and driving. But I'm in the parking lot of our apartment complex. I can see the frickin apartment." Well, they ended up impounding his truck. For a DUI in the parking lot? Why are they going to impound your truck? Well, it was because he ended up having paraphernalia on him. Bye. Bye, Felicia. Bye. I told you before: "I'm not about that life." Done. Done.

So I moved home for six months. I went back to Florida for two weeks to put in my notice and to take my car and all my belongings—everything I brought with me to Florida fit in a car, so everything to go back fit in a car. That was the fastest trip ever from Florida to Michigan.

When I moved here for those six months, I worked at Nauty's as a waitress and at Domino's on Sherman. Delivering pizza in the Heights? Whoo. That was interesting. I was never worried except for one delivery one time, because you were not allowed to go in the home. Of anybody. It didn't matter if you were in Shores in those beautiful mansions or whatever. Didn't matter. You were not allowed to go in the home. Well, at this one guy's house, I knock on the door—and I always take one or two steps back just as courtesy; I'm not going to be all up on your door. But this guy, he's looking around, he's looking around, and finally he's like, "You need to come inside." "I'm not allowed to come inside." "Either you come inside, or I'm not payin for my pizza." "Okay, then I guess you're not gettin your pizza, man. I'm out. I can't. I'm not supposed to come inside." "I don't handle business outside. You need to come in." And he was a big guy—stocky. I ended up taking a step in the door with one foot and was like, "This is as far as I will come. Alright? Cool. Bye. Bye." Oh, I hated it. Oh I hated it. But I did it. Six months, I did it.

So I was back. I had those two jobs. It was more or less to teach my boyfriend a lesson, like, "You can't keep doing this. If you want any quality of life with me, you need to stop and grow up. Now!" I was here for six months, he came up to make up, and we made Ian. I moved back to Florida in November of oh-seven.

When I moved back, I got a job as a preschool teacher—with kids three and up, because I couldn't do poopy diapers—but I ended up having pregnancy complications, so I had to quit.

I hadn't been there three months yet to get my ninety days, so they had to terminate me. Then I was in the hospital with Ian for nine and a half weeks. I had Ian, they ended up hiring me back, and I ended up working there for three years. And to look back and be like, "You know what? I did three years of it, and I helped those kids start on the right path"—that was a good experience. I've got a lot of their moms on my Facebook, and it's just like, "Wow, these kids are excelling." But, well, in the process of working there, it was time for review, and my raise was eleven cents. I told them, "I'm better than this. I can't. I can't. I've got a family now. It's not just me and this guy. It's the three of us."

We bought a house, and we got pregnant with our second—our little girl. She was my housewarming gift; that's what we said. She was conceived on our first weekend in the house.

I went to school then to become a medical assistant. I gave up my weekends. I went to school Saturdays and Sundays for eight hours and worked Monday-through-Friday forty-plus and did what I had to do, and I graduated valedictorian of my class. Then Maya came—that was all perfect. I got hired right out of extern and worked at a clinic for two years, then I left and went to a bigger group where I just excelled further, and that's how ear, nose and throat became my niche—I love it.

I'm a weirdo. I can't get enough: ear wax, boogers, sinus infections, mucus. Head and neck cancer is interesting to me. Doing endoscopies—fiber-optic scopes up the nose to look at the vocal cords and all of that? That's so interesting to me. Ears and how they work. The mechanics behind them and how crystals that don't belong in certain aspects can get in there and cause you to feel like you're spinning? I can fix that. I know how to fix that. You know what I'm saying? That is cool, and I like having that power. I love educating people on how to spray your nose the right way. I just love it. It gets me excited. I was excited to go to work. I wanted to go to work. I couldn't get enough of it.

This is where it gets a little sticky. I had went out with my girl-friend on a Saturday night to The Dallas Bull. My friend is actually friends with Brantley Gilbert's band, and he was playing at the Florida State Fairgrounds, and after they play they go to this particular bar—The Dallas Bull. That's why we were there. I had the kids taken care of for the night, and she and I decide that we were hungry afterwards, so we go up to the Waffle House (also known as the "Awful Waffle"). We just sit down, we just order, and my boyfriend's texting me: "Guess I'm gonna lock the door cause apparently you found somewhere else to stay tonight." I'm like, "Have I ever given you a reason to not trust me? Are you being serious right now?" So I call him up. I'm like, "Dude, what? I'm at the Waffle House with Sherry. Here. Frickin talk to her." And he hangs up. Wouldn't answer my phone calls. Wouldn't answer my text messages. I say, "Sherry, we gotta go." We get our food to go, and she takes me home.

I get home. I walk in the bedroom. He's in the bedroom, and I blurt out, "What the fuck is your problem?" I am so mad at this point. We had this sleigh bed, and I'm white knuckled gripping the end of the bed: "What the fuck is your problem?" He just says, "What are you talking about?" I'm like, "Really?" His response is, "You're drunk. Don't talk to me. You're drunk. You can't talk to me."

He starts getting dressed—out of his pajamas, into real clothes. I ask, reasonably, "Where the fuck are you going?" He says, "I'm leaving." "No you're not." "Yes I am." I'm standing there in front of the door, and I wouldn't move. "You're gonna have to move me." "Oh, I can." "I know you can. Do it. Let's see you move me. Let's go." So we struggled there.

Then he gets out in the living room. And I have this problem when I get really excited: my mouth will salivate, and I'll spit at you. Well, at this point, I'm angry. And I'm yelling at him. And I'm spitting. And he's like, "Quit fucking spitting at me." So I cover my mouth and go, "ruh-ruh-ruh-ruh-ruh-ruh-ruh-ruh." Like a little chihuahua, right? I'd stop and wipe my hand off and I'd do it again. I just kept going. Finally, he looks at me and he goes, "I'm fucking done with you." I said, "You're done with me?" He said, "I'm fucking done with you." "Oh, well in that case, let me get that door for you." I open the door for him, let him out. He left. No idea where he went.

I call my mom in just this frenzy, and after I talk to her for a little while I decide, "You know what? No, no. He's done? Fine. Be done. I'm done too." I got all my kids's birth certificates, packed each of us three or four pairs of clothes, and I left. I put the dog in my car, because I don't know where Dan is. I went up an hour north to get my kids from the friend of mine they were staying with. (Good friend. Tammy. She actually set up the GoFundMe when Ian got his cancer and everything.)

Well, then Dan's calling me, "You better not be drunk right now." "I'm not. I am so not." "I'm calling the cops. You took my car." "Nope. It's not your car. It's your dad's car—that I paid for. But okay, we'll say it's yours. Sure." "Well I wanna see my kids." My friend was like, "They're not going home."

I call my mom again, "Mom, I need three one-way tickets. Tonight. I'm coming home. Tonight." "Okay. Alright. See you later." We get everything planned. We're good to go. Leaving out of Tampa at five-thirty.

I go back to the house. My keychain is on the table. The only thing that was remaining on my keychain was my mother's house key. He took my key to my Kia, my house key, my mailbox key. Everything. All I had on my keychain was the key to my mother's house. Alright. I'm like, "Where's my jewelry box?" "You can have that back when I get to see my kids." "It's not that important to me then. It's just stuff." I go back in the kids's rooms; I grab all their school stuff, because they had already started school. I try to get everything that I think they'll really need. And not one time did he ask me, "Please don't go. Let's talk about this. Let's work this out." Nope. "Bye." "Okay, bye."

Eleven years together. He had proposed that first year when I was down there, and then again when I moved back, but he wouldn't follow through with it because I wouldn't take his last name alone. I'm like, "I'm a Deiters. I've got it tattooed on my frickin back, you know? Get outta here. It can be Deitiers hyphen Hurregers all day long, yes, but it will not be just your last name. Sorry. I can't. I can't. Times have changed. I don't have to if I don't want to. If I don't want to take your last name, I don't have to take your last name. If I wanted to change my last name to Jingleheimersmith, then that's what I'm gonna do, okay?" He didn't like that.

I left. It's the middle of the night—early, early morning by now. The kids are like, "Where are we going, Mom?" I tell them, "We're gonna go to Michigan and surprise Me-me for her birthday." Me-me is my grandma, their great grandma. I told them, "Her birthday was Friday, but her party's tomorrow. We are gonna go and surprise her." We got in Tammy's car, and away we went.

How I know that it was meant to be: I have flown multiple times with my children, just me and them. Never once when Dan would bring us to the airport did they offer him an assisting boarding pass to get us through security and to help us with our bags to our gate. Nothing. Never one time in my life did they ever offer him this. Well, my girlfriend Tammy's with us at the airport. We had one suitcase between the three of us, plus our backpacks—with one-way tickets. The lady at check-in looks at me, looks at my kids, looks at Tammy, looks back at us, looks at Tammy again, and she goes, "Would you like an assisting boarding pass?" Tammy looks at me, and I point to the sky and go, "Dude, that's all I can tell you." She goes, "Yep. I know. Yes. Let's do it."

Tammy gets us to our gate. We get on the plane. It is packed. We're all the way in the back. They go to turn the plane on—to get it started. The lights go out and come back on. "Ladies and gentlemen, we're gonna have to deboard the plane." Fuck. All I keep thinking is, "He knows I'm here. He's called the cops, and I'm gonna get arrested for trying to take my kids."

We deboard, and I'm looking like a crazy woman. You would think I was a crackhead looking for my next fix. My kids are like, "You alright mom?" I'm like, "Yeah I'm good I'm good. Let's go get some food." I'm trying to keep them busy, trying to keep me busy. We're supposed to go from Tampa to Chicago, then from Chicago to Grand Rapids. We were supposed to be in Grand Rapids at eleven forty-five that night. We were supposed to wake up the next morning in my mom's house—and now I don't know if we'll even make it out of Florida. We get some food, and then over the loudspeaker they announce, "Ladies and gentlemen, we are so sorry for this inconvenience. Due to this delay, Southwest will put you up in Chicago, and then you'll fly out from Chicago to your destinations. Please wait until your name is called to come up to the desk and make new reservations." I tell the kids, "Alright you guys, sit right here." I've got them in the seats closest to the little desk. Finally they call me up and they're like, "Melissa?" "Yep." "Here are six hundred dollars in vouchers for your hotel and for the final leg of your journey." "Alright."

W e got to Muskegon, and we ain't going back. Ian still hasn't gotten used to saying "pop." I explain it to him, "Honey, nobody up here is gonna understand what that soda stuff is. Up here you gotta say 'pop.' " But we're good.

We got back here and I was actually offered a job that Wednesday to be a school bus driver. I told them, "God bless you," and they were like, "No, really. We love your personality and what you're about. You're so positive. You could come in here any day you want and work for us."

Then the following week, my mom needed her car fixed, so we go to Discount Tire—they offer me a job there. I actually did work there. I was slinging tires for about two weeks. That was a really nasty job. It's hard. It is a very physical job. You have your tires that range from itty-bitty that go on a tractor to low-profiles that go on a sports car to those big mamma-jammas that go on the big souped-up trucks. They're very heavy. I'm taking tires that are wider than my arm span and picking them up, rolling them up my body, then I have to turn, then step up onto another tire to get them on a shelf. They got two and a half weeks out of me, and I called and said, "I'm not coming in today." They asked, "Why not?" I said, "Cause my body can't handle it, man. My hips are popping out. I can't do this. I'm tired." But I was a tire slinger for about two weeks.

My dad actually knows the physician that I work for now. My dad used to take the guy out on charter fishing expeditions in Lake Michigan, and it came up that his office needed a medical assistant. I went in, applied for the job, and he called me back within an hour, "Hey, we'll offer you this." "Well, pay me this and I'll see you tomorrow." "You got a deal." "Awesome." I've been there since October. It's not ears, but it's a job.

So with Ian and all of that stuff. He got diagnosed in August of '14. It started with a bump on his head. It started out the size of a nickel. It was on the side of his head, and we thought that he had just slipped and fell. He was swinging between my bed and my dresser, then all of a sudden he came out and he was like, "Mom, I hit my head on the wall. I've got a goose egg." "You want some ice?" "No, I'm alright. I'm good, I'm good." Away he goes.

Well, two weeks later it's still there. I'm thinking, "How many goose eggs hang out that long?" I called the pediatrician, explained to him what's going on, and he told me, "Ah, you know, don't worry about it. How's he acting?" I tell him, "Normal. Like Ian." He says, "Ah, don't worry about it. Just keep an eye on it." Okay.

By April it had grown from three-point-something to four-point-something—in centimeters. At that point, we were letting his hair grow out, because kids can be mean. We went for a CT scan that just showed fluid, like it was just retaining fluid. Then, at the end of July, he was complaining about a sore throat. I'm like, "Alright, I'm taking you to the doctor."

So we walk into the pediatrician. They call Ian back, and he stands up and he gets in front of me and it's the right side of his neck—it looks like somebody just took grapes and papier-mâchéd them right to his neck. I'm like, "Whoa whoa whoa. That is new. That is new. Overnight new." We go back there and they run a strep and the doctor comes in and he says, "Melissa, you're going to be the happiest mom in the world who has a kid with swollen lymph nodes. He's got strep. But I'm not happy with that bump. I want to send you to a craniomaxillofacial specialist in Tampa."

We go there, and this woman is amazing. Oh my goodness. She does all the cleft palates, and when babies are born and they have issues with how their heads are growing and with the plates and everything, she goes in and fixes them. She is just amazing. So we go in and she says, "Wow, that is a nasty bump. Can you move it?" Ian goes, "Yeah!" He grabs it and is moving it all around. She's like, "Well that's kinda...oh, okay buddy. That's awesome." (Then that was his parlor trick for like ever—"Watch. It moves, it moves!") She goes, "I want you guys to get an MRI." "Alright, cool. You got it."

That next week, we go in for the MRI, and we got the personal phone call: "The bump lit up. The lymph nodes lit up. We're gonna need you to get some bloodwork done." "Okay. You got it. Whatever you say." So we go do it—we get the bloodwork done. They call me personally again. Monday. The doctor on the phone goes, "So bloodwork's normal. Just wanna do a biopsy though, see what's goin on in that bump."

Well, they told me the bloodwork was normal, but there's this LD—lactate dehydrogenase—basically the bad stuff in your blood. His LD was six hundred and ninety-five. So we go in, and they take two chunks out of that bump. It came back atypical cells and lymphoma. They can't determine leukemia versus lymphoma until they do a bone marrow biopsy, and then once they do that, there's this magical number: twenty-five. This is how it was explained to me: if it's over twenty-five, it's leukemia; if it's under twenty-five, it's lymphoma. His came back, and it was way over twenty-five. It was leukemia.

When we got the news, it was: "I need you guys to come tonight. I need you to pack a bag. I need you to get to St. Joseph's Children's Hospital right now. An oncology/hematology team is waiting for you. It will be a direct admit." "Okay, okay. Um. Can you repeat that please?" I hand Dan the phone. He takes the phone; I collapse to the floor. I can't do that right now. There's a time and a place, but now is not that time or that place.

But if that's what you have to do? Fine. I've got this. I packed us a bag for me and him, packed my daughter a bag to go to her grandparents' house. I mean, go go go go go go go.

That's the craziest thing. Through all of this: as a parent—yes—it sucks. But there's one parent that can handle it, and there's one that can't. There always is, and there will always be. That's just the way it is. Even if they're both acting like they're both good and they've got this, one of them doesn't. Okay? Bottom line: I was always the heavy—all of the doctors appointments, all of the overnight stays, everything. And I understand: you have to make a living, you have to provide for us. But you know what? I need to do the same thing. Why can't this be fifty-fifty? Why is it always on me? So with him telling me that he was done this last August and me moving on and moving back up here and everything? In time, it was coming.

Once we moved, he had no idea where we were, so he's calling me, "Can you guys just come home? Can you just come over and we'll talk?" "It is too late. That ship has sailed." "What do you mean?" "That ship has sailed. It's too late. We're not there anymore." "You're already in fucking Michigan? Are you fucking kidding me blah-blah-blah-blah?" "Yep. Mmm'kay, are ya done? Cause ya told me you were done...Uh-huh. Okay. Keep yelling. It's fine, but whatever." So, yeah. It is what it is.

But you know what? I'm doing great. Life is good. I'm good. Over the years, I've met a lot of really cool people. I've got a lot of people that have made amazing footprints in my life. There's other ones that it's like, "Man, I wish the wind would blow and you'd just be gone." It is what it is, you know?

I went to MCC before I decided to move away and join the circus. I wanted to go to Western. I wanted to teach. I wanted to do a double major in Science and English. That sounds really weird, right? But that's what I wanted: Science and English. Because I love them both. I wanted to go to Western. I wanted to get my bachelor's and then my master's and then go to the east coast. I wanted to get my doctorate and then teach at an Ivy League school. That was my plan.

Much different now. I love the medical field. I wouldn't trade it for anything. I'm still young enough that, once my kids get a little bit older, I'm going to take the MCATs, and I'm going to pursue being a doctor. That is what I want to do. I don't know if I would necessarily want to be a surgeon, but they kind of go hand in hand, so at this point, I'm looking at a good thirteen years of school. I look at that and I think about it and I realize, "Ooh, I'm gonna be fifty." But if that's something that I'm still pursuing into that stage of life? Okay. That's fine by me. As long as I do it. I'll get there.

I'm glad I went the path I did. I've been around a little bit. I've seen some things that most people probably never do. So when I look at what's happening out there and then I compare it to what I see on the news, it's like the media in this country just tells us what they want us to know. It's like the tail wagging the dog. People get so distracted by stuff like all this talk about building The Wall, but in the meantime, Flint and their gross water? It's still happening.

That's still happening, but people are just like, "Okay, what's the next thing, what's the next thing, what's the next thing?"

What we should be saying is, "No, let's get back to the basics." I am all about helping another country out. Awesome. But you know what? Our country's going down the shit hole. What about our kids that are on the streets? What about our homeless people? What about our vets? We're going to take refugees from another country because they're being treated like crap—that's great—but what are we doing for the people who fought for us to be here? We're not doing a daggone thing.

I feel like we could be doing so much more, but we're not. And it needs to start local. It needs to start here and grow from there. I'll use Muskegon County as a prime example. You've got all these schools here that are empty—just sitting there rotting. For what reason? Make it a state-funded whatever. Find that one percent in America that's keeping America going, and have them start helping fund these places. Turn them into kitchenettes, or make them into shelters for our homeless vets. Do something for these guys who have gone out and sacrificed their lives for us.

I just moved back at the tail end when all the political stuff was winding down, and there was a woman that was running from Lansing: came from nothing, struggled, made herself who she is now, knows what it's like to be low-income. I don't remember her name, and I don't even know if she even won, but we need more people like that. And even with someone like her, I'll tell you what I worry about: I worry about people getting into office and getting brainwashed and taking the power to their head. Don't take everybody's money and put it into some other government-funded blah-blah-blah of "how many hairs does a cat shed in a year?" Who cares? Put it into something that's going to matter. Put it back into our education system. Give it back to the teachers—because dammit, they're the ones that are making the upcoming generation. If you're in office, you're supposed to be in that position to help people;

you're not in that position to better your pockets. Turn around and help those other people.

Because people are people. I don't care if you're purple, pink, yellow, green, blue—I don't care. You are a person. You have the same insides that I do. You put your socks on one foot at a time, and you sit down to poop. Everybody does these things, okay? Nobody is better than anybody else.

So what do I think about what's going on? You're not supposed to talk about politics in a bar. You are not supposed to talk about politics, and you cannot talk about religion in a bar. But okay, here we go anyway: I don't know what I think about Trump. I'm still up in the air. It's still up in the air. I think some of the things that he's doing are great. It's great that he's demanding answers and not just letting things sit and wait. I hate sit and wait. Get it done. If you want this to happen, make this happen. Take a vote right now. Right now.

Full disclosure though: I didn't vote this year. I had just got back to Muskegon, and in Michigan you had to be registered so many days before the election, and I couldn't do an absentee ballot for Florida because my physical address was no longer down there. But who would I have voted for? Myself. Absolutely. Myself. I've got great ideas. I told my mom, "Let me get in there. Let me get in there. Let me get hold of it." Because things have to change. I get fired up with this stuff. Things have to change.

MIKE AGAIN

"Here in America, We The People always have the final word."

—Donald J. Trump

I wouldn't read this if I were you. As a formality, a book like this one must have a postscript that ties up all the loose ends. It's just that, if all those loose ends couldn't be tied up over the course of the preceding 83,994 words, I promise you that they will not be tied up over the next 2247.

That said, if any confusion remains about the source of those 83,994 words, an acknowledgement and an explanation might prove useful.

Acknowledgement: The words you have read are not mine, but are those of the participants, each of whom lent a name to a chapter. Certain sensitive details were eliminated and certain opinions were softened at their individual request, but the ideas, stories, and actual phrases that make up the text of this book came not from my head, but from each of theirs in turn.

Explanation: From March through May of 2017, I sat down with seventeen Muskegon County residents for casual recorded chats. My task was simply to get out of the way and let my neighbors speak their minds, then to piece together the resulting oral histories into something that resembled a coherent narrative.

Was the pool of participants skewed in any way? Of course it was. It consists almost entirely of my former classmates, their parents, and their friends. Judge for yourself whether or not a sanitation engineer, a non-profit administrator, a factory owner, a shop floor guy, a poor boy/rich girl Christian couple, a good cop, an older shop floor guy, a transient ex-con, a widowed Rotarian, a judge, my aunt, an old-school tech entrepreneur, a technocrat, a salesman, an electrician, and a single mom offer a reasonable cross-section of the population.

As to the content, might an authorial interjection here or some thick description there have been useful in helping to clarify some essential historical or demographic detail? Maybe. Maybe it would have been useful for you to know that the Muskegon Mall was in operation from 1976 until 2001, or that overall crime in the county has been falling for the past fifteen years, or that William was the judge who sentenced Kurt to prison, or that I met Tony when he solicited me for "gas money" on Western Avenue while I waited for my wife to finish up her class at Bill's daughter-in-law's yoga studio, or that Jon's police funeral cortege stretched on for damn near the full length of the isthmus bubble of North Muskegon. Maybe. Still, I thought it best just to stay out of the way and let the stories tell themselves.

Okay, fine, but shouldn't I have at least preceded each chapter with a detailed refutation of every factual inaccuracy offered by the speaker? Perhaps. Anecdotal explanations for social ills can hardly be checked against Wikipedia, but all dates of plant closings and other such events were, in fact, verified before making their way into the final text. As for other possible points of contention, I could track down no record of Muskegon Heights' 2012 precinct totals, but in 2016, Donald Trump received 177 of the 3631 ballots cast there. The reader is encouraged to engage in further sleuthing at their leisure.

Alright, but then what about my opinion? Shouldn't I have spared you the necessity of reflecting on the preceding pages by offering you a nice little two-page lesson in what you really ought to think about all of these inscrutable semi-urban Midwestern-ers? No. The purpose of this project was neither to make sweeping judgements, nor to editorialize every nuance of every individual's autobiography. I remind the reader that, at times, the things people say over burgers and beers may not contain the truth, the whole truth, and nothing but the truth, and that that's part of the point of all this. I acknowledge the contributions of the participants while endorsing none as the sole arbiter of unvarnished wisdom.

A second but by no means secondary acknowledgement is also in order: to Belorussian Nobel Laureate Svetlana Alexievich. Without her influence, the idea to compile a book using such a method likely never would have entered my head, and certainly would not have entered in time for me to assemble the preceding portrait of my once-and-future hometown in the early months of The Age of Trump.

Because make no mistake, this was a portrait. This is not a work of documentary journalism, but a work of art. It is a perspec-tive containing seventeen perspectives, and I have no doubt that the resulting picture would be altered by adding an eighteenth, further altered by adding a nineteenth, and so on. The lines may be colored in and the shadows may fall more or less where the laws of nature dictate they should, but I repeat: this is not the thing in itself. It is merely a seventeen-sided representation of a hundred seventy thousand-sided object situated in a ten million-sided object situated in a three hundred twenty million-sided object. I cannot draw out America with a book. This book can only claim to offer seventeen disparate glances at it.

An eighteenth view, however, permeates these pages, and it is mine. I solicited the participants. I directed the interviews. I edited the results into something readable. I decided which half of what they told me stayed just between them and me. Although my general sensibilities were offended by some and my standards of truth and common sense were affronted by others, I came away from each conversation with the felling that I had spoken to an invariably good-hearted, inevitably flawed human being. You know, like people. I like them all without exception or caveat. I only hope my touch-up of their lines captured as best as could be captured the unique voice of each personality. I meant it when I said that it's past time for everyone to really get to know the neighbors again.

As I also said, if the preceding hundreds of pages could not distill the meaning and importance of all this, then I certainly cannot do it in five or six. Were I to be invited back onto another meticulously-organized Russian daytime political talk show, I could now ramble on for hours about the problems and prejudices and questions and misunderstandings of Trump supporters and of Trump opponents and of Trump wait-and-seers alike, but I still could not sum up in a pithy russophone soundbite exactly why Trump happened, and I certainly could not predict what Trump may yet portend, either for the people of Muskegon or for the people of Moscow.

That's an ending that we will all do our little part to write. We collectively decide whether this thing ends in a bang or a whimper. For those who hope for the whimper, I hope that this was a useful tool in better understanding who Trump's voters are, what they wanted, what they want, and how a hundred thousand of them spread across the upper Midwest might be peeled off in 2020. For those who hope for a bang, I hope that this was a useful tool in better understanding who Trump's skeptics are, what their concerns are, and how dramatically most of them differ from the crying college student caricatured on *Hannity* (which most Trump voters never watch anyway). If it is necessary for me to say this, I will say it: I hope (but do not pray) for the whimper.

I voted for Hillary—and went through the hassle of obtaining an absentee ballot and sending it from Moscow to a Blue Wall state—

because I felt it important to demonstrate that Donald Trump did not represent my country and did not represent my younger self's neighbors, and I felt it strongly enough that I considered it necessary to make my marginal voice one more in the overwhelming chorus of sanity and decency that would resound across the land on November 8, 2016. Had John Kasich won the Republican nomination, I may have gone through the motions of voting, but I probably would have just done what I did while in China in November 2012: trust my country and trust my old neighbors and trust the polls to get it right without my participation in the process, and then live (abroad) with the same old boring old consequences of elections in a country protected by two centuries of accrued inertia in its political norms and cultural institutions.

No longer. The shock of the 2016 election was not that Donald Trump won—it was that he could be in a position to win. The surprise was not that one hundred thousand people spread across Wisconsin, Michigan, and Pennsylvania so radically altered the course of human affairs, but that in a country of three hundred million mostly decent people, a man who promised to annihilate decency could top thirty percent. Were there idiots and assholes who voted for Donald Trump? Certainly. But there are not 62,985,106 of them. Had there been only 62,885,105 Trump voters, Hillary Clinton may have become president, but the frustrations and misunderstandings and prejudices and calculations and fears and hopes that persuaded even that many of your neighbors to lend their individual voice to this con artist would have remained.

Because for most residents, it does not feel like morning in Muskegon. Over the course of this project, I spoke to exactly one person who had an unabashedly optimistic view of the area's progress: Jonathan, a gay technocrat prepared to sacrifice ideological purity to the greater good of constituents' interests. If, as my former graduate school classmates in New York and my returned Peace Corps volunteer friends in Washington maintain, the future belongs to Jonathan, then I rejoice, for then the future belongs to me too.

I am not rejoicing. Unlike the hot takes in my ears (podcasts) and in front of my eyes (endless Twitter), few of the neighbors with whom I spoke had anything specific to say about healthcare policy minutia or about Deputy Attorney General recusals or about Islamic Revolutionary Guard Corps ambitions. Those details are important—they are the real work of Washington—but in this moment, the fate of the nation turns on simpler stuff.

For the most part, nothing Trump has done (or has failed to do) has yet affected any of his supporters' lives in any material way, nor has it really touched most of his detractors'. Sooner or later, empty under secretary offices and outright assaults on democratic norms are bound to produce some tangible result, but for now, life goes on as normal: one day to the next. Some of my neighbors' November 7 selves may well have been shocked into action by what is happening here and now, but here and now has arrived so gradually that it's all but impossible to remember. Like normal people, my neighbors are still most concerned about their work, their children, their mortgages, their aging parents' health, their new car, this weekend's plans, and the Tigers' struggling bullpen. On the whole, their political allegiances have more to do with general perceptions of identity—informed by a shared clip here and a habit of mind there—than they have to do with a scrupulous evaluation of Congressional Budget Office scores or Brookings Institution reports. All were expert in their corner of the world. Most were satisfied with where they are in life. Several were skeptical of the media in a general way. Half were eager to talk sports. Fewer were eager to talk politics. Two or three had anything substantive to say about President Trump's specific action in any specific policy area.

As some of those specifics are filled in (or left blank) in specific ways over the next four years, it is possible that a few million of our Trump-supporting neighbors will turn away in disillusion. Really, who in the preceding pages would vote to prolong our national embarrassment once it has become clear that not even a reality TV boss has the power or inclination to reduce insurance premiums, nor to feed the hungry, nor to juice up Amtrak's wi-fI routers, nor to Build The Wall, nor to curb America's use of military force abroad, nor to kick scumbag sisters off welfare, nor to foster a strong judiciary, nor to expedite the emigration process for ThaI brides, nor to make America's innumerable Muskegons nicer places to live? Then again, how many will blame any failures on the obstruction of politically correct elites, or cry that the liberal media invented the latest witch hunt, or reason that Ruth Bader Ginsberg looks like she could keel over at any minute, or bank on taking their still-promised tax cut to the bank, or respond in genuine fear to the angry dark faces on their newsfeed, or solemnly swear that it is the duty of every true patriot to defend the nation against the existential threat of Elizabeth Warren, or feel leery about booting a wartime Commander in Chief?

I cannot answer that question, though it will be answered. As the voice at the end of this chapter, I can only voice my concern: that the continued lack of results will not lead back towards heated debate over marginal tax rates, but forward to something worse. Disillusion followed by disillusion does not usually effect technocratic consensus. "A plague on all their houses" is not the cry of a healthy body politic. This story is far from over.

June 21, 2017

Made in the USA
Middletown, DE
20 August 2018